Time Abundance

Time Abundance

Rethinking Wealth in a Post-Work Society

Elian Varo

Mindful Pages

Published in 2025

ISBN: 9789371342469 (PB)
ISBN: 9789371343916 (eBook)

Published by

Mindful Pages
Imprint of Alpha Editions LLC
312 W. 2nd St #1834
Casper, WY 82601, USA

This book was developed using advanced writing tools to support the drafting and ideation process. All content has been thoughtfully curated, refined, and reviewed to ensure quality and relevance.

Content

Introduction
The Clock Is Not God

Time has long been spoken of as the ultimate currency, encapsulated neatly in the familiar phrase, "time is money." But what if this metaphor, so deeply embedded in modern consciousness, has led us astray? What if, rather than being merely incomplete, it distorts our understanding of what wealth truly is? Perhaps real wealth isn't measured in wages earned or bank balances swollen by long hours, but rather in our ability to shape our days—our energy, our attention, our very awareness—free from the confines of transactional demands. This book argues for just such a reframing. It proposes a radical, yet quietly intuitive, shift: from the pursuit of financial capital to the cultivation of temporal sovereignty—the capacity to choose how we spend our lives. An idea both timeless and timely, and never more necessary than it is today.

We stand at a curious juncture in human history. Labour, once the bedrock of civilisation and personal identity alike, is becoming optional. Machines—clever, untiring, and increasingly autonomous—are displacing human effort at a scale and speed our ancestors could hardly have imagined. The age-old model of trading hours for income is beginning to fray. For some, it has already collapsed. And yet, strangely, the societal pressure to justify one's existence through labour has not diminished; if anything, it has intensified. The result is a strange cultural dissonance. On the one hand, time is more abundant than ever. On the other, we are more shackled to it—measuring, maximising, monetising—than any prior generation. Might it be, then, that true luxury in this brave new world lies not in surplus productivity, nor even in riches, but in time itself? In the ability to live fully, to pause, to wonder, to engage life not as a race, but as a rhythm.

This book extends you a simple but powerful offer: the possibility of time freedom. In a landscape where long-standing economic orthodoxies are being quietly dismantled, and where traditional structures of toil are steadily giving way, the truest wealth may no longer be held in assets but expressed in autonomy. For centuries, this kind of freedom has been hidden beneath layers of necessity—cultural imperatives, historical patterns, economic coercion. Somewhere along the way, we began to live not for ourselves, but for our jobs. We became subject to a temporal regime that promised prosperity, but often delivered exhaustion instead.

Yet, there is an exit—if we are willing to reimagine our relationship with time. Not as a limited asset to be consumed or managed, nor as a task to be conquered. Time, properly understood, is something far richer. It is a field, not a funnel—a living space in which the human soul may stretch out, breathe, and belong. True abundance is not about extracting more from each hour, but about rethinking what those hours are for. Wealth, then, becomes less a matter of acquisition, and more one of alignment—with values, with presence, with purpose.

Unlike the myriad self-help guides that promise to help you get more done in less time, this book offers no such efficiencies. It is not concerned with squeezing more from the day. It is, instead, an appeal to live differently—to be differently. To unfasten yourself from the tyranny of ticking clocks and endless tasks. In the world that is slowly emerging, the ability to command your own time may prove to be the greatest privilege of all. But with that privilege comes a question: how do we step into such freedom without collapsing into anxiety or listlessness? How do we learn to rest without guilt, to enjoy without agenda, to inhabit the present moment without needing to monetise it?

This, in essence, is the invitation of *Time Abundance*: to reconsider time not merely as a schedule, but as a sacred dimension of human existence. Across the pages that follow, we'll walk together through a thorough, and at times unsettling, inquiry. We'll dismantle the myths that keep us tethered to overwork and over-identification with output. We'll question the moral overtones we attach to busyness, and the ways we've come to equate productivity with virtue. We'll look back—towards the agricultural rhythms that first structured our days, and the industrial systems that cemented our servitude to the clock. And from there, we'll look forward, towards a vision of life that privileges presence over pace.

But the task is not purely intellectual. To reclaim time, we must also engage emotionally and spiritually. We must reckon with our discomfort around stillness, and our suspicion of leisure. We must confront the quiet panic that rises when the noise of activity ceases. And yet, we must do so not merely to critique the status quo, but to imagine something better. A life where time is not measured in deliverables, but in depth. A world where we might grow, love, create—not in the margins of our schedules, but in the centre of our days.

At its heart, *Time Abundance* is not just a meditation on the luxury of free time. It is a manifesto for the return of our attention and energy to their rightful owners—ourselves. It marks a turning point, a chance to redefine what it means to lead a good life in an age that worships productivity. No longer must our worth be tallied by how many tasks we complete or how busy we appear. Instead, our value can begin to be rooted in how fully we inhabit our moments—how richly we live, rather than how much we produce.

Importantly, this is no call for escapism. It is not about running away from the world, but stepping more fully into it—with eyes open and spirit awake. Not less engaged, but more deeply so. The goal is not to do nothing, but to do what matters—on your terms, in your time. The future we're imagining here isn't one devoid of work, but one overflowing with life. And that future, though not yet fully realised, is already making itself known.

Let me be clear: this book is not a roadmap to traditional success. It won't teach you how to climb higher, earn more, or optimise faster. What it offers is both subtler and more profound: an invitation to rethink what success even means. To venture into the wide, open terrain of time freedom—a landscape where your days are governed not by external demands but by inner rhythms, intrinsic motivations, and personal meaning.

The questions at the heart of this book are among the oldest known to us. What is time, really? How does it shape who we become, what we value, how we relate to one another? Can we ever be truly free within time, or only from it? And if we could reclaim our hours, our days, our lives—what might we discover waiting there? The answers won't be handed to you as prescriptions. Instead, they'll unfold as provocations, as tools, as glimpses of possibility for those prepared to walk this path.

In a culture so relentlessly fixated on doing, we must relearn the art of being. In a system that prizes ceaseless output, we must dare to desire more life, not just more labour. Time freedom is not the fantasy of the privileged few; it is, or ought to be, a shared birthright. But to claim it, we must first liberate ourselves from the deeply held narratives that equate worth with work. We must take back the most essential of liberties: to live on our own terms, by our own cadence, with our own clarity of purpose.

This book is not simply about time. It is about reclaiming life—fully, tenderly, boldly. Welcome to *Time Abundance.*

Chapter 1
The Invention of Time Poverty

Time, in its earliest incarnations, moved in concert with the earth—measured not by devices, but by the shifting light, the changing seasons, the cyclical patterns of nature. It was communal, ambient, lived. But over centuries, something shifted. What was once an intuitive, organic rhythm slowly became regimented, repackaged, and eventually sold back to us as a finite resource to be budgeted and bartered. Time ceased to be something we lived within and became something we were told to manage.

The transformation was not accidental. It unfolded in stages—first through the structuring impulses of early civilisation, then through technological ingenuity, and finally, most insidiously, through the imperatives of capitalism. Where once the sun dictated the day's pace, we now obey clocks and calendars forged not in nature, but in factories and offices. Time, as we now experience it, bears little resemblance to its original form.

At the heart of this shift lies a pervasive and quietly corrosive belief: that time is scarce, that we are always running out of it, and that only through labour—through the monetisation of our minutes—can we justify our existence. This belief, so deeply embedded in the modern psyche, has a name: time poverty. It suggests that we never have enough time, that every day is a deficit to be resolved rather than a space to be lived.

But this, let us be clear, is a fiction—a carefully constructed illusion built atop centuries of increasingly rigid time discipline. From the agrarian calendars of early farmers to the relentless synchronisation of factory bells and digital alerts, we have inherited a worldview in which time is no longer a shared human experience but a metric of control. This chapter seeks to prise open that narrative and expose its scaffolding.

Consider, for a moment, the agrarian era. Time then was expansive, dictated by the rhythms of the land. Work followed daylight and the seasons, and though certainly not without hardship, life maintained a kind of temporal elasticity. There were pauses, rituals, festivals—moments where productivity ceded to presence. Contrast that with the industrial age, where time was chopped into hourly units, sold by the piece, and monitored with exacting precision. The very language of the era—"time is money," "killing time," "wasting time"—betrays a worldview in which time is no longer lived, but spent, traded, and lost.

It's not just the systems that changed, but our very sense of self. As we internalised the clock, we began to measure our worth by output, by deadlines met and goals achieved. Time became a measure of morality; to be idle was to be irresponsible. Even leisure was repurposed—rebranded as "recharging" so one might return to productivity renewed. In such a landscape, is it any wonder we feel perpetually behind?

Yet, buried within all this structure, this compulsion to optimise, there remains a flicker of something older—something gentler. The sense that time need not always be tracked or tamed. That perhaps, beneath the overlays of economic necessity, time is still what it once was: a space, a medium, a shared human inheritance. To believe otherwise is to accept a version of life that reduces our days to spreadsheets and stopwatches.

This chapter is not a nostalgic yearning for some lost golden age. Nor is it a naïve dismissal of the demands of contemporary life. But it is an attempt to reckon honestly with the cost of this collective belief in time poverty. If we are to reclaim our relationship with time, we must first understand how we came to view it as something to be conquered. We must look unflinchingly at the systems that shaped this view—and ask, with sincerity and courage, whether they still deserve to govern us.

From Sundials to Timesheets

In the early days of civilisation, time was largely shaped by the cycles of nature. The agrarian calendar marked the seasons, the ebb and flow of harvest, and the rhythm of work determined by the sun's arc across the sky. People lived in synchrony with their environment, their daily tasks aligned with the natural progression of the day. While these tasks could be demanding, they were not imposed by any abstract system; they were grounded in real-world necessity, in the demands of survival. Life had a rhythm that was defined not by the clock, but by nature itself, an organic and cyclical way of being.

The advent of the sundial, a device that could measure the passing of time through the movement of the sun, represented the first steps toward structuring time beyond nature's flow. While the sundial itself didn't dictate work hours, it introduced the idea that time could be measured, divided, and used as a standard. Yet it was still linked to the natural world, its usage reflecting the world's inherent cycles. The leap to something more rigid came with the rise of industrialisation.

With the Industrial Revolution, time took on a more mechanical and transactional nature. The rise of the factory system, where workers were expected to be present for precise hours of the day, gave birth to a new era in which time was dictated by the clock. The clock, once a tool for the wealthy, became ubiquitous. The introduction of time sheets and factory whistles now dictated the boundaries of human activity. Time, in the industrial era, was no longer tied to natural cycles but became the ultimate currency, a resource to be measured and maximised. Workers were no longer free to align their efforts with the rhythm of nature but were tethered to the demands of a machine, with hours specified down to the minute. This mechanical view of time shifted not only the way work was organised but also the way we viewed ourselves: *we* became the machines, governed by the same tick-tock precision.

In this era, time was commodified in the strictest sense. It was a measure of human productivity, and thus, human worth was determined by how much time one could sell, how much one could "produce" within those hours. The factory clock became the invisible ruler of human existence, and the individual's sense of value became increasingly tied to their ability to *fill* those hours with work. This time discipline permeated not just work but also leisure, as the notion of having time "off" was slowly replaced with the need to "make use of" that time, to find ways to maximise it, to *do* something with it.

Scarcity Scripts and the Fear of Stillness

The legacy of industrial time discipline extends far beyond the factory floor. It has embedded itself in the very way we think about time, our relationship with it, and, ultimately, ourselves. In modern life, we are not merely bound by schedules—we are bound by the unspoken belief that we must *earn* our right to rest, to pause, to simply *be*. Rest has become synonymous with laziness; stillness with failure. These internalised beliefs about time—the so-called "scarcity scripts"—are rooted in centuries of cultural conditioning. We have been taught to believe that time is scarce and that we are morally obligated to "fill" it. The very idea that we can *afford* to do nothing, to rest without guilt, feels foreign and, for many, shameful.

These psychological frameworks, inherited from an era where labour and time were directly connected, create an almost visceral fear of idleness. The thought of doing nothing—of resting without a clear, productive outcome—evokes deep anxiety. In a world that constantly pushes us to achieve, to produce, and to demonstrate our worth, the pause, the gap, the moment of stillness becomes a threat. Stillness, in this context, becomes an enemy to productivity, to success, and ultimately to self-worth. In a sense, we have internalised the factory model of time discipline to such an extent that we are unable to disconnect from it, even when we are free from its external constraints. It has shaped our very identity, embedding the belief that the value of our time can only be measured by how much we are *doing.* To rest, to allow ourselves the luxury of stillness, is to risk being perceived as unproductive, as unworthy, as "lazy."

Yet, in truth, the fear of stillness is not only psychological—it is also deeply societal. From the earliest days of industrialisation, work and productivity became the defining pillars of identity. This equation of value with activity—what I call the "scarcity script"—has shaped everything from our educational systems to our media, where messages of hustle culture, endless growth, and "grinding" dominate. The pervasive notion that time must always be filled with purpose and output has led us to view time as a commodity, and by doing so, we have stripped it of its richness and potential for personal rejuvenation. The irony is that we have become so focused on the scarcity of time that we have forgotten to question the true value of what we're spending it on. This chapter will delve deeper into these internalised beliefs, offering a framework for unlearning the fear of stillness and finding the courage to rest without guilt.

What We Talk About When We Talk About Time

The language we use to discuss time—terms like *spending*, *wasting*, *investing*, and *saving*—speaks volumes about how we view our relationship with it. These metaphors frame our experience of temporality as a transaction, an exchange in which time is an asset to be managed, optimised, and, ultimately, exploited. Time is something to be *spent* wisely, *invested* in the right places, and *saved* for later use. Even the term "time management" reveals the transactional nature of how we view time: as something that must be controlled, maximised, and optimised.

Take, for instance, the term *wasting time.* The very notion that time can be "wasted" implies that there is an inherent value to every passing moment, that each second must be spent in a productive or valuable way. It evokes the image of time slipping through our fingers, lost forever, with no way to recover it. Yet, the term itself betrays a narrow, scarcity-driven understanding of time—one that disregards the notion that time *spent* in reflection, in rest, or in pure enjoyment has intrinsic worth beyond its productivity. In truth, these "wasted" moments may be the most restorative and creatively enriching experiences we can have.

On the other hand, the metaphor of *investing* time suggests that every action or interaction is calculated, measured, and geared towards a return, whether it's financial or personal. We are encouraged to treat time as a resource to be optimised and leveraged. And yet, this "investment" mentality often leads us to overlook the joy of the present moment, the simple satisfaction of being alive in time, without the constant pressure to *do* or *achieve.*

These metaphors, deeply ingrained in our collective consciousness, reinforce the scarcity mindset around time. They present time as a finite resource that must be "used" or "saved" in order to maintain its value, and in doing so, they frame rest, leisure, and spontaneity as indulgences, rather than essential components of a balanced, fulfilled life. To truly embrace time abundance, we must break free from these linguistic and conceptual traps. We must learn to reclaim time from the strictures of transaction and begin to understand it not as something to be controlled, but as a space to be inhabited fully, a gift to be cherished rather than bartered.

This chapter is an invitation to reimagine the way we understand time. It will explore how our historical relationship with time has led us to construct a life in which we are constantly tethered to the clock, bound by the demands of productivity and the relentless pursuit of efficiency. But it will also offer a vision of what is possible when we free ourselves from these artificial constraints, allowing us to experience time as something more expansive and meaningful than we have ever been taught to believe. Time is not a resource to be consumed; it is a domain to be explored, to be savoured, to be *lived.* And it is time we reclaimed it.

The Mythology of Busyness

In modern society, to be busy is to be virtuous. The phrase "I'm too busy" has become the default response to any inquiry about one's wellbeing, and increasingly, the busier we are, the more valuable we seem. From CEOs to students, from stay-at-home parents to artists, the constant narrative of busyness has woven itself into the very fabric of our identity. In a world driven by the relentless pursuit of productivity, the idea that being busy is inherently noble has taken root deeply within our collective psyche. But beneath this surface, the mythology of busyness not only masks deeper anxieties but also shields us from confronting the lack of meaning and systemic inefficiencies that plague our everyday lives. What is busyness really about? Is it a sign of success, or a convenient veil for insecurity, dissatisfaction, and societal pressures?

The roots of this "busyness worship" lie in the industrial age, when productivity became the cornerstone of both individual success and national progress. With the rise of the factory system and the deskilling of labour, time became a commodity—something to be measured, maximised, and leveraged for economic output. From there, an association formed in Western cultures: productivity became equated with moral worth. It was no longer about *doing* something meaningful, but *doing* something—anything, in fact—that would yield measurable results. To be constantly occupied, constantly working, was to be virtuous, responsible, and, in the eyes of many, indispensable.

Yet this belief persists long after the industrial system has receded into the background of our economies. Today, in an era where many of the tasks we once took for granted can be automated or outsourced, the myth of busyness is more pervasive than ever. We live in a culture where the value of our time is measured not by what we achieve in that time, but by how much we occupy ourselves. The phrase "I'm busy" has transformed into a status symbol, a form of social currency. But what does it truly signify? Is it a reflection of meaningful work, or is it just a mask for something far more troubling?

The Busyness Illusion: Masking Anxiety and Lack of Meaning

To understand the mythology of busyness, we must first interrogate the underlying reasons we are so compelled to maintain the illusion of constant activity. The truth is, busyness often functions as a coping mechanism. The faster we move, the less time we have to reflect on the underlying emptiness that may be festering within us. If we keep our minds preoccupied with tasks, emails, meetings, and to-do lists, we never have to confront the uncomfortable questions of meaning and purpose. In this way, busyness is a shield, protecting us from deeper anxieties that we may not even be aware of.

This is particularly evident when we look at the psychological toll that busyness can take on individuals. In the modern workplace, particularly in high-pressure environments, busyness has become a cultural norm. Employees are expected not just to perform well, but to be constantly *engaged*, *on* at all times, and *available*. In many industries, the expectation of perpetual busyness has created a cycle of stress, burnout, and anxiety. Studies have shown that workers in hyper-competitive sectors, such as finance or tech, report higher levels of stress and mental health issues than those in less demanding fields. The myth that busyness equals success often leads to the false belief that being overworked is a sign of competence and importance, when in reality it can be a symptom of poor time management, ineffective systems, or unhealthy work cultures.

Take, for example, the rise of "hustle culture." This popularised mindset elevates the state of constant activity to something that is almost sacred. The idea that "sleep is for the weak" or that "you need to grind 24/7 to make it" has become a mantra for a generation. Yet this culture, far from promoting meaningful work, breeds exhaustion and dissatisfaction. It is no coincidence that the very same generation of entrepreneurs and creatives that peddle these ideas often face burnout, depression, and a sense of disillusionment with the very systems they champion. In short, the busyness myth is a paradox: while it promises success and fulfilment, it often delivers anxiety and fatigue.

Furthermore, busyness can serve as a distraction from existential questions that, while uncomfortable, are crucial to human wellbeing. What am I actually working towards? What does this work mean for my life and the world around me? These questions are easily swept under the rug when we're too busy to pause and reflect. In a culture that celebrates "getting things done" rather than questioning what is truly worth doing, busyness becomes an evasive strategy. We avoid confronting the uncomfortable possibility that the things we are filling our time with may not matter in the grand scheme of our lives, that our daily activity might be ultimately meaningless.

The Moral Fallacy: Productivity as a Measure of Worth

The idea that productivity is inherently moral is one of the most pernicious aspects of the mythology of busyness. It implies that the more you do, the more worthy you are. This equation of activity with virtue runs deep in Western thought, embedded in religious, philosophical, and economic systems. From Protestant work ethics to the glorification of overwork in capitalist societies, there has been a long-standing belief that "good" people work hard, while "bad" people are idle. The more you accomplish, the more *you* accomplish, the greater your value—both to society and to yourself.

This ideology, deeply ingrained in our social structures, distorts our understanding of what it means to live a meaningful life. It suggests that work is an intrinsic good, and that leisure—especially unstructured leisure—is a waste. As a result, we develop an unhealthy relationship with both our work and our rest. For instance, many people experience deep guilt when they take time off, even for activities like relaxation or self-care, because they are taught to view rest as a moral failing, an indulgence that detracts from the "real" work that they are supposed to be doing. The implication here is clear: only through *doing*—through busy, measurable activity—can we prove our worthiness. And yet, this logic is profoundly flawed.

Psychologist and author Tim Kreider's reflection on this in his essay *The "Busy" Trap* illustrates this cultural phenomenon perfectly. He writes, "Busyness serves as a kind of hedge against emptiness." The more we do, the less we have to confront the emptiness of a life filled with pointless activity, with a lack of fulfilment. The moralisation of productivity is not only an ethical misstep, but a dangerous one, because it undermines our capacity to live intentionally, to choose our activities with purpose and care. It forces us into a cycle of activity for its own sake—pushing us away from those quiet moments that can bring clarity, creativity, and meaning.

Unpacking the Myth: A New Perspective on Busyness

So, if busyness is not inherently virtuous, and if productivity does not equal moral worth, what does this mean for our relationship with time and work? What happens when we begin to see busyness for what it truly is: a social construct, a myth that serves to distract us from the deeper needs of our lives?

The first step is recognising that our value does not lie in our productivity. Our worth is not measured by how much we do, but by how we *are* in the world. To resist the mythology of busyness is to recognise that there is an inherent dignity in stillness, in rest, and in slow, intentional work. We need to reframe our relationship with time—not as a commodity to be spent or wasted, but as a canvas on which to create lives of meaning, joy, and presence. This shift in thinking requires us to dismantle the cultural pressures that equate busyness with virtue, and instead, embrace a worldview that honours quality over quantity, depth over breadth.

It's also crucial to question the systems that demand busyness in the first place. The myth of busyness is perpetuated not just by social norms, but by systemic inefficiencies that demand more from workers without delivering true value in return. From corporate structures that value face-time over meaningful contributions, to educational systems that prize "overwork" over holistic development, our institutions often reward busyness at the expense of actual progress. If we are to break free from the mythology of busyness, we must also call for systems that prioritise genuine, meaningful work—work that fosters well-being, personal growth, and societal benefit.

The Call for Mindful Living

The mythology of busyness is a deeply ingrained cultural narrative that equates our self-worth with the quantity of our activity. It convinces us that the more we do, the more virtuous we become. But as we've seen, busyness often masks deeper anxieties and unacknowledged dissatisfaction, and it is not the marker of true success or moral worth. To break free from this illusion requires us to reimagine the role of work and time in our lives—not as something to be constantly maximised or filled, but as something to be lived intentionally. In doing so, we move towards a more meaningful relationship with both our work and our rest, where productivity is valued not for its own sake, but as a tool for achieving a more fulfilling, balanced life.

The Mythology of Busyness

In modern society, to be busy is to be virtuous. The phrase "I'm too busy" has become the default response to any inquiry about one's wellbeing, and increasingly, the busier we are, the more valuable we seem. From CEOs to students, from stay-at-home parents to artists, the constant narrative of busyness has woven itself into the very fabric of our identity. In a world driven by the relentless pursuit of productivity, the idea that being busy is inherently noble has taken root deeply within our collective psyche. But beneath this surface, the mythology of busyness not only masks deeper anxieties but also shields us from confronting the lack of meaning and systemic inefficiencies that plague our everyday lives. What is busyness really about? Is it a sign of success, or a convenient veil for insecurity, dissatisfaction, and societal pressures?

The roots of this "busyness worship" lie in the industrial age, when productivity became the cornerstone of both individual success and national progress. With the rise of the factory system and the deskilling of labour, time became a commodity—something to be measured, maximised, and leveraged for economic output. From there, an association formed in Western cultures: productivity became equated with moral worth. It was no longer about *doing* something meaningful, but *doing* something—anything, in fact—that would yield measurable results. To be constantly occupied, constantly working, was to be virtuous, responsible, and, in the eyes of many, indispensable.

Yet this belief persists long after the industrial system has receded into the background of our economies. Today, in an era where many of the tasks we once took for granted can be automated or outsourced, the myth of busyness is more pervasive than ever. We live in a culture where the value of our time is measured not by what we achieve in that time, but by how much we occupy ourselves. The phrase "I'm busy" has transformed into a status symbol, a form of social currency. But what does it truly signify? Is it a reflection of meaningful work, or is it just a mask for something far more troubling?

The Busyness Illusion: Masking Anxiety and Lack of Meaning

To understand the mythology of busyness, we must first interrogate the underlying reasons we are so compelled to maintain the illusion of constant activity. The truth is, busyness often functions as a coping mechanism. The faster we move, the less time we have to reflect on the underlying emptiness that may be festering within us. If we keep our minds preoccupied with tasks, emails, meetings, and to-do lists, we never have to confront the uncomfortable questions of meaning and purpose. In this way, busyness is a shield, protecting us from deeper anxieties that we may not even be aware of.

This is particularly evident when we look at the psychological toll that busyness can take on individuals. In the modern workplace, particularly in high-pressure environments, busyness has become a cultural norm. Employees are expected not just to perform well, but to be constantly *engaged*, *on* at all times, and *available*. In many industries, the expectation of perpetual busyness has created a cycle of stress, burnout, and anxiety. Studies have shown that workers in hyper-competitive sectors, such as finance or tech, report higher levels of stress and mental health issues than those in less demanding fields. The myth that busyness equals success often leads to the false belief that being overworked is a sign of competence and importance, when in reality it can be a symptom of poor time management, ineffective systems, or unhealthy work cultures.

Take, for example, the rise of "hustle culture." This popularised mindset elevates the state of constant activity to something that is almost sacred. The idea that "sleep is for the weak" or that "you need to grind 24/7 to make it" has become a mantra for a generation. Yet this culture, far from promoting meaningful work, breeds exhaustion and dissatisfaction. It is no coincidence that the very same generation of entrepreneurs and creatives that peddle these ideas often face burnout, depression, and a sense of disillusionment with the very systems they champion. In short, the busyness myth is a paradox: while it promises success and fulfilment, it often delivers anxiety and fatigue.

Furthermore, busyness can serve as a distraction from existential questions that, while uncomfortable, are crucial to human wellbeing. What am I actually working towards? What does this work mean for my life and the world around me? These questions are easily swept under the rug when we're too busy to pause and reflect. In a culture that celebrates "getting things done" rather than questioning what is truly worth doing, busyness becomes an evasive strategy. We avoid confronting the uncomfortable possibility that the things we are filling our time with may not matter in the grand scheme of our lives, that our daily activity might be ultimately meaningless.

The Moral Fallacy: Productivity as a Measure of Worth

The idea that productivity is inherently moral is one of the most pernicious aspects of the mythology of busyness. It implies that the more you do, the more worthy you are. This equation of activity with virtue runs deep in Western thought, embedded in religious, philosophical, and economic systems. From Protestant work ethics to the glorification of overwork in capitalist societies, there has been a long-standing belief that "good" people work hard, while "bad" people are idle. The more you accomplish, the more *you* accomplish, the greater your value—both to society and to yourself.

This ideology, deeply ingrained in our social structures, distorts our understanding of what it means to live a meaningful life. It suggests that work is an intrinsic good, and that leisure—especially unstructured leisure—is a waste. As a result, we develop an unhealthy relationship with both our work and our rest. For instance, many people experience deep guilt when they take time off, even for activities like relaxation or self-care, because they are taught to view rest as a moral failing, an indulgence that detracts from the "real" work that they are supposed to be doing. The implication here is clear: only through *doing*—through busy, measurable activity—can we prove our worthiness. And yet, this logic is profoundly flawed.

Psychologist and author Tim Kreider's reflection on this in his essay *The "Busy" Trap* illustrates this cultural phenomenon perfectly. He writes, "Busyness serves as a kind of hedge against emptiness." The more we do, the less we have to confront the emptiness of a life filled with pointless activity, with a lack of fulfilment. The moralisation of productivity is not only an ethical misstep, but a dangerous one, because it undermines our capacity to live intentionally, to choose our activities with purpose and care. It forces us into a cycle of activity for its own sake—pushing us away from those quiet moments that can bring clarity, creativity, and meaning.

Unpacking the Myth: A New Perspective on Busyness

So, if busyness is not inherently virtuous, and if productivity does not equal moral worth, what does this mean for our relationship with time and work? What happens when we begin to see busyness for what it truly is: a social construct, a myth that serves to distract us from the deeper needs of our lives?

The first step is recognising that our value does not lie in our productivity. Our worth is not measured by how much we do, but by how we *are* in the world. To resist the mythology of busyness is to recognise that there is an inherent dignity in stillness, in rest, and in slow, intentional work. We need to reframe our relationship with time—not as a commodity to be spent or wasted, but as a canvas on which to create lives of meaning, joy, and presence. This shift in thinking requires us to dismantle the cultural pressures that equate busyness with virtue, and instead, embrace a worldview that honours quality over quantity, depth over breadth.

It's also crucial to question the systems that demand busyness in the first place. The myth of busyness is perpetuated not just by social norms, but by systemic inefficiencies that demand more from workers without delivering true value in return. From corporate structures that value face-time over meaningful contributions, to educational systems that prize "overwork" over holistic development, our institutions often reward busyness at the expense of actual progress. If we are to break free from the mythology of busyness, we must also call for systems that prioritise genuine, meaningful work—work that fosters well-being, personal growth, and societal benefit.

Conclusion: The Call for Mindful Living

The mythology of busyness is a deeply ingrained cultural narrative that equates our self-worth with the quantity of our activity. It convinces us that the more we do, the more virtuous we become. But as we've seen, busyness often masks deeper anxieties and unacknowledged dissatisfaction, and it is not the marker of true success or moral worth. To break free from this illusion requires us to reimagine the role of work and time in our lives—not as something to be constantly maximised or filled, but as something to be lived intentionally. In doing so, we move towards a more meaningful relationship with both our work and our rest, where productivity is valued not for its own sake, but as a tool for achieving a more fulfilling, balanced life.

From Sundials to Timesheets

The measurement of time is one of the most profound transformations in human history—one so deeply embedded in our daily lives that we scarcely pause to reflect on its origins. Time, once a natural, cyclical force tied to the rhythms of the earth, has gradually been redefined as something to be controlled, measured, and optimised. From the earliest days of civilisation, when our ancestors relied on the sun's path across the sky to structure their days, to the rise of the industrial time clock that now governs the rhythm of modern life, time has evolved from an organic concept to a commodity. This transformation is not merely technological; it reflects the changing ways in which we, as individuals and societies, relate to work, rest, and ultimately, existence itself. Understanding this evolution is crucial not only for appreciating the historical trajectory of time discipline but for recognising the ways in which these artificial constructs continue to dictate our lives.

The transition from agrarian time systems, governed by the cycles of nature, to the mechanised timekeeping of the industrial era marks one of the most significant shifts in human history. It wasn't just the introduction of clocks or the formalisation of hours; it was the imposition of an entirely new relationship with time itself—a relationship that would come to define the modern working world. Time, once seen as something to flow with, became something to be measured, optimised, and above all, controlled.

The Agrarian Cycle: Time in Harmony with Nature

Before the industrial era, the primary markers of time were natural: the rising and setting of the sun, the changing seasons, and the ebb and flow of agricultural tasks. In agrarian societies, work was dictated by the seasons, the cycles of planting, harvesting, and rest. While the lives of farmers and labourers were undoubtedly demanding, their time was not governed by an arbitrary set of hours imposed from without, but by the rhythms of nature itself. The day began with the sunrise and ended with the setting sun, and the flow of work adapted to the environmental conditions, not to the ticking of a clock.

For example, during harvest season, workdays were longer, extending into the evening, while during winter, shorter daylight hours allowed for more rest. Time was divided according to necessity, with natural processes determining both the work and the rest periods. There was no universal "standard" workday, no rigid timetable of when to start or finish a task. Time was lived through, not controlled. This kind of time awareness, which is now often referred to as *seasonal* or *natural time*, had a far more flexible, human scale.

It's important to note that even in agrarian societies, the concept of time wasn't entirely unstructured. The rhythms of communal labour, religious observances, and the needs of the harvest did impose a kind of time discipline. Yet, it was not the cold, impersonal mechanism of the clock that governed this discipline. Instead, it was the community's shared understanding of nature's cycles—marked by the phases of the moon, the passage of seasons, and the growth of crops—that determined when work could be undertaken and when it must cease.

This system of time was still far more attuned to the natural world, and arguably more humane, than the mechanised constructs that would soon emerge. But it was also not without its stresses, particularly in times of famine or poor harvests. However, even during these difficult periods, the imposition of time was fundamentally different from the rigid constraints that would come with the rise of the industrial time clock.

The Industrial Revolution: The Birth of the Time Clock

The transition from agrarian time to industrial time was not merely the adoption of new tools, but a fundamental shift in the nature of labour and life itself. With the rise of factories, time became both a means of organisation and a tool of control. The agricultural rhythm of life, with its natural ebb and flow, was replaced by the clock—the mechanical and impersonal device that would govern the lives of workers from dawn until dusk.

The introduction of the time clock in factories was revolutionary, but not necessarily in the way that was immediately beneficial to workers. In an agricultural economy, time was divided by need and nature; in the industrial system, time became the property of the employer, with workers required to adhere to a set number of hours that would be strictly monitored. The famous phrase "time is money" was born out of this period, with time becoming an economic asset rather than a natural resource. Workers were no longer paid for the value of their labour or the output of their work, but for the number of hours they spent in a factory or workshop. The clock, which had once been a tool for personal organisation, became a tool for systemic control.

The invention of the time clock—and the advent of timekeeping practices—became essential to industrial production. Time was now fragmented, quantified, and segmented into hourly units that could be measured, regulated, and optimised. The factory whistle signalled the beginning and end of work, and the precise marking of time became synonymous with productivity. With this new structure came a fundamental shift in the way people understood the value of their labour and, by extension, their lives. Time was no longer something one could flow with or adapt to; it was something that needed to be controlled and filled.

This system marked the beginning of what we now recognise as the "nine-to-five" workday, and the notion that work time should be strictly separated from personal or leisure time. The division of life into neatly packaged, segmented units of time would shape the experience of work for generations. The factory worker, then, became a symbol of modern life, tethered to the clock and constantly pressured to maximise productivity.

The Impact of Time Discipline on Society

The industrialisation of time created a new, highly regimented approach to daily life that remains with us today. The imposition of artificial time systems—whether in factories, schools, or even governmental offices—had profound implications for how society functioned. The rise of "clock time" created a clear distinction between work time and personal time, which was not present in earlier agrarian societies.

For one, time became a commodity—something to be exchanged and traded. As the workday became regimented, the focus shifted to making the most out of every minute. Efficiency, productivity, and optimisation became the guiding principles of work, even if the actual results did not align with these goals. This was particularly evident in the early days of factory work, when workers were expected to work at the pace of machines, often with minimal rest or opportunity for reflection. The notion that time was inherently valuable became entrenched in society, with less and less attention given to how time could be spent meaningfully, creatively, or at rest.

This mentality continued to dominate Western cultures throughout the 19th and 20th centuries, as the time discipline of the factory spread across all sectors of life. In the post-industrial era, the imposition of "clock time" has evolved into what we now recognise as the culture of overwork and burnout. Our lives are dictated by an incessant need to fill every moment with some form of task or productivity, driven by the myth that we must always be doing something to prove our worth.

Today, this artificial structure of time continues to impact not just how we work, but how we experience life. It drives the culture of constant activity and productivity that defines modern society—whether it is the pursuit of academic success, career advancement, or the need to always be available in a hyper-connected world. The sense of urgency and efficiency that we associate with "doing" permeates everything, from our work to our social interactions. The pressures of living in a society governed by artificial constructs of time are immense. Our relationship with time has shifted from being something organic and cyclical to something that is rigid, transactional, and ever-demanding.

The Future: Reclaiming Time

The question we must ask ourselves today is: can we ever return to a more harmonious, natural understanding of time? Can we create systems that allow for the organic flow of life, or are we forever bound by the ticking of the clock?

As we enter an era where AI and automation have the potential to radically change how work is organised, it is possible—perhaps even essential—that we revisit our relationship with time. Instead of living by rigid schedules and prescribed hours, we could begin to reclaim the natural, seasonal rhythms that once governed our days. We could embrace flexibility and adaptability, acknowledging that the human experience of time is not something that can be reduced to mechanical efficiency.

The evolution of time, from the sundial to the timesheet, has been a story of shifting human needs, technological progress, and the growing dominance of systems that dictate our lives. Yet it is not just a history of oppression, but also a story of possibility. As we gain the power to rewrite the rules of time, perhaps we can find new ways to experience it—one that is less about regulation and more about presence. The future of time, after all, may just be about reintroducing the human element into the equation.

Scarcity Scripts and the Fear of Stillness

In a world increasingly defined by the demand for constant productivity and activity, there exists a pervasive belief that rest—especially unstructured, idle rest—is both indulgent and morally suspect. To be idle, to *do nothing*, is often equated with a lack of discipline, drive, or ambition. The mere thought of allowing ourselves the luxury of time without a task to complete can stir feelings of guilt, anxiety, or shame. But why has such a deeply ingrained cultural framework emerged, and why does it persist so strongly in the face of evidence that downtime and stillness are essential for mental health, creativity, and long-term productivity?

At the heart of this issue lies what I call *scarcity scripts*—internalised beliefs and assumptions about time, worth, and activity that distort our understanding of what it means to live a fulfilling life. These scripts, inherited from generations past, are woven into the fabric of modern society, shaping the way we think about time, effort, and the value of our lives. They are psychological frameworks that have taught us to fear stillness and associate it with worthlessness, idleness, or failure. However, this is a mythology that deserves to be dismantled. The first step towards reclaiming a balanced, meaningful relationship with time is recognising and challenging these scripts.

The Psychological Roots of Scarcity

The concept of *scarcity* is central to the modern experience of time. In economic theory, scarcity refers to the fundamental problem that resources are limited and must be allocated efficiently. Yet, this economic model has been projected onto our relationship with time itself. Just as we have been taught to optimise material resources, we are now conditioned to optimise time—every moment must be accounted for, every hour "used" in a productive way. In many ways, we have internalised the idea that time, like money, is finite and must be maximised or saved for future use.

The roots of these scarcity scripts can be traced back to early economic structures, where time itself was a commodity. In agrarian societies, time was naturally divided between periods of labour and rest, dictated by the seasons, the daylight hours, and the rhythms of nature. But with the rise of industrialisation, time became increasingly regimented. Factory work, with its emphasis on fixed hours and productivity, ushered in an era where the value of a person's labour was tied directly to the number of hours they could work. The idea of time as a scarce resource was solidified in the consciousness of both the working and middle classes, where time could not be "wasted" on non-productive activities.

By the time the knowledge economy emerged, this internalised notion of time as a finite resource had taken hold. The idea that time must be allocated to tasks with measurable outcomes has become deeply ingrained in modern consciousness. The same people who grew up learning the value of hard work and productivity are now unable to sit still without feeling the weight of guilt or inadequacy. This internalised pressure to be constantly productive—whether through work, exercise, or constant self-improvement—leaves no room for rest, reflection, or simply being present.

The Fear of Stillness: A Modern Epidemic

One of the most insidious consequences of these scarcity scripts is the fear of stillness, a fear that permeates our daily lives. The idea that doing nothing is a form of failure or laziness has become so widespread that it often goes unquestioned. Yet, this fear of stillness, while deeply cultural, is not innate. It is learned—a product of centuries of societal conditioning that has equated stillness with weakness, worthlessness, and moral failure.

This fear can be traced back to the moral and cultural narratives embedded in the work ethic. From Protestant Christianity's emphasis on industriousness and thrift, to the capitalist ideal of the "self-made" person who is constantly striving to achieve, the dominant cultural messages have long been that rest is something to be earned, not a natural or necessary state of being. If one is not working, one is seen as *not* contributing to society, and by extension, one is not contributing to their own success. The American dream, for example, has long been built on the notion that hard work is the path to success and that leisure or inactivity is reserved for the wealthy elite, rather than a human right for all.

In practical terms, this fear manifests in various ways. Take, for instance, the way many people approach their weekends or vacations. Rather than viewing these as opportunities for rest, recovery, and rejuvenation, many feel compelled to fill every moment with an activity. This can range from catching up on chores to engaging in an endless stream of social media, exercising, or consuming content—anything that can be "counted" as productive. The same impulse that drives people to overwork also compels them to over-schedule their free time, leaving no space for what might be the most restorative activity of all: *nothing*. This constant state of striving has been linked to higher levels of anxiety, depression, and burnout, as people exhaust themselves in pursuit of a productivity ideal that offers no real emotional or spiritual fulfilment.

The fear of stillness is not just a personal struggle—it is a societal problem. We live in a culture that constantly reinforces the need to *do*, and this imperative to be constantly active is amplified by the digital age. Our smartphones, social media, and work emails never stop pinging, ensuring that we are always "on." This never-ending flow of information reinforces the idea that there is always something that needs to be done, that we can never afford to stop. But paradoxically, this state of perpetual motion leads us further away from meaningful action. It diminishes our capacity to be present, to cultivate relationships, or to engage in the deep, reflective work that truly nourishes us. In our quest for productivity, we often forgo the very things that make life worth living.

The Psychological Toll of Scarcity Scripts

The consequences of living within the confines of scarcity scripts and fearing stillness are profound. They contribute not only to chronic stress and burnout but also to a sense of existential emptiness. We may find ourselves questioning: "What am I really working towards?" In a society that elevates "doing" above "being," we lose sight of the inherent value of rest and reflection. We forget that human beings are not machines designed to produce endlessly, but complex creatures whose lives are enriched by stillness, by moments of introspection, and by the simple act of being present.

Psychologists and sociologists have pointed out that this overemphasis on productivity is, in part, a response to the fear of facing uncomfortable emotions or confronting deeper questions about the meaning of life. Stillness forces us to slow down, to look inward, and often, to face the things we've been avoiding. Whether it's confronting our own mortality, addressing unresolved emotional issues, or simply acknowledging the dissonance between our ideals and our reality, stillness allows us to pause and ask life's more challenging questions. Yet for many, the fear of this confrontation is too great. As a result, people fill their lives with noise—both literal and metaphorical—as a way of avoiding the discomfort of stillness. But in doing so, they forfeit the opportunity for the kind of personal growth and clarity that only arises through moments of deep introspection and rest.

The psychological toll is not just individual. These scarcity scripts and the associated fear of stillness have broader social consequences. They perpetuate a cycle of overwork and burnout, feeding into corporate cultures that demand constant productivity from employees, without regard for their well-being. Organisations that operate under the assumption that workers must always be "doing" to be valuable contribute to a society where mental health crises are endemic, and work-life balance is a distant ideal.

Breaking the Cycle: Reclaiming Rest and Meaning

The antidote to this cultural and psychological trap lies in reimagining our relationship with time and value. The first step is recognising that rest is not a luxury or an indulgence, but a necessity for mental health, creativity, and long-term productivity. In fact, research has shown that rest and downtime are essential for cognitive function, emotional regulation, and problem-solving. The notion that we must be constantly productive in order to be worthy is a fallacy—one that harms both our wellbeing and our ability to contribute meaningfully to the world.

Reclaiming rest requires actively challenging the scarcity scripts that have been internalised over generations. It means giving ourselves permission to do nothing, to pause, and to simply *be*. This does not mean abandoning responsibility or ambition, but rather recognising that our value does not lie in the number of tasks we can complete or the hours we can work. Our worth is intrinsic, independent of our productivity. Learning to rest without guilt is a radical act of self-acceptance and self-care—one that honours our humanity and acknowledges our need for balance.

The fear of stillness, like all fears, can be overcome. But it requires a shift in mindset, one that places value not just on doing, but on being. When we embrace stillness, we reclaim our time, our health, and our sense of purpose. It is only through this radical reimagining of how we relate to time and work that we can begin to create lives that are not just productive, but meaningful.

What We Talk About When We Talk About Time

Time is one of the most fundamental and yet elusive concepts in human experience. It governs our lives, shapes our identities, and dictates the way we interact with the world around us. But what is fascinating—and often overlooked—is the language we use to talk about time. The metaphors we employ to describe time influence not only how we understand it, but how we experience it. From "spending" time to "investing" it, the words we choose reinforce certain beliefs about time's value, its scarcity, and its role in shaping our lives. These metaphors are not just linguistic flourishes; they are deeply embedded in our cultural consciousness and reflect long-standing assumptions about what is worth doing with our limited hours on this earth.

At the heart of this is a paradox: time, in its essence, is both the most precious and the most abundant resource we have. And yet, the language we use around it often leads us to treat it as if it is endlessly fleeting, constantly slipping through our fingers. We are constantly encouraged to "make the most of it," to "save it," to "invest" it wisely, as though it is a limited currency—one that must be guarded and accounted for at all costs. But where does this perspective come from, and how does it shape our lives?

The Currency of Time: Spending, Wasting, and Saving

One of the most ubiquitous metaphors for time is that of *spending*. We talk about time as if it were money, a finite resource that can be "spent" on various activities, whether productive or not. This metaphor is so ingrained in our thinking that it often goes unquestioned, despite its inherent implications. If time is something we spend, it must also be something we *lose*—the notion of waste is implicit in the concept of spending. Just as we can waste money by spending it frivolously, we can waste time by spending it on activities deemed unproductive or unnecessary.

But what does it mean to "spend" time? In the most straightforward sense, it implies that time is something we give away, something that diminishes as we use it. And just like money, there is an underlying assumption that we must be careful not to spend it too recklessly. The result is a pervasive sense of urgency, a need to ensure that every moment counts. Time becomes something we are always in danger of running out of, an account that must be carefully managed.

Yet, *spending* time is not inherently wasteful. It all depends on how we view the transaction. If we regard time spent on leisure, creativity, or rest as a worthy expenditure, then we expand our definition of "spending" to include activities that nourish us, even if they don't yield immediate or tangible results. But the dominant cultural narrative surrounding time tends to equate productivity with worth, often pushing us to view time spent on non-task-oriented activities as a "loss." In this sense, time becomes a commodity, to be maximised and carefully guarded.

Take, for example, the way we talk about "wasting" time. The very phrase carries a negative judgement about the value of what we are doing. Wasting time suggests that we are engaging in something frivolous, unimportant, or lazy. It carries with it a moral implication, as though our worth is diminished when we choose not to engage in tasks that society deems valuable or necessary. Yet, there is an irony here—many of the most enriching, life-affirming experiences happen precisely in moments of "wasted" time. The long conversations with a friend, the afternoon spent reading a book that takes us out of the world, or the hours spent doing nothing at all. These moments, often considered "wasted," are often where we find meaning, creativity, and joy.

The concept of *saving* time follows a similar line of thought. We speak of saving time as if it were a finite resource that must be preserved for later use. In modern life, time-saving devices and techniques—whether in the form of digital tools, efficient workflows, or life hacks—are sold as the ultimate solution to our overloaded schedules. But what are we saving time for? The implication here is that time must be "used" for something—saved up in order to be spent later. This leads to an interesting paradox: in our efforts to save time, we may find that we are actually spending it in ways that reduce our capacity for meaningful rest or reflection. We may be *saving* time in one area of our life, only to *spend* it frantically elsewhere, without ever fully experiencing the "saved" moments for what they are.

Investing Time: The Logic of Productivity

Another powerful metaphor that shapes our understanding of time is the idea of *investing* time. To invest time, we assume that it will return dividends—whether in the form of personal growth, career advancement, or relationships. The idea of investing in something implies a future payoff, a return on the time spent. This metaphor is closely tied to the modern worldview that time, like money, should be used for future gain. The more time we "invest," the more we expect to receive in return.

The concept of investing time is particularly prominent in professional and educational spheres, where time spent working, learning, or networking is often viewed as an investment in one's future. The assumption is that every hour of effort will eventually lead to greater rewards. This metaphor is central to the capitalist ethos, where time is money, and time spent working is viewed as an investment in success.

However, this metaphor also carries its own set of risks. The notion of "investing" time creates an implicit pressure to always be working towards something, to always be focused on the future rather than the present. In our desire to "get ahead," we may lose sight of the value of the present moment, of the simple act of being, rather than always striving, achieving, or accumulating. When time is viewed solely as an investment, it reduces our ability to appreciate the time we have now, to savour the act of living for its own sake, not because it is tied to an outcome.

This relentless focus on the future can also lead to burnout, as we continually defer gratification and personal fulfilment in favour of future goals. The pressure to always "make the most" of our time can overwhelm us, leading to a state of constant busyness where we are never fully present in the moment. In this way, the metaphor of investing time, though powerful, may also reinforce a cycle of anxiety and stress, driving us to neglect the restorative power of rest, play, and reflection.

The Implications of Temporal Metaphors

The metaphors we use for time have a profound impact on how we experience it. When we view time as something to be spent, saved, or invested, we are implicitly adopting a view of time as a limited, scarce resource—something that must be accounted for at every turn. This perspective encourages a constant sense of urgency, pushing us to measure our value in terms of how much we do rather than who we are. The result is a culture of busyness, where time is constantly filled with tasks, goals, and productivity, leaving little room for spontaneity, rest, or reflection.

The impact of these metaphors is not just intellectual or emotional—it is also deeply social. The language we use around time shapes the structures of our workplaces, our educational systems, and our cultural norms. It influences how we approach work-life balance, how we structure our days, and even how we interact with others. The metaphors of time—whether spending, wasting, or investing—reinforce certain societal expectations about how we should live our lives. In this way, the language we use is not neutral; it actively shapes the way we experience the world and our place within it.

Reimagining Time: From Scarcity to Abundance

One of the most powerful tools for transforming our relationship with time is to reimagine the metaphors we use to describe it. What if, instead of "spending" time, we thought of it as *experiencing* time? What if we stopped thinking of time as a resource to be maximised, and instead saw it as an expansive space in which we can simply *be*, without the constant pressure to do or achieve? What if we embraced the idea that rest, leisure, and stillness are not wasted moments but essential parts of a life well-lived?

To truly reclaim time from the scarcity mindset, we must change the way we speak about it. Instead of viewing time as something to be spent or invested, we can begin to think of it as a canvas upon which we can create, explore, and live fully. Time is not a resource to be used up, but a gift to be savoured and cherished. When we shift our metaphors, we shift our experience of time itself—allowing us to live more freely, more meaningfully, and with greater presence in the moment.

By rethinking the language we use around time, we can transform our relationship with it. Instead of viewing time as a limited commodity, we can start to see it as an abundant resource—one that is ours to shape, to enjoy, and to use in ways that bring us true fulfilment.

Chapter 2
The End of Earning As We Know It

The world of work, once so firmly rooted in the grind of necessity, now finds itself on shifting sands. The long-standing equation that equates labour with livelihood—that survival demands struggle—may well be approaching its epilogue. With automation growing ever more sophisticated, artificial intelligence steadily encroaching upon tasks once thought uniquely human, and bold experiments in economic frameworks like universal basic income gaining traction, the traditional scaffolding of "earning a living" is beginning to crack. What once seemed immutable—that worth must be proven through labour—is now up for re-examination.

Work, for generations, was more than just a means to survive. It was our moral compass, our social anchor, our primary mode of identity. From the stories we're told as children to the milestones that mark adulthood, effort and industriousness have been cast as virtues, while toil has been painted as noble, even redemptive. To work was to contribute, to count, to claim one's rightful place in the world. But now, as the mechanics of economic survival become less entangled with human sweat and more entwined with algorithmic precision, the entire construct begins to wobble.

And with that wobble comes a profound discomfort. What becomes of selfhood when pay is no longer tethered to effort? How do we define our value in a world that no longer requires our labour? These are not abstract musings—they cut to the bone of identity, of purpose, of meaning. Particularly in more affluent parts of the world, where the cushion of technological advancement grows thicker by the year, the very foundations of personal and collective worth are being redrawn.

This chapter ventures into that terrain—the emotional tremors, the psychological upheaval, and the societal reckoning that accompany a decoupling of effort from earning. We will confront head-on the dogma that equates struggle with legitimacy. And we'll consider the uneasy silence that can follow when one's role in the economic machinery is no longer the defining thread of life.

For some, this shift will feel like a long-awaited liberation. Finally—at last—the freedom to step off the treadmill and breathe. To define a life by one's own measures rather than the demands of a job description. But for others, the change will be disorienting, even distressing. The routines that once anchored the day, the titles that offered identity, the work that once structured selfhood—all now potentially obsolete. And when that scaffolding falls away, what's left?

The decline of the rigid, industrial-era model—the regimented nine-to-five, the lifelong profession, the notion of "a job for life"—is not a forecast but a present reality. It is happening. Slowly in some places, more swiftly in others. Yet the implications are only beginning to be understood. If work no longer dictates who we are, then who, exactly, are we?

These are not idle speculations; they demand urgent attention. The architecture of society is being reshaped not just by machines, but by the values we attach to time, contribution, and human dignity. As earning detaches from effort, as roles shift and blur, we are being called—perhaps forced—to ask deeper questions about the human condition. And there is no turning back.

Beyond the Paycheck Paradigm

One of the most deeply ingrained assumptions of modern capitalism is that survival is inherently linked to work. The idea that we must earn a living by exchanging our time for money has shaped the very structure of our lives. Our days are divided between hours of work, which pay for the necessities of living, and brief moments of rest or leisure, which feel like rewards for a job well done. Yet, this structure is increasingly being dismantled. With the rise of automation and artificial intelligence, many jobs that were once considered essential to the functioning of society are now being performed by machines or algorithms. What does it mean when human labour is no longer the linchpin of economic survival?

The emotional residue left behind when income is no longer tied to effort is profound. For centuries, we have been conditioned to associate work with worthiness. Our identity has been shaped around our occupations: the title on our business cards, the tasks we perform, the hours we put in. Without these markers, who are we? If we no longer have to work to survive, what happens to the part of us that has always believed that our value lies in our productivity? The transition from a work-centric life to a more time-rich existence, where earning is decoupled from effort, can trigger a deep sense of disorientation.

This shift, while liberating for many, can also lead to a sense of loss. Without the framework of work to provide structure and meaning, individuals may feel adrift. This is particularly true in societies where work is not only the means of survival but also a source of status, identity, and social connection. In such contexts, the end of earning through toil can feel like the disintegration of the self.

Status, Identity, and the Role of Work

Work has long served as the primary scaffold of identity. It defines not only how we spend our time but also how we are seen by others. The titles we hold—be it doctor, teacher, engineer, or executive—are more than mere labels; they are a reflection of our societal value. In many ways, the work we do is the lens through which we view ourselves, and it is also how we are judged by society. When that relationship shifts or disappears entirely, what remains?

The end of earning through toil challenges the very foundations of identity. For decades, work has not just been a means to an end; it has been the axis around which our lives turn. Our sense of accomplishment, our social status, and even our self-esteem have been tightly bound to our jobs. This is particularly true in cultures that emphasise achievement, productivity, and competition. The belief that "we are what we do" is ingrained in much of the world's social and economic structure. But as automation continues to replace human labour, the question emerges: who are we when the thing we do to make a living is no longer available?

For some, the loss of work may lead to a crisis of meaning. Without work to provide identity, individuals may feel they are no longer contributing to society, leading to feelings of insignificance or purposelessness. This is especially true in cultures where productivity and achievement are deeply valued. The prospect of not working, or not working in the traditional sense, can feel uncomfortable, even unworthy. The anxiety that comes with the loss of work-related status is a very real psychological barrier to embracing a world where work no longer defines us.

Yet, for others, this new reality may offer a profound opportunity for liberation. With the disappearance of traditional work structures, people are free to redefine themselves. They are no longer beholden to the expectations of the corporate world or the 9-to-5 grind. They are free to explore new forms of meaning, whether through creativity, leisure, community involvement, or the pursuit of passion projects that were once sidelined in the race for economic survival. In this sense, the end of earning as we know it opens the door to a more holistic understanding of identity—one that is not confined by the boundaries of job titles, deadlines, or KPIs.

Who Are You When You're Not Working?

Perhaps the most profound question that arises from this shift is: *Who are you when you're not working?* In a world where work has been the defining feature of our existence, this question forces us to confront the very essence of our identity. If we are no longer defined by the work we do, how do we define ourselves?

For many, this question may be unsettling. Without the constant reference point of a job, a title, or a set of responsibilities, who are we beneath the surface? This is a question that demands introspection, and for many, it may prompt a period of existential crisis. It is not easy to shed the skin of a lifetime of work-based identity. For decades, we have been told that our worth is measured by what we achieve and how much we contribute to society. But when that equation is no longer valid, what remains?

In a world where the traditional notion of earning through work is increasingly obsolete, we are forced to confront the notion of self-worth without the old markers of productivity. This invites a deeper exploration of who we are beyond our work. Are we defined solely by our economic output, or do we have inherent value as individuals, regardless of our ability to produce? This is the existential crossroads that many will face as the nature of work and earning continues to evolve.

The answer to this question may lie in a more expansive, compassionate understanding of identity—one that does not hinge solely on work, but instead embraces the full complexity of human experience. It may require us to redefine what it means to be "successful" and to acknowledge that our value is not tied to the hours we spend working, but to the quality of our lives in all their facets: relationships, passions, creativity, leisure, and personal growth.

The Path Forward

As we look to a future where earning no longer requires toil, we must consider how we can embrace these shifts in a way that honours both the potential for personal liberation and the need for social stability. It is a future that offers profound opportunities for self-discovery, creativity, and the cultivation of meaningful lives. But it is also a future that will require us to rethink the very foundations of our identity and our understanding of worth.

In the pages that follow, we will explore the psychological, emotional, and societal dimensions of this transformation—examining both the challenges and the possibilities that arise when we let go of the old paradigm of earning through effort. For some, this will be a time of crisis; for others, it will be a time of liberation. But for all of us, it will be a time of profound change—one that offers the opportunity to create a new relationship with work, with time, and with ourselves.

The Rise of Decentralised Income

For centuries, the relationship between work and income has been relatively straightforward: to earn money, you must work. Whether through manual labour, intellectual exertion, or creative output, the act of working was seen as the necessary—and only—path to economic survival. This foundational principle of modern economies, which has shaped our social contracts, legal frameworks, and personal identities, is now undergoing a radical transformation.

New economic models are rapidly emerging, decoupling income from labour in ways that challenge the deeply ingrained assumptions of work, value, and wealth. Concepts such as Universal Basic Income (UBI), royalties, Decentralised Autonomous Organisations (DAOs), and AI-driven monetisation are reshaping the nature of economic participation and presenting alternative pathways to income generation. As traditional employment structures give way to a more fluid, decentralised economy, the very notion of "earning" is evolving, raising critical questions about how we value human labour, who has access to wealth, and what it means to live a life of purpose in a world where the necessity of toil is diminishing.

This chapter explores the rise of decentralised income models, examining how they disrupt old systems, rewrite societal assumptions about work, and introduce new ethical, philosophical, and practical questions about the future of wealth distribution.

Basic Income: A Radical Shift in Economic Philosophy

Perhaps the most talked-about concept in the decoupling of income from labour is *Universal Basic Income* (UBI). The idea is deceptively simple: every citizen receives a fixed, unconditional sum of money from the government, regardless of employment status, wealth, or background. UBI is not a new concept—it has roots in philosophical thought dating back to Thomas Paine in the 18th century, who argued for a basic income as a means to provide economic freedom to all citizens. Yet, it is only in recent decades that the idea has gained serious traction, particularly as automation and artificial intelligence have increasingly displaced human labour.

Supporters of UBI argue that it is not just an economic necessity but a moral one. With technological advancements automating large swathes of the labour market, the old model of earning a living through paid work is becoming obsolete for many. Those who are displaced by these technologies often find themselves in precarious, underpaid, or insecure forms of employment. UBI, proponents claim, would provide economic security, empowering individuals to pursue education, entrepreneurship, caregiving, or creative endeavours without the constant pressure of having to earn a living through traditional work.

Yet, UBI also raises significant concerns. Critics argue that it would create disincentives for work, eroding the work ethic that has underpinned modern economies. Some worry that it could lead to inflation, as governments print more money to fund these payments. Others fear it would simply be a band-aid solution to deeper structural issues, such as income inequality and the underemployment caused by automation. Despite these concerns, UBI remains a central idea in the evolving discourse on the future of income and work. The question is no longer *whether* UBI is possible, but *how* it will be implemented and what the implications will be for the labour market and social structures.

Royalties: Redefining Value Through Creative Ownership

Another avenue through which income is being decentralised is the system of royalties, particularly in the context of intellectual property and creative industries. For generations, income from creative work has been tied to the labour of production—musicians, writers, artists, and inventors created value that was exchanged for payment in the form of wages, advances, or project-based fees. However, with the rise of digital technologies and the globalisation of markets, the possibility of earning income through royalties has expanded dramatically.

Royalties, in essence, allow creators to continue earning from their work long after it has been produced. For instance, a musician can continue to earn money from a song long after it has been recorded and released. Similarly, a writer may continue to receive royalties from books, while a software developer can earn from licensing agreements or subscription models. In this system, income is not tied to the immediate, manual effort of the creator; it is generated through the ongoing consumption of their work.

The growth of platforms like Patreon, Kickstarter, and Spotify has made it possible for individuals to monetise their creative work in ways that were once impossible. Artists and creators no longer need to rely on traditional gatekeepers—publishers, labels, or production companies—to access markets and earn money. Instead, they can interact directly with their audience, creating more personalised, diverse, and sustainable income streams. This model challenges the old paradigm of work where value is produced only through direct labour and provides a more sustainable, ongoing way for people to earn from their creativity.

However, the rise of royalties also introduces complexities. The streaming platforms that dominate the music, film, and publishing industries are often criticised for the way they distribute royalties, with the bulk of earnings funnelled to large companies rather than individual creators. Furthermore, the continual income stream offered by royalties can also raise questions about the relationship between intellectual property and public good, particularly when vast profits are generated from works that may be easily replicated or altered without consent.

DAOs: Decentralised Autonomous Organisations and Collective Income Models

The concept of Decentralised Autonomous Organisations (DAOs) is one of the most fascinating—and disruptive—emerging models of economic participation. A DAO is an organisational structure that operates entirely on a blockchain, with decisions made collectively by its members through smart contracts. These organisations are not governed by a traditional hierarchical structure but by a set of coded rules that automatically execute decisions based on consensus among members. DAOs allow for the creation of entirely new economic systems where income is not tied to individual labour but to the collective efforts of the group.

DAOs are already being used in the cryptocurrency space to fund projects, make investments, and allocate resources without the need for centralised authorities or traditional corporate structures. The members of a DAO can vote on projects or investments, and income generated from these collective actions is distributed according to predetermined rules. For example, a DAO might pool resources to develop a new piece of software or a digital art collection, and profits from the venture would be shared among the contributors, not based on the number of hours worked but on their contributions and ownership stakes.

The rise of DAOs challenges the traditional notion of labour as something that must be compensated on an individual basis. Instead, they offer a model where collective ownership and decision-making take precedence. This model has the potential to reshape industries from finance to entertainment, providing more equitable opportunities for those who traditionally have had little access to economic power. However, DAOs also raise new questions about governance, accountability, and how collective decisions are made. Who is ultimately responsible for the success or failure of a DAO? How can fairness be ensured in a system where decisions are made by those with the most resources or influence?

AI Monetisation: The New Frontier of Income Generation

Artificial Intelligence (AI) has become one of the most potent forces in the decoupling of income from traditional labour. From predictive analytics and content creation tools to fully automated systems in finance and retail, AI is increasingly capable of performing tasks that once required human intervention. As AI becomes more integrated into the economy, new opportunities for income generation are emerging that are not tied to human labour in the traditional sense.

One such model is AI-driven monetisation, where individuals and companies can earn income through the deployment of AI systems. This includes everything from creating AI-powered applications that generate revenue through subscriptions or advertising, to leveraging AI tools for more efficient decision-making in businesses. In this model, individuals or organisations can "monetise" AI technology itself, earning passive income as the AI continues to perform tasks, optimise processes, or generate content.

The idea of AI as an income-generating tool raises fascinating ethical questions. As AI takes over more tasks traditionally performed by humans, will the income generated by AI systems be distributed to those who own the technology or to the wider public? Could the monetisation of AI lead to a society where the vast majority of income is concentrated in the hands of those who control these technologies? Or will AI enable more people to create value and generate income on their own terms, bypassing the traditional systems of employment and labour?

Decoupling Income from Labour: What It Means for Society

The decentralisation of income, whether through basic income, royalties, DAOs, or AI, signals the emergence of a new economic reality—one in which the old ties between income and labour are loosened. This decoupling could have profound implications for how we define work, wealth, and social value.

On one hand, these models offer the potential for greater economic equality, as they allow more people to generate income through means other than traditional employment. They also provide opportunities for personal freedom, enabling individuals to pursue creative, intellectual, or social projects without the pressure to "earn" their living through the 9-to-5 grind.

However, they also raise significant challenges, particularly in terms of governance, fairness, and the distribution of wealth. The question of who controls the new income-generating systems and how wealth is distributed remains central to the conversation about the future of work. If decentralised income models are to be truly transformative, they must be designed in ways that ensure inclusivity, fairness, and accessibility for all.

As these new models of income continue to evolve, the nature of work—and the role it plays in our lives—will continue to shift. What will it mean to live in a world where income is no longer tied to labour? How will our relationships with money, status, and identity change when work is no longer the primary means of survival? These are the questions that will define the next phase of economic evolution.

Beyond the Paycheck Paradigm

For as long as human societies have existed in their current form, work has been synonymous with survival. From agrarian societies to the rise of industrial economies, the belief that *to survive is to work* has been a cornerstone of economic thought, social structures, and personal identity. The most basic understanding of the relationship between labour and income has been that we exchange our time and energy for a paycheck. Whether in the form of wages, salaries, or even self-generated income, the idea that money is earned only through effort has been deeply ingrained in both our collective and individual consciousness.

However, this assumption is rapidly being called into question. With the rise of automation, artificial intelligence, and the growing conversation around Universal Basic Income (UBI), the fundamental connection between work and income is beginning to unravel. For the first time in history, a growing number of people can theoretically survive without participating in the traditional labour market. This decoupling of income from toil raises essential questions about how we understand work, wealth, and value, and what it means for our personal identities and the way we interact with the world.

The transition away from a system where survival is directly tied to labour creates emotional, psychological, and societal complexities. What happens when the work we do no longer defines our worth? When the act of earning a living is no longer intrinsically linked to effort, how do we reconcile this with a lifetime of cultural conditioning that equates income with hard work? This article examines the profound shifts occurring in the economic landscape, interrogating the emotional residue left behind when income is no longer tied to toil. In doing so, we explore the broader implications of these changes on our sense of self, our purpose, and our role in society.

The Long Shadow of Toil: How We Got Here

To understand the emotional impact of decoupling income from effort, it's essential to look at how the concept of *earning a living* became so deeply entwined with notions of personal worth. Historically, the idea that labour is the only legitimate means of securing income is rooted in both the rise of capitalism and the

Protestant work ethic. The industrial revolution solidified the notion that individuals must sell their time for wages. As society transitioned from agrarian to industrial economies, this shift was not only a matter of economic organisation but also moral philosophy. The Protestant ethic, which emphasised hard work, frugality, and thrift as evidence of virtue, reinforced the belief that effort was the key to success and moral rectitude.

This association between work and worth has persisted throughout the modern era. In the 20th century, as economic growth, technological advancement, and consumerism spread across the globe, the belief that we must earn our way to survival became universal. Work was the mechanism by which we contributed to society, raised families, and gained social mobility. It was the currency through which we proved our value, not just to others but to ourselves. The more we worked, the more we were rewarded, and the more we were recognised as worthy members of society.

However, this model has always had its flaws. For all the promises of security and opportunity, the connection between work and income has often been tenuous for those at the margins of the economy. Inequality, lack of access to well-paying jobs, and the strain of precarious work have meant that many people never fully experience the rewards of labour. At the same time, for those in more secure employment, the weight of constant productivity and the erosion of personal time have led to the rise of burnout and a crisis of meaning.

Now, however, with the advent of new economic models, the very relationship between work and income is being called into question. *What does it mean when income is no longer tied to toil?*

The Emotional Residue: Guilt, Anxiety, and the Loss of Purpose

The possibility of earning without direct labour is liberating, yet it is also unsettling. A generation raised to believe that work is the bedrock of identity and survival now finds itself facing a new reality in which that foundation is eroding. For many, the notion that they could survive without having to work for every penny challenges an entire worldview built around the idea that our value is derived from our effort.

The psychological fallout from this shift is profound. In many ways, the emotional residue left behind when income is decoupled from effort can be likened to a loss of self-worth. For much of our lives, work has provided us not only with sustenance but also with structure and identity. It is no small thing to have that foundation disrupted, and the resulting confusion or discomfort is often palpable. If we no longer have to labour for income, how do we find meaning in our lives? What replaces the constant quest for productivity, achievement, and external validation?

For some, the emotional impact is a sense of *emptiness*. The work that once structured their days no longer provides purpose, leaving a vacuum that is difficult to fill. The loss of daily tasks, of the grind, can lead to an identity crisis—who are we if not the sum of our work and the income we earn from it? Without the daily ritual of work, it can be challenging to feel productive, significant, or worthy. The idea of being paid without effort can even trigger feelings of guilt or shame. *Is it morally right to receive income without contributing?* This question lingers for many, reflecting the deep-seated belief that work is both a personal duty and a moral obligation.

For others, this decoupling may lead to *anxiety*. When income is no longer linked to labour, it can feel as though everything is up for grabs. If our security is no longer guaranteed by our ability to work, what does the future hold? The destabilisation of economic models designed around labour can trigger fears about the long-term sustainability of such systems. If people no longer need to work, what becomes of economic productivity, social cohesion, or the functioning of communities? The challenge of finding new, equitable ways to distribute resources without relying on traditional forms of work looms large.

Yet, for some, this new reality presents the possibility of *freedom*. The absence of the daily struggle for survival allows people to explore new avenues of self-expression, creativity, and personal growth. No longer tethered to jobs that offer limited fulfilment, they can pursue passions, invest in their communities, or focus on personal development. The idea that work should no longer be a burden, but an opportunity for personal flourishing, is both radical and liberating. For these individuals, the loss of the paycheck paradigm is not a loss at all, but a new beginning—one where income is decoupled from effort, allowing for a more holistic approach to life.

Reimagining the Self: Identity Beyond Work

At the core of the emotional dissonance surrounding this shift is the question of identity. Who are we when we are not defined by the work we do? For centuries, work has not only been the means of survival but also a primary source of identity. The notion of "being a worker," "a professional," or "an expert" has shaped how we relate to ourselves and others. Work is the lens through which we view our role in society, and without it, we are left to confront a new, often uncomfortable question: *Who am I without my job?*

This question is not just philosophical—it is existential. Many of us have constructed our identities around the notion of work, tying our sense of purpose and self-worth to the labour we provide. Without that reference point, we are forced to reckon with our value in different terms.

The idea that identity can be free of occupation is difficult to conceptualise for many. How can we be valuable members of society if we are not contributing through work? How do we measure success if it is no longer based on climbing the career ladder or accumulating wealth through labour? These questions are at the heart of the ongoing conversation about the future of work and income in a world where survival no longer requires toil.

In the absence of traditional work, there is a chance to explore identity in new ways—through creativity, community, learning, and personal growth. The removal of the paycheck paradigm allows for a more expansive, diverse conception of self, where work is not the only means of self-actualisation. Instead, *living* becomes the focus—whether through the pursuit of passions, the cultivation of relationships, or the exploration of new intellectual frontiers.

Yet, as liberating as this prospect may seem, it also requires us to confront our dependency on work as a source of meaning. If we are to move beyond the paycheck paradigm, we must consider how to reframe our relationship with time and value—one that is no longer measured by hours worked, but by the richness of life we lead.

A New Economic Reality

As we move further away from the idea that survival must be earned through toil, we are faced with both challenges and opportunities. The decoupling of income from labour is not a simple transition; it is a profound rethinking of how we define value, worth, and contribution in our society. It forces us to confront deep questions about identity, purpose, and the future of work. It asks us to rethink the very systems that have defined our lives for centuries.

Ultimately, the end of the paycheck paradigm does not signify the end of work—it signifies a transformation in the way we view work and its role in our lives. As we navigate this shift, we must also embrace new models of living—ones that recognise the value of human potential in all its forms, not just through the labour we provide. This is not just an economic transformation; it is a personal, cultural, and societal revolution, one that challenges us to live and work in ways that are more aligned with the complexities and possibilities of our human experience.

Status, Identity, and the Role of Work

For centuries, the concept of work has been intrinsically tied to identity. The question "What do you do?" is often the first we ask when meeting someone new, not just out of curiosity but because, for much of modern history, it's been the most telling indicator of a person's social standing, economic value, and even moral character. From the highest echelons of professional achievement to the dignity of manual labour, work has served as the scaffolding of identity—shaping how we view ourselves and how society perceives us. But what happens when the work that has for so long defined us becomes optional, or even irrelevant, in a world where automation and new economic models are reshaping the very foundations of labour?

The decoupling of income from traditional work presents both an existential challenge and an unprecedented opportunity. For some, the loss of work as a central element of their identity can trigger a crisis—anxiety, uncertainty, and a sense of meaninglessness flood in where once there was clear purpose. For others, it can signal liberation—a chance to redefine themselves beyond the narrow confines of labour and consumption. As new economic models such as Universal Basic Income (UBI), automation, and the rise of decentralised income begin to gain traction, the social and psychological implications of this shift are becoming more apparent.

This chapter explores how work serves as a pillar of personal identity, the deep emotional and psychological effects of losing this anchor, and the opportunities for reinvention that lie ahead. It is an exploration of how the erosion of work as the primary determinant of identity can lead to both personal crises and profound liberation, depending on the way we engage with these shifts.

Work as Identity: The Historical Roots of the Connection

To understand the profound impact that the decoupling of work from identity may have, we must first examine the historical relationship between labour and selfhood. The association of work with identity is deeply rooted in Western economic thought. The development of the modern work ethic, particularly in the context of capitalism, framed work as a moral virtue. This belief was championed by figures such as Max Weber, whose seminal work *The Protestant Ethic and the Spirit of Capitalism* (1905) argued that the Protestant work ethic, with its emphasis on hard work, thrift, and productivity, played a critical role in the rise of capitalism. This ethic embedded the idea that not only was work necessary for survival, but that it was morally virtuous, a means of demonstrating personal responsibility and contributing to the common good.

Over time, this idea permeated every level of society, becoming the primary means by which individuals measured their own worth and how others evaluated them. In the industrial age, as people moved from agricultural work to factory-based labour, the need to show that one was contributing to the economy became even more critical. Employment became the primary way of gaining respect and social status. From the millworker to the manager, from the teacher to the doctor, work defined individuals not only economically but socially, shaping their relationships, their ambitions, and their self-esteem.

In more recent decades, the shift from the factory to the knowledge economy has only deepened this connection. Occupations are now more varied and often require more extensive education, skills, and expertise, creating new ways for individuals to elevate their status through professional achievement. Careers became not just a means of earning but the primary means of defining self-worth. A person's job often became synonymous with their identity: *"I am a lawyer," "I am a teacher," "I am a CEO."*

This cultural and psychological emphasis on work has created a framework where personal identity and status are largely constructed around professional roles. The phrase "what you do" has a far greater weight than "who you are," and as such, work has long been a source of both pride and anxiety. Our entire social contract, with its structure of rights, responsibilities, and relationships, has been built around the centrality of labour. But what happens when this structure begins to crumble?

The Crisis of Identity: Work as the Loss of Self

For those who have spent their entire lives defined by their job, the erosion of the traditional work model can be a profound existential crisis. Imagine a person who has spent decades climbing the corporate ladder or dedicating themselves to their profession. For these individuals, their work has been their identity—it is what they do, what they excel at, and what others admire. Their self-worth has been directly tied to their productivity, their expertise, and their career trajectory. Now, imagine that this traditional form of work is no longer necessary or, at worst, obsolete. The emotional fallout of this shift can be considerable.

The loss of a professional identity can lead to feelings of *worthlessness* and *anxiety*, as individuals find themselves struggling to redefine who they are without the career that once defined them. This is particularly acute for those in high-status positions, where success is not only a personal achievement but also a public one. The prospect of losing this source of identity can evoke feelings of confusion, even despair. What remains when you are no longer "the doctor," "the executive," or "the expert"? What is left when your job is no longer your identity?

This crisis of self can be exacerbated by societal expectations. Work is not only a personal endeavour but a social contract. We are taught to view hard work as virtuous and laziness as morally questionable. When a person no longer works in the traditional sense, especially if their income is no longer tied to direct labour, they may feel disconnected from these societal norms, potentially facing feelings of guilt or shame. The emotional and psychological toll of such a transition can manifest in stress, depression, and a sense of purposelessness.

In a world where the value of work is often tied to personal achievement and external validation, the decoupling of work from identity poses a fundamental challenge to our understanding of self-worth. How do we define ourselves when the traditional markers of success are no longer relevant?

The Path to Liberation: Identity Beyond Work

Yet, while the loss of work as a central reference point for identity can create a crisis, it also offers an unprecedented opportunity for liberation. If our identity is no longer anchored to our jobs, it opens up vast possibilities for reinvention and self-discovery. No longer confined by the constraints of an occupation, individuals have the potential to pursue a wider array of interests, passions, and talents that were previously sidelined by the demands of work. For some, the absence of the daily grind may enable a deeper connection to self, leading to more authentic and fulfilling lives.

This new freedom can be profoundly empowering. Without the social pressure to conform to traditional work structures, individuals can redefine what success looks like for them. *What if our worth is not determined by how many hours we work or how much money we make?* What if our value is inherent, not transactional? This shift in perspective can allow for a more holistic view of self-identity—one that encompasses not only work but also creativity, relationships, personal growth, and community engagement.

The loss of a job or career as a primary source of identity also opens up the possibility for more equitable social models. The decoupling of survival from work challenges the assumption that income must be earned through labour, allowing for new economic systems, such as Universal Basic Income (UBI), to be considered. These systems not only provide financial security but also pave the way for a society where the focus shifts from work to personal fulfilment and contribution in other forms.

In this new reality, people can pursue meaningful activities that do not conform to the traditional notions of work. It can allow for the pursuit of art, education, care work, or even rest, all of which contribute to personal well-being and societal health. The idea that we are defined by our productivity is being replaced by a more expansive view of identity—one where worth is not defined by external measures but by the intrinsic value we bring to the world through our presence, creativity, and relationships.

The Future of Identity and Work

The end of work as the primary determinant of identity represents a significant turning point in the human experience. As new economic models continue to evolve, the opportunity to redefine the relationship between work and self will be both a challenge and a chance for growth. While many will inevitably experience the emotional fallout of losing a central source of identity, others will see this shift as an opportunity to embrace a new, more flexible, and liberated conception of self.

For society at large, this evolution demands a rethinking of how we construct meaning and value in our lives. As we move away from work-based models of identity, we will need to develop new ways to foster a sense of purpose and belonging. Rather than defining ourselves by what we do, we must find ways to define ourselves by who we are—by our creativity, compassion, curiosity, and engagement with the world.

Ultimately, this shift holds the potential to transform not just individual lives but entire cultures. By shedding the traditional links between work and self-worth, we can create a world where people are free to explore their full potential without the constraints of outdated work models. In doing so, we may find that work is no longer the defining feature of who we are—but that we are, in fact, much more than what we do.

Who Are You When You're Not Working?

In a world built on the logic of productivity and toil, where identity is often synonymous with occupation, the question *Who are you when you're not working?* demands both introspection and courage. For much of human history, work has been the foundational structure of life. It defines our roles, gives us a sense of purpose, and often dictates how we interact with the world. Whether we are professionals, creatives, or service workers, the work we do shapes not just our daily routine but also how we see ourselves and how we are seen by others. The structure of work is so embedded in our society that we rarely pause to consider what happens when it is no longer the primary source of our identity.

But the landscape is changing. As automation and artificial intelligence increasingly replace human labour, and as alternative economic models like Universal Basic Income (UBI) and decentralised income structures gain traction, the question arises: *If I'm no longer defined by my job, what is left?*

This question invites a profound exploration of selfhood, one that compels us to step outside the comfortable boundaries of titles, deadlines, and key performance indicators (KPIs). It forces us to confront the truth that our identities, as they are often conceived, may be fragile constructs tied to an outdated economic model. In a world where our roles in the economy are rapidly evolving, we must grapple with the possibility that our worth is not—and should never have been—tied to what we do for a living.

This article delves into the heart of that question, exploring the emotional and psychological ramifications of a life no longer defined by work. It examines how modern culture has constructed the idea of *work as identity*, and what it means for us when we are faced with the opportunity to redefine ourselves without the constraints of occupational labels. More importantly, it offers a framework for how we might navigate this shift with intention, allowing us to reconnect with a more authentic sense of self and purpose.

Work and the Construction of Identity

At the core of modern societal structure lies the belief that who we are is fundamentally connected to the work we do. From childhood, we are conditioned to define ourselves by our occupations. The standard social greeting at a gathering is invariably, *"What do you do?"* This question isn't just a simple inquiry; it's a shortcut to understanding a person's role in society and, implicitly, their value. Our careers have come to function as the scaffolding of our identities. The titles we hold, the jobs we perform, and the roles we take on become markers of who we are.

This connection between work and identity is not merely societal convention; it is also deeply psychological. According to psychologists like Erik Erikson, work plays a crucial role in the development of self-esteem, as it often represents a manifestation of our skills, competencies, and ambitions. Moreover, the psychological notion of "role identity" suggests that we derive our sense of self from the roles we occupy in society. The more we invest in those roles, the more they become part of our internal self-concept. This relationship between work and identity is particularly pronounced in the context of what is known as "status anxiety"—a term coined by the late philosopher Alain de Botton, which describes the fear of being judged based on our social standing and professional success.

Historically, this relationship has been integral to the structuring of society. In the industrial era, for example, work served as the primary means of social mobility. A person's labour not only provided for their family but also determined their social class, their place in the community, and their prospects for future generations. In today's capitalist economies, while social mobility has become more fluid, the idea that work is a primary source of self-worth persists. Jobs offer financial independence, social recognition, and often a deep sense of accomplishment. In a sense, our identities become bound to our jobs—whether as an executive, a teacher, a scientist, or a labourer—because they give us a way to show our value to the world.

But what happens when work is no longer central to one's sense of self, either because of economic upheavals, technological change, or a societal shift toward models like UBI, where survival is not tethered to one's job? The loss of work as a key component of identity can feel like losing an anchor, an existential crisis where one must confront the discomfort of not knowing how to define themselves.

The Psychological Toll: Crisis of Identity and Meaning

For those who have spent their lives defining themselves through their work, the loss of that framework can lead to a deep sense of emptiness. The psychological toll can be profound. When the thing that once gave us purpose is stripped away, we are left to ask, *Who am I, really?*

In a world where work is no longer the defining feature of life, this shift can trigger a *crisis of identity*. The individual whose life has been oriented around work may struggle to navigate a sense of self that does not rely on a professional role. This can manifest as a sense of aimlessness, a lack of direction, or even feelings of worthlessness. After all, if our work no longer provides the structural foundation for who we are, what is left?

This is where the emotional residue of decoupling work from identity becomes most evident. *What if I'm no longer "good enough" if I'm not working?* For many, the concept of worthiness is inextricably linked to productivity. The more we produce, the more we contribute, the more we matter. To suddenly be faced with the possibility of *not* working—of not earning through toil—forces us to confront an uncomfortable question: *Am I still valuable?*

In some cases, this loss can create a profound sense of *disorientation*. Without work to structure the day, what fills the vacuum? It is in this moment of emptiness that the cultural narratives surrounding work become starkly visible. We are told that "success" comes through effort, through labour, through striving. But when that effort is no longer required, or when survival no longer depends on it, those familiar narratives start to lose their grip.

The Path to Liberation: Rediscovering Meaning Beyond Work

Yet, while the dissolution of work's hold on our identities may create a crisis, it also offers the possibility of profound liberation. What happens when we are no longer bound by the expectations of what work *should* look like, when the pressures of meeting deadlines, earning money, and achieving professional milestones are removed? The answer is that we are free to rediscover who we are without the constraints of occupational labels.

The end of work as identity opens the door to a more expansive understanding of selfhood. It invites us to consider a person's value not in terms of productivity but in terms of the richness of their existence. Without the need to define ourselves by a job title, we can explore other aspects of who we are—our passions, our relationships, our creativity, our spirituality. In a way, we become free to live authentically, shedding the roles that were once imposed upon us and engaging more fully with the world as individuals, rather than workers.

This liberation also offers the opportunity to recalibrate our social norms. If we are no longer defined by what we do for a living, then the societal pressure to be constantly "productive" begins to dissipate. We can begin to value rest, reflection, and play as vital components of a full life, rather than seeing them as indulgences or failures of character. The possibility for reinvention becomes not just a personal journey, but a collective one, as societies rethink how to define success and how to measure human value.

The liberation from work as identity also enables us to reshape our relationships with one another. Without the constant pressure to "achieve" through work, we can prioritise relationships, emotional growth, and well-being. The demand for constant output diminishes, allowing for more authentic connections and greater attention to what truly matters. In this space, identity can be constructed on our own terms, rather than being dictated by the economy.

A Future Beyond Work: The New Identity

The decoupling of work from identity represents one of the most significant cultural shifts of the 21st century. As automation, artificial intelligence, and alternative income models reshape the labour market, the notion that we are defined by our jobs will slowly give way to a more holistic understanding of self. This shift forces us to ask the question: *What is the essence of who we are, beyond what we do?*

To move beyond work as identity, we must embrace a more fluid, expansive view of human potential—one that values creativity, connection, and personal growth as much as productivity. We must learn to see ourselves not as products of our labour but as complex, multi-dimensional beings with limitless capacity for meaning-making and fulfilment. This is the challenge, and the opportunity, that lies before us as we redefine what it means to be human in a world where work is no longer the defining feature of life.

In this new world, we must find new ways to fill the vacuum left by the absence of work. We must be brave enough to explore who we truly are when we are no longer "doing" for the sake of survival. And perhaps, in doing so, we will discover that, in the absence of work, we can finally become who we were always meant to be.

Chapter 3: Time as the New Capital

The world we live in is changing. For generations, we have measured our worth through the lens of labour—our jobs, the hours spent working, and the income generated by those hours. Time was always thought of as a finite resource, a commodity to be traded for money, productivity, or status. But as automation, artificial intelligence, and new economic models slowly decouple income from toil, the very concept of time is undergoing a radical transformation. Time, in the post-work world, is no longer just something to be spent; it is becoming an asset—a currency that, when invested wisely, can yield dividends of meaning, fulfilment, and connection.

The shift from work as the central axis of life to time as the new capital is not merely economic—it is philosophical, psychological, and deeply personal. This chapter explores the idea of *time as capital*—a shift from seeing time as something to be measured by productivity to seeing it as something to be *invested*. It introduces the concept of a *time-investment portfolio*, where the experiences we curate, the relationships we cultivate, and the meaning we create compound over time, providing returns far greater than monetary wealth. As the concept of work continues to evolve and the traditional models of earning and survival fade, we must learn to navigate this new paradigm where time, not money, becomes the ultimate measure of value.

The central tension at the heart of this chapter lies in distinguishing between what we might call *passive leisure*—the endless consumption of entertainment, distractions, and mindless activities—and *active freedom*, the intentional, mindful use of our time to cultivate a life of purpose and authenticity. In a world full of distractions and constant connectivity, the difference between these two is crucial. While passive leisure may provide short-term satisfaction, it can ultimately drain our vitality and sense of self. True freedom, on the other hand, comes from the active, conscious decision to invest our time in what truly matters—whether that is deepening our relationships, pursuing creative endeavours, or simply being present in the moment.

But perhaps the most pressing issue in this new world of time capital is the question of *attention.* In an economy where everything—from social media to streaming services—is designed to capture our focus, attention has become the ultimate finite resource. Just as financial capital must be allocated wisely, so too must our attention. In a world of constant distractions, reclaiming our attention is perhaps the most vital step toward a more authentic, meaningful life. By investing our attention in what truly matters, we can begin to cultivate a life that is rich not just in hours, but in substance.

This chapter, then, is about recognising the value of time as something more than a unit of exchange. It is about shifting our mindset from one of scarcity to one of abundance—a recognition that time, when spent intentionally, becomes the key to not only a fulfilling life but a life that is truly ours to design. The stakes are high. As the traditional structures of work and productivity fade, we have the opportunity to redefine what it means to live a successful, meaningful life. And it all begins with the way we think about and invest our time.

The Portfolio of Presence

When we think about wealth, we typically think about money—assets accumulated through work, savings, and investments. But as traditional notions of work and earning evolve, time has emerged as the new currency, and the way we invest it will define the next era of personal fulfilment. In the same way that a financial portfolio is built to grow in value over time, so too can we curate a *time-investment portfolio*—a collection of experiences, relationships, and pursuits that, when deliberately chosen, compound joy, purpose, and satisfaction over time.

This portfolio does not consist of monetary assets but rather of moments and actions that enrich our lives and align with our core values. Just as financial investments grow through compound interest, the time we invest in relationships, personal growth, creativity, and well-being accumulates over time, leading to a richer, more fulfilling life. *Experience* becomes the asset that appreciates most significantly in this new paradigm. The more time we spend in meaningful pursuits—whether through learning, nurturing relationships, or pursuing passions—the more these investments grow, enriching our overall well-being.

For example, consider the time invested in a long-term friendship. While time spent on the surface—small talk, casual hangouts, or social media exchanges—may provide temporary enjoyment, it is the deeper, more intentional interactions that build the foundation of a meaningful relationship. The shared experiences, the emotional support, the personal growth that comes from truly knowing and being known by another person—these are the investments that compound over time, creating a lasting connection that enhances both parties' sense of fulfilment and purpose.

The same principle applies to other areas of life. The time we dedicate to learning a new skill, engaging in creative expression, or reflecting on our values adds to the portfolio of presence that shapes our identity. Unlike financial wealth, which is often measured by external markers like income or assets, the value of our time-investment portfolio is measured by the depth of our experiences, the strength of our relationships, and the richness of our lives. Time, when consciously invested, can create wealth in the form of personal growth, emotional well-being, and intellectual enrichment.

This shift requires a fundamental change in how we view time. Instead of seeing it as a finite resource to be "spent" or "saved," we must learn to see it as a tool for cultivation. The question is no longer *How much time do I have?* but rather *How am I choosing to invest it?* The difference between these two perspectives is what separates a life lived reactively—caught in the endless cycle of work, obligations, and distractions—from a life lived intentionally, where time is a precious resource that contributes to a larger vision of who we are and who we want to become.

Freedom vs. Leisure

The distinction between *freedom* and *leisure* is critical in a world where time is emerging as the new capital. On the surface, leisure might appear to be a form of freedom—an escape from the pressures of work, a chance to relax and recharge. However, a closer examination reveals that not all leisure is created equal. *Passive leisure*—the consumption of entertainment, the scrolling of social media, or the endless binge-watching of television—can mimic rest, but it rarely leads to true rejuvenation or fulfilment. In fact, it can often leave us feeling more drained, disconnected, and disengaged from our own lives.

True *freedom*, on the other hand, is an active form of engagement with time. It is the intentional use of our hours and days in ways that are aligned with our values and passions. Active freedom is about making choices that reflect who we are and who we wish to be. It is not about avoiding work or responsibility but about creating the space to live authentically. This can be found in anything from creative expression to volunteerism, from time spent in nature to building deep, meaningful relationships. Freedom, in this sense, is the freedom to *choose*—to craft a life that feels rich and aligned with our deeper purposes.

The modern world has made it all too easy to confuse passive leisure with freedom. The constant stream of entertainment and distraction available at our fingertips offers the illusion of choice and freedom but often leads to a more profound sense of disconnection and dissatisfaction. In a time when we have the potential to reclaim our lives from the shackles of traditional work models, it is critical to distinguish between these two forms of time use. Freedom lies not in passivity but in the deliberate, active shaping of our lives around what matters most.

The Currency of Attention

In a post-work world, perhaps the most valuable commodity is no longer time itself but *attention*. We live in an age of constant distraction, where every ping of a notification, every new email, and every social media post vies for our focus. As attention becomes the ultimate scarce resource, reclaiming it becomes essential to living authentically. Just as we must be strategic with our financial capital, we must also be intentional with where we allocate our attention.

Attention, unlike time, is a finite resource. We cannot pay attention to everything, and the things we choose to focus on will define the quality of our lives. In the past, our attention was often dictated by the demands of work. Now, in a world where work is less central to our survival, we have the opportunity to choose what we direct our focus toward. The ability to control and direct our attention is key to living a life of meaning. This means being conscious of what draws our focus—whether it is external stimuli like the media, or internal distractions like stress or self-doubt—and learning to invest our attention in ways that align with our deepest values.

Reclaiming attention is not just about avoiding distraction, though that is certainly part of it. It's about shifting from a reactive state of constant multitasking to a more intentional, present way of being. When we direct our attention mindfully, we enhance our ability to experience life more fully, to connect more deeply with others, and to engage with the world in a way that feels purposeful and rewarding. This is the true currency of the post-work era—the ability to reclaim and direct our attention in ways that compound the richness of our lives.

In a world where time has become the new capital, how we choose to invest it will shape the future of our personal and collective well-being. The shift from work as identity to time as capital requires us to rethink our relationship with time, leisure, attention, and freedom. The opportunities for meaningful, authentic living are greater than ever, but they demand a conscious, intentional approach to how we spend our hours and direct our focus. In this new landscape, time is not just something to be *spent*—it is something to be *invested*, with returns that come in the form of deeper connections, more meaningful experiences, and a richer, more fulfilling life.

The Emotional Economy of Hours

In an age where productivity is often measured in hours worked, the relentless drive for more has become a defining feature of modern existence. The typical refrain is that time is money—hours spent working, hours used for something productive, are hours that contribute to the fabric of our success. Yet, increasingly, this view is being challenged by a more subtle, yet profoundly important notion: *What if the true wealth of our lives isn't determined by the quantity of time we spend, but by the emotional quality of how we live each hour?* This shift from a focus on the quantity of hours worked to the emotional and psychological richness of the hours we live represents the crux of a new "emotional economy."

The idea that wealth is not just the sum of money earned, but the emotional depth experienced during the hours of our lives, is a radical departure from how we've been taught to think. It calls into question the entire framework of work and success—one that has long tied personal value and societal status to the number of hours worked and the output achieved. Instead, it asks us to reconsider what truly constitutes a "wealthy" life. Is it merely surviving and accumulating more hours, or is it finding joy, meaning, and satisfaction in the way we invest our time? This is a question that invites profound reflection, one that speaks to the heart of what it means to live authentically, in alignment with our deepest needs and values.

This concept draws deeply from fields such as positive psychology and affective neuroscience, both of which have explored the emotional underpinnings of well-being and the powerful role emotions play in shaping our experience of time. Positive psychology, particularly, emphasises human flourishing and the idea that emotional richness—rather than productivity or achievement—is the true measure of a successful life. Similarly, affective neuroscience has demonstrated how emotions are not just reactions to our environment, but active forces that shape how we experience time itself, influencing everything from our perception of the passing hours to our sense of vitality.

The *emotional economy of hours* is a framework that asks us to move beyond counting hours and to start considering their quality. How are we investing our hours—not just in terms of doing, but in terms of being? How can we intentionally spend our time in ways that bring joy, meaning, and fulfilment? The emotional currency of our hours is not spent in the same way as a financial one—it doesn't require an exchange of effort or toil, but rather a deeper connection with the present, with others, and with our own well-being.

The Portfolio of Presence

The concept of a *portfolio* is traditionally tied to finance—a collection of investments, each contributing to an overall increase in wealth. In the emotional economy, however, we can think of our time as a portfolio too, but one that consists of moments rather than monetary assets. This portfolio isn't about accumulating hours in a day, but about consciously investing in moments that enhance the richness of our experience. Just as a financial portfolio grows through diverse investments, a time-investment portfolio thrives on the diversity of experiences we choose to invest in.

The portfolio of presence consists of the people, experiences, and activities that we invest in—those that bring us joy, fulfilment, and a deep sense of meaning. These are the moments where we are not simply passing time, but truly living it. In this context, we might invest in a meaningful conversation with a close friend, a day spent in nature, a quiet moment of reflection, or time spent pursuing creative passions. Each of these moments adds to the value of our portfolio in ways that can't always be quantified but are deeply felt.

The investment in relationships, for example, is one of the most significant and high-yielding ways to spend time. Research consistently shows that social connection is among the strongest predictors of happiness and well-being. Investing time in nurturing relationships compounds joy over time, much like interest on an investment. We gain not only the immediate satisfaction of connection but also long-term emotional security and meaning. It's these types of investments that create a rich, fulfilling life—not hours spent in endless meetings or grinding away at tasks that, while productive, might not contribute to our overall sense of well-being.

Additionally, the time we spend engaging in activities that align with our values and passions also adds significant emotional value. Whether through creative pursuits, intellectual exploration, or personal growth, these hours of self-expression and growth contribute to an authentic sense of fulfilment. The compound interest here is a deeper sense of self-worth, purpose, and alignment with our true desires.

In this emotional economy, there is no "return on investment" in the traditional sense of profit. Instead, the yield is emotional richness—more joy, more contentment, more vitality. The time we spend on these investments creates a life that is not only lived but deeply experienced, not merely survived but truly savoured.

Freedom vs. Leisure

In discussions about time, the terms *freedom* and *leisure* are often used interchangeably. But in the emotional economy, a critical distinction must be made between the two. The idea of *leisure* in our modern context is often tied to the idea of passive consumption: sitting in front of the television, scrolling through social media, or playing video games. While these activities can provide short-term distraction, they are rarely fulfilling in the deeper, emotional sense. Passive leisure might give the illusion of rest or freedom, but it often leaves us feeling drained, disconnected, and dissatisfied. In fact, research in positive psychology and affective neuroscience shows that activities such as mindlessly consuming entertainment can lower our levels of happiness, particularly when they displace more meaningful, active forms of engagement.

Active freedom, on the other hand, is a different kind of time use altogether. It's about intentionally choosing how to spend your hours in ways that resonate with your values, bring you joy, and foster personal growth. Active freedom allows you to be fully present in the moment, deeply engaged in life. It could be spending time with loved ones, pursuing creative projects, exploring nature, or engaging in deep, reflective thought. Active freedom is about choice, autonomy, and the conscious decision to direct your time in ways that align with what truly matters to you. It's an investment in your emotional and psychological wealth, one that enhances your vitality and brings a sense of purpose.

This distinction is central to understanding the emotional economy of hours. True freedom is not about the absence of work or responsibility; it's about the freedom to engage in life on your own terms, in ways that align with your core values and foster joy. Leisure, when it is passive and driven by external demands or distractions, can drain us. But freedom—when it is actively chosen and intentionally crafted—replenishes us, bringing us closer to the life we want to live.

The Currency of Attention

In the emotional economy of hours, perhaps the most precious resource is *attention*. In a world of endless distractions—push notifications, news feeds, emails, and entertainment—our attention is constantly under siege. It has become the ultimate finite resource, one that must be carefully guarded and allocated if we are to live authentically and meaningfully.

Attention, unlike time, cannot be regained once it is spent. It's the one resource that once diverted, cannot be recaptured. This is where the emotional economy differs significantly from traditional economic models. In the traditional system, time and money are seen as commodities that can be earned, spent, or saved. But attention, when lost, is gone. And yet, despite its scarcity, we often squander it on fleeting distractions, mistaking them for rest or fulfilment.

To reclaim our attention is to take control of our emotional wealth. The more attention we give to meaningful experiences—those that foster connection, growth, and authenticity—the more emotionally rich our lives become. The act of reclaiming our attention is not simply a matter of turning off notifications or cutting out distractions; it's about engaging with the world on a deeper level, choosing where to direct our focus in ways that contribute to our well-being.

For instance, mindfulness practices—whether through meditation, focused breathing, or simply being present in a conversation—allow us to restore and redirect our attention in ways that enhance our emotional quality of life. The more we are able to focus on what truly matters, the more fulfilling our experiences become, compounding joy and satisfaction over time.

Investing Time, Investing Emotion

In this new world of time as the new capital, the way we invest our hours is no longer about just getting through the day or accumulating moments of leisure. It's about recognising that the quality of our time—the emotional richness of each hour—is what truly matters. By intentionally investing our time in experiences, relationships, and activities that align with our deepest values, we can create a life that is not only rich in hours but rich in emotional and psychological fulfilment. Time, when used intentionally, becomes more than a unit of survival; it becomes the currency of a life well-lived. The wealth we seek is not measured in the hours we survive, but in the joy and meaning we cultivate within them.

The Portfolio of Presence

Time, once considered merely a unit of measurement, is rapidly evolving into a currency more valuable than any banknote or stock portfolio. In a world that constantly pushes the notion of "time is money," it is easy to fall into the trap of treating time like a commodity to be rationed and spent efficiently. We obsess over productivity, multitasking, and the quantification of every hour, trying to stretch the minutes and seconds to meet the demands of work, family, and personal goals. Yet, this relentless pursuit of efficiency often misses the deeper potential that time holds—its ability to compound not just wealth, but meaning, joy, and fulfilment. This is where the *time-investment portfolio* comes in: a conceptual framework that reimagines wealth not as the quantity of time spent, but the emotional and experiential value we derive from each moment.

The portfolio of presence is not just about measuring time, but investing it in experiences, relationships, and pursuits that offer long-term emotional returns. Just as a financial portfolio is carefully balanced across different assets to optimise growth, so too can we invest our time in a variety of ways that compound personal satisfaction, mental well-being, and a sense of connection. This new way of thinking challenges the idea that we should "spend" time as we do money. Instead, it asks us to consider the possibility that time, invested with intention, can yield an emotional wealth that grows exponentially.

This idea draws from both positive psychology and the science of human flourishing. Studies in these fields suggest that the quality of our emotional experiences significantly impacts our overall well-being and life satisfaction. In essence, the time we invest in our relationships, passions, and personal growth generates compound interest that increases our sense of purpose and joy over time. In contrast, time spent solely on transactional or obligatory tasks can often leave us feeling drained, disconnected, and unfulfilled.

Therefore, the real question becomes: *How are we choosing to invest our time?*

Time as an Asset

At its core, the portfolio of presence invites us to see time as an asset—something that can be strategically allocated for the maximum emotional return. This shift in perspective is profound. We are so accustomed to thinking about time in terms of labour and productivity that it can be difficult to imagine it as something that can be "invested" in ways that deepen our lives rather than merely filling the hours. And yet, research from fields like affective neuroscience reveals that our brains do not simply process time in terms of the passage of minutes and hours, but also by the emotional richness we experience within those moments. The more emotionally significant an experience, the more likely it is to enrich our overall well-being.

Consider, for example, the experience of travel. While it's easy to think of time spent in a new city or country as "wasted" if it doesn't directly result in productivity or income, the emotional value derived from such an experience can be immense. The connections made, the perspectives gained, the joy of exploration—these moments accumulate over time, enriching our personal portfolio in ways that contribute to our happiness and life satisfaction. In contrast, time spent in work meetings or scrolling through social media might not offer the same emotional returns, no matter how many hours are "invested."

The real challenge, then, is not in finding more time, but in understanding how to direct the time we already have toward experiences that deepen our emotional and psychological lives. A well-curated time portfolio includes a balance of relationships, learning, creativity, and rest—activities that nurture not just the body, but the mind and soul. These investments, though intangible, are often the most valuable, providing long-term dividends that can last far beyond the fleeting satisfaction of material success.

Experiences: The Currency of Joy

One of the most powerful assets in the time-investment portfolio is experience. Unlike material wealth, which often has diminishing returns as it grows, experiences—particularly those that foster personal growth and connection—tend to compound in value over time. Positive psychology research consistently shows that people derive greater satisfaction from experiences than from possessions. This is because experiences, unlike material goods, have an emotional richness that deepens over time. Think of a trip to a far-off place: the memories, stories, and relationships formed during that time often become more meaningful the longer they are reflected upon, creating a lasting sense of joy that continues to enrich your life long after the trip itself has ended.

Investing in experiences doesn't require extravagant or expensive activities. It can be as simple as spending quality time with loved ones, engaging in a hobby, or pursuing something creative. The key is that these moments offer opportunities for *presence*—a deeper engagement with the world and with ourselves. When we invest in such experiences, we don't just accumulate memories; we build emotional wealth that enhances our capacity for joy, fulfilment, and resilience in the future.

Take, for example, the power of shared experiences. A study published in *Psychological Science* revealed that shared experiences, such as attending concerts or travelling with friends, significantly boost happiness levels. This is because these experiences create bonds that are reinforced over time, compounding joy with each new shared memory. In contrast, time spent in isolation or on passive consumption doesn't create the same emotional returns. Experiences that foster connection are key to building a valuable emotional portfolio.

Relationships: The Foundation of Emotional Capital

If experiences are the currency of joy, relationships are the foundational assets upon which the time-investment portfolio is built. The importance of relationships in shaping happiness and well-being cannot be overstated. Human beings are social creatures, and our sense of identity and fulfilment is deeply intertwined with the people we share our lives with. Investing time in cultivating relationships, whether with family, friends, colleagues, or partners, yields emotional dividends that surpass the returns of any material asset.

The science behind this is clear. Research from Harvard's *Grant Study*—one of the longest-running studies of human development—has shown that the quality of our relationships is the single greatest predictor of long-term happiness. The study, which has tracked the lives of 724 men for over 75 years, found that those who invested in close, supportive relationships were not only happier but healthier, more resilient, and longer-lived. Conversely, those who neglected relationships or faced social isolation were more prone to depression, physical illness, and premature death.

When we invest our time in relationships, we are not simply spending it; we are building emotional wealth. Each moment spent nurturing a relationship—whether through conversation, shared activities, or emotional support—adds to our portfolio of presence. These connections provide not only immediate comfort and joy but long-term security, offering emotional sustenance through life's inevitable ups and downs. In a world that increasingly values individual achievement and success, it is essential to remember that relationships are the real cornerstone of a fulfilling life.

Meaning: The Long-Term Yield

In addition to experiences and relationships, meaning is perhaps the most profound asset in the time-investment portfolio. The search for meaning, defined as a sense of purpose or significance in life, is what gives our lives direction and coherence. Studies in existential psychology and neuroscience suggest that meaning is integral to human well-being. When we feel that our lives have purpose, we experience greater satisfaction, resilience, and mental health. Meaning is not something that can be acquired through external achievements or possessions; it is created through the choices we make and the ways in which we engage with the world.

Investing time in activities that align with our values—whether through work, volunteering, creative expression, or activism—yields long-term emotional dividends. These investments do not provide immediate rewards but compound over time, creating a life that feels significant and fulfilling. The pursuit of meaning is not about ticking boxes or accumulating accomplishments; it is about making choices that reflect our deepest aspirations and desires.

Take, for example, the work of Viktor Frankl, a psychiatrist and Holocaust survivor whose book *Man's Search for Meaning* has influenced generations of readers. Frankl argued that meaning is not found in external success or pleasure, but in how we choose to engage with suffering and hardship. In this sense, meaning is a kind of emotional wealth that is built through the way we live our lives, the choices we make, and the legacies we leave. Investing time in creating meaning—whether in work, relationships, or personal pursuits—yields a return that transcends material wealth.

The Emotional Return on Investment

The portfolio of presence isn't about how much time we have; it's about how we choose to invest it. When we shift our perspective from time as a finite resource to time as an emotional asset, we begin to recognise the true value of our lives. The experiences we have, the relationships we nurture, and the meaning we create over time compound to yield a wealth that cannot be measured in hours or dollars, but in the richness of our emotional and psychological well-being.

In the end, this new way of thinking challenges us to reconsider how we define a "wealthy" life. It asks us to move beyond the idea that success is measured by what we do and instead, to evaluate our lives based on the emotional and relational wealth we accumulate. The more consciously we invest our time in experiences, relationships, and meaning, the richer and more fulfilling our lives will become. And in a world that is constantly pushing us to accumulate more, perhaps the most revolutionary thing we can do is to invest in what truly matters: *our presence.*

Freedom vs. Leisure

In the landscape of modern life, *leisure* has often been presented as the pinnacle of freedom. From the early days of industrialisation, when labour became both a necessity and a burden, to today's era of automation and the rise of the gig economy, leisure has been marketed as the ultimate escape from the shackles of work. Yet, as the boundaries between work and non-work blur, it's becoming increasingly clear that there is a critical distinction between *passive leisure*—the kind of downtime that requires little effort—and the *active freedom* that results from intentional, purposeful use of time. In fact, the latter is what sustains us, fosters growth, and cultivates deeper fulfilment.

The dichotomy between these two concepts—passive leisure and active freedom—speaks to a broader cultural shift in how we perceive and manage our time. The notion that relaxation and leisure are synonymous with freedom is, for many, a falsehood that hides the deeper needs of the human spirit. While passive leisure, such as binge-watching television or scrolling through social media, may feel like a necessary reprieve from the stresses of daily life, it can paradoxically leave us feeling empty, anxious, and disconnected. On the other hand, active freedom—spending time in ways that are intentionally aligned with our values, passions, and relationships—has the potential to rejuvenate us in a way that passive leisure never can.

This article seeks to distinguish between these two forms of time use, exploring how they affect our emotional and psychological well-being. By reimagining *freedom* not as mere idleness but as a mindful engagement with time, we can begin to create lives that are not only more fulfilling but also more sustainable. Rather than relying on passive distractions to fill the void left by a work-centred life, we can take active control of our hours and shape them in ways that bring joy, meaning, and vitality.

The Illusion of Passive Leisure

We live in a world saturated with options for passive leisure. Our smartphones and streaming platforms are designed to offer continuous, frictionless entertainment, making it easy to fill any moment with distractions. The idea of *taking a break* has, in many cases, become synonymous with disengagement from the present moment—scrolling through Instagram, watching the latest TV series, or playing video games. This kind of leisure is appealing because it requires minimal effort. It is passive, accessible, and often seen as a reward for enduring the pressures of work.

However, this type of leisure can be misleading. At first glance, it may seem like rest, but it often leaves us feeling more drained than before. Research in positive psychology has shown that while passive leisure can provide temporary relief, it rarely fosters long-term well-being. For example, a study published in the *Journal of Personality and Social Psychology* found that passive entertainment—such as watching television—had little impact on overall happiness or life satisfaction, particularly when it became habitual. It may offer short bursts of distraction, but it doesn't contribute to any lasting emotional growth or development.

The issue with passive leisure is that it often fills time without filling our emotional or psychological needs. It serves as an escape from discomfort, but it doesn't actively engage our minds or bodies in ways that nourish them. In many cases, it leaves us feeling more disconnected from ourselves and others, particularly when we've spent hours absorbed in something that provides no personal meaning or value. Over time, this can lead to what psychologists call *hedonic adaptation*—the diminishing return of pleasure from repeated consumption of the same activity. What initially offers us relief can, over time, feel like a hollow pursuit, further feeding our sense of emptiness rather than fulfilling us.

The danger of passive leisure is that it can disguise itself as freedom. It provides temporary relief, but it doesn't empower us to act intentionally or move us closer to what we value. It traps us in cycles of passive consumption, preventing us from engaging with life in a meaningful way. Thus, the idea that "freedom" equals "leisure" needs a reevaluation, as it often leads us away from true freedom, which lies in our ability to make deliberate, conscious choices about how we spend our time.

Active Freedom: The Power of Intentional Time Use

If passive leisure is about escape, *active freedom* is about engagement. It is the art of using time not merely to distract or disengage but to deepen one's connection with the world. Active freedom is an intentional form of time use—one that aligns with personal values, fosters relationships, cultivates creativity, and supports well-being. It's about being present and choosing activities that reflect who we are and what we truly need, rather than following societal scripts of "rest" that are disconnected from our inner world.

Consider, for example, a day spent in nature. The simple act of walking through a forest, hiking up a mountain, or sitting by the sea may not seem like a traditional form of rest, but it has a profound impact on our mental and emotional health. Research shows that time spent outdoors can significantly reduce stress, improve mood, and boost cognitive function. The benefit comes not from the lack of activity, but from the alignment of the activity with our need for relaxation, connection with nature, and physical movement. Active freedom, in this case, is not about doing nothing, but about intentionally engaging with an environment that nurtures the mind and body.

Similarly, spending time with loved ones, engaging in meaningful conversations, or participating in a community activity can yield a type of emotional satisfaction that passive leisure cannot match. These moments build and deepen relationships, foster connection, and contribute to a sense of belonging—all of which are essential for long-term happiness. According to a landmark study by the *Harvard Study of Adult Development*, strong social connections are a key predictor of happiness and longevity. In contrast to the fleeting satisfaction provided by passive leisure, these activities create emotional richness that compounds over time.

Active freedom also requires a level of mindfulness—a conscious awareness of how time is spent and what we wish to gain from it. Unlike passive leisure, which often happens unconsciously, active freedom asks us to reflect on how we are using our hours and to make intentional decisions about how we want to engage with the world. It may involve activities that are physically demanding or intellectually challenging, but the key difference is that these activities are aligned with our values and passions. They energise us, inspire us, and offer a deeper sense of fulfilment than mindless entertainment ever could.

The Role of Autonomy in Active Freedom

One of the central components of active freedom is autonomy—the ability to make choices that align with our personal goals and values. Autonomy is linked to increased well-being, as it allows individuals to live in ways that feel authentic and self-directed. When we exercise autonomy, we are not following external dictates about how we should spend our time; instead, we are choosing what feels most meaningful to us.

This concept is supported by self-determination theory, a psychological framework that suggests people have three basic psychological needs: competence, autonomy, and relatedness. The more we can satisfy these needs through our activities, the more likely we are to experience intrinsic motivation and long-lasting happiness. Active freedom, then, is a direct expression of autonomy—it is the deliberate act of choosing how to spend our time in ways that fulfil these psychological needs.

The contrast between autonomy and passivity is stark. While passive leisure can feel like a break from the demands of life, it often strips us of our sense of agency. We may feel like we are "escaping" from the pressures of work, but in doing so, we are also surrendering our control over how we spend our time. In contrast, active freedom places the power of choice back in our hands. It empowers us to craft a life that is rich, meaningful, and aligned with our values.

The Impact of Technology on Time Use

In today's hyper-connected world, technology plays a significant role in shaping how we experience both leisure and freedom. On the one hand, digital tools can enhance our freedom by providing access to information, creative outlets, and opportunities for social connection. On the other hand, the constant barrage of notifications, emails, and social media updates can quickly turn passive leisure into a trap of distraction and depletion.

The rise of "doomscrolling"—the act of endlessly consuming negative news on social media—illustrates how technology can often encourage passive leisure rather than active engagement. While these activities may momentarily fill time, they don't nourish our emotional or psychological needs. In fact, studies have shown that excessive use of social media can lead to increased feelings of anxiety, depression, and isolation. In contrast, when we use technology to pursue passions, connect with others authentically, or engage in personal growth (e.g., taking online courses, participating in creative forums, or reading enriching content), it becomes a tool for active freedom rather than passive consumption.

The Freedom to Choose: Cultivating a Life of Active Engagement

The fundamental distinction between freedom and leisure lies in the agency we hold over our time. True freedom is not simply about having time to "rest" or "relax," but about the ability to choose how we spend our time in ways that contribute to our well-being. It is about being able to use our hours not only to unwind but to engage with the world in ways that are meaningful, enriching, and aligned with our values.

Active freedom is an invitation to engage more deeply with life, to choose activities that foster connection, creativity, and personal growth. It requires us to step outside the passive consumption of entertainment and take control of how we spend our hours. In doing so, we open up the possibility for a more fulfilling, intentional life—one where freedom is not merely the absence of work, but the presence of choice, engagement, and purpose.

Ultimately, the distinction between passive leisure and active freedom is about living consciously. It's about recognising that time is not simply something to be filled, but something to be invested. How we choose to spend our time matters. By cultivating active freedom and being intentional with our leisure, we can begin to build lives that are not only richer in experience, but also in meaning, joy, and emotional fulfilment.

The Currency of Attention

In the vast landscape of our daily lives, one resource is steadily becoming the most valuable of all: *attention.* It is the thread that weaves together our experiences, governs our interactions, and shapes the quality of our lives. Yet, in the post-work era, where the traditional structures of labour and productivity are being upended by automation, digital technologies, and new economic models, attention has transformed into the ultimate *finite resource.* No longer just something that fuels our productivity, attention is now the most precious commodity, one that, if not carefully managed, slips through our fingers—leaving us overwhelmed, distracted, and disconnected from our true selves.

While time is often regarded as our most valuable asset, it is the way we direct and allocate our attention that determines the quality of our time. We can spend hours in a day, yet if our attention is scattered or hijacked by external forces, we may feel that we have squandered those hours. In a world increasingly dominated by technology, social media, and a constant flood of information, reclaiming our attention is not just a matter of efficiency—it is essential for a meaningful, authentic life. The shift from a world centred on work to one of post-work freedom has created both a challenge and an opportunity: to learn how to invest our attention in ways that lead to more profound, fulfilling experiences.

This article explores the significance of attention in the post-work world, where its value has never been higher. We will examine how the pervasive distractions of modern life threaten to diminish our capacity for deep focus, and how reclaiming this attention can lead to more authentic, engaged living. Drawing from scientific research in neuroscience, psychology, and philosophy, we will see how the intentional cultivation of attention offers not just a way to cope with modern life, but a path to greater joy, creativity, and self-understanding.

The Economics of Attention

The idea that attention is a finite resource is not a new one. In fact, it's one that has been explored in depth by numerous scholars, particularly in the fields of psychology and economics. The term *attention economy* was first coined by psychologist Herbert A. Simon in the late 1970s, when he observed that in a world of information abundance, "a wealth of information creates a poverty of attention." Simon's observation was prescient, as it foreshadowed the current state of our digital world, where attention is the most sought-after commodity by tech companies, advertisers, and media creators alike.

Today, attention is bought, sold, and traded on a massive scale. Social media platforms, search engines, and streaming services design their products to capture and retain our attention, often using sophisticated algorithms that exploit the most primal aspects of human psychology. These companies rely on *continuous engagement*—a never-ending cycle of notifications, updates, and content designed to pull us back in, minute after minute. The result is that our attention is increasingly fragmented, pulled in multiple directions at once, with no real opportunity to focus deeply on any one thing.

But why is attention so valuable? The answer lies in the fact that attention is the gateway to experience. What we pay attention to shapes what we see, hear, feel, and understand. As neuroscientist John Maunsell explains, "Attention is the mechanism that allows us to select from the vast array of stimuli around us those things that are most relevant to our goals and well-being." In this sense, attention is not just the passive reception of stimuli; it is an active process of engagement. The more we invest in something, the more it becomes a part of our lived experience. In a world where time is increasingly unstructured and open-ended, attention has emerged as the means by which we create value from the hours we have.

This realisation is particularly urgent in the context of the post-work world, where the traditional markers of success—employment, income, and status—are no longer as tightly linked to survival or personal fulfilment. In this shifting landscape, how we choose to direct our attention becomes the primary factor in creating meaning in our lives. If attention is the currency, then the way we spend it—whether in pursuits of creativity, learning, relationships, or rest—determines the quality of the life we lead.

The Dangers of Distracted Attention

While attention is now widely recognised as a precious commodity, the modern world presents significant challenges to its preservation. The constant barrage of stimuli we face each day is designed to capture and hold our attention, often without us realising it. A study conducted by the National Center for Biotechnology Information (NCBI) found that 65% of smartphone users check their phones within five minutes of waking up, and more than 80% check their phones within 30 minutes of going to bed. This constant checking isn't just a habit; it's a response to a world where our attention is constantly solicited.

This state of continuous partial attention—where we are constantly multitasking and shifting our focus between various demands—has profound consequences. Research in neuroscience has shown that our brains are not designed to multitask efficiently. When we switch our attention from one task to another, our cognitive resources are depleted, leading to a phenomenon known as *cognitive overload.* This cognitive strain not only reduces our ability to perform complex tasks but also diminishes our capacity to experience and enjoy the present moment.

This constant state of distraction comes with significant emotional costs. Studies in affective neuroscience show that people who are frequently interrupted or distracted experience higher levels of stress, lower levels of well-being, and a diminished sense of personal accomplishment. The emotional exhaustion that comes from living in a world where attention is constantly divided leads to burnout, a feeling of disconnection, and ultimately, a life that feels fragmented and unfulfilled. Rather than fully immersing ourselves in the present, we spend our time hopping from one distraction to the next, never fully engaging with the world or with ourselves.

It is easy to mistake passive engagement with digital media as relaxation or rest, but in many cases, it is more akin to *emotional depletion.* Mindlessly scrolling through social media or watching hours of television may feel like leisure, but it does little to recharge us. In fact, it often leaves us feeling empty, anxious, and disconnected. In this sense, we must distinguish between mere *escapism*—the temporary relief we get from consuming entertainment—and true *rest*, which requires a deeper form of attention that nurtures our mental and emotional health.

Reclaiming Attention for Authentic Living

To reclaim our attention is to reclaim our lives. The process begins with recognising that, in the post-work world, attention is our most powerful tool for creating meaning and fulfilment. In a time when productivity is no longer the sole measure of success, the ability to direct and focus our attention becomes a means of crafting a life that is not just productive but rich in emotional and psychological wealth.

Reclaiming attention begins with conscious awareness. It requires an intentional decision to cut through the noise and distractions that constantly seek our focus. Mindfulness practices, for example, are an effective tool for bringing attention back to the present moment, helping us cultivate a deeper awareness of our thoughts, feelings, and surroundings. Research from the University of California, Davis, has shown that mindfulness not only reduces stress but also enhances our capacity to focus, improves memory, and increases emotional regulation. By becoming more mindful of how we spend our time and where we direct our attention, we begin to break free from the habitual distractions that fragment our lives.

Another key aspect of reclaiming attention is recognising the importance of deep, focused engagement in our activities. Whether we are working, learning, or spending time with loved ones, the ability to immerse ourselves in the task at hand leads to greater satisfaction and well-being. The concept of *flow*, as described by psychologist Mihaly Csikszentmihalyi, refers to the state of deep immersion in an activity that is both challenging and rewarding. In this state, attention is fully engaged, and time seems to disappear. Achieving flow in our daily lives, whether through creative work, hobbies, or meaningful conversations, provides a sense of accomplishment and joy that passive leisure can never replicate.

The final step in reclaiming attention involves designing a life that protects and values this precious resource. This means being intentional about the digital tools we use, setting boundaries around screen time, and creating space for activities that allow us to engage deeply with the world. It also means prioritising real-world connections and experiences over virtual ones—recognising that true connection requires not just being physically present, but also fully attentive and emotionally engaged.

Attention as the Gateway to Authenticity

In the post-work world, attention is the bridge between who we are and who we want to become. The way we choose to direct our focus shapes our reality, influencing how we experience each moment and, ultimately, how we construct meaning in our lives. By reclaiming our attention from the distractions that constantly demand it, we not only enhance our ability to live authentically but also create a richer, more fulfilling existence.

Attention is more than a resource; it is the lens through which we experience and engage with the world. In a time of unprecedented change, the ability to focus and direct our attention has become the ultimate skill for living well. When we invest our attention intentionally, we invest in a life that is deeply connected, meaningful, and true to our values. This is the new currency of the post-work era—a resource that, when wisely reclaimed, offers not just a life of productivity, but a life of true richness and fulfilment.

Chapter 4
Deprogramming the Productivity Complex

In the culture we inhabit today, productivity has taken on a near-sacred status—not merely a marker of efficiency, but a barometer of virtue. The more we accomplish, the more deserving we are, or so the prevailing logic goes. From early schooling to our professional lives, the message is drilled in with quiet persistence: your value lies in your output. Busyness becomes a badge of honour, while idleness—or even rest—is treated with suspicion. Yet this dogged pursuit of productivity, once seen as aspirational, now increasingly feels brittle. Fractured. At times, plainly destructive.

Ours is a society that no longer merely values productivity—it venerates it. But beneath this glossy idol lies something more troubling: what might be called the productivity complex. It's the unspoken conviction that a life is only worthwhile insofar as it produces. Not only is this ideology deeply internalised, it often operates beneath our awareness—surfacing, for example, in those pangs of guilt that accompany a moment of doing absolutely nothing. A quiet afternoon, an unstructured weekend, a blank calendar—these should be gifts. Yet more often, they feel like failures.

In this chapter, we turn our attention to this quietly corrosive belief system. We'll examine how the relentless drumbeat of doing has seeped into our inner lives, convincing us that rest is indulgent, even shameful. We'll also ask how we might unlearn it—how we can gently, yet deliberately, begin to peel away this programming and invite in a gentler rhythm. A rhythm not measured by output, but by presence.

At the heart of this unlearning is a rather uncomfortable fact: doing nothing has become, for many, an act of rebellion. Not because it's radical in form, but because of how it makes us feel—ill at ease, self-critical, exposed. There's a nameable shame that surfaces in those spaces where we are not "accomplishing" something. Why? What have we lost that makes stillness feel like a threat?

We'll trace the roots of that discomfort—psychological, social, even neurological—and begin to craft a more forgiving relationship with time. Part of that shift involves dismantling the cult of efficiency and embracing what might be called the art of elegant sufficiency. Not "doing more with less," as the corporate cliché goes, but doing enough—with care, with intention, with breathing room. It's an art, after all, to know when something is enough.

Indeed, slowness, often miscast as laziness or lack of ambition, might just be one of the most crucial skills of our time. In a world increasingly governed by speed—faster communication, faster transactions, faster lives—our capacity to resist that tempo, to reclaim some measure of autonomy over our time, becomes a quiet act of resistance. A necessary one.

What we're exploring here is not simply a new productivity hack or lifestyle tweak, but a shift in how we relate to life itself. A way of working—and more importantly, of being—that is guided not by the compulsion to maximise, but by the desire to pay attention. To live with a sense of sufficiency, to prioritise depth over breadth, to choose stillness over noise when the moment calls for it.

Reclaiming our time, then, is not just about efficiency. It's about dignity. It's about stepping off the wheel long enough to ask what we truly value, and how we want to spend the fleeting hours that are ours to claim. Not in endless striving, but in presence. Not in accumulation, but in meaning.

The Shame of Doing Nothing

In a world that worships action, the notion of doing "nothing" has become one of the most shame-inducing concepts in modern culture. From childhood, we are conditioned to think that the value of our time is directly proportional to what we produce during it. Whether it's a report at work, an exam at school, or a to-do list at home, our time must be filled with productive activities, or it is deemed wasted. The concept of unstructured time—time spent without direct productivity—can feel like a failure, both to ourselves and in the eyes of society.

This pervasive belief that we must always be busy is deeply ingrained in the cultural narrative of success. In fact, it is so ingrained that it has become an almost subconscious reflex. The "hustle culture," which glorifies being busy at all times, has led many to believe that resting or simply being present is indulgent, lazy, or even morally wrong. The shame of doing nothing, of being idle, is so strong that it has led to a widespread inability to embrace true rest. But this shame response is not just cultural; it is physiological. Our nervous systems have been conditioned to equate stillness with unworthiness. The brain, trained by years of cultural messaging, often responds to inactivity with a sense of anxiety or guilt.

This shame is not only unproductive, it is detrimental to our health. Research in neuroscience and psychology suggests that chronic stress, often linked to a constant drive for productivity, can have long-term negative effects on both our physical and mental well-being. The pressure to perform, to keep pushing forward at all costs, leads to burnout, anxiety, and depression. Ironically, in a culture that prizes productivity, our health and happiness are often the first casualties. We must, therefore, learn how to recondition our nervous systems to embrace *doing nothing*—to reclaim unstructured time as a legitimate, necessary part of life, not something to be feared or avoided.

Reconditioning the nervous system requires patience and practice. One of the first steps in this process is understanding that *stillness*—whether through meditation, mindful walking, or simply sitting in silence—does not need to be filled with productivity to be valuable.

Learning to rest, to truly disengage from the demands of life, is an essential part of self-care and well-being. This chapter will offer practical tools to help us break free from the tyranny of busyness, allowing us to feel comfortable with unstructured time and to understand its crucial role in our emotional and psychological health.

From Efficiency to Elegance

The concept of *elegance* is often associated with beauty, refinement, and simplicity. But in the context of time, elegance can be seen as the art of doing just enough. Efficiency—pushed to its extreme—has become a form of *hyper-activity*, constantly seeking to optimise every second, every minute, every task. While efficiency can certainly have its place, when taken to its extreme, it becomes a constant race against time, leaving no room for presence, for reflection, or for creativity.

What we need, instead, is the art of *elegant sufficiency*. This idea is rooted in the belief that we don't need to do everything, and we certainly don't need to do everything perfectly. Elegance in time use involves knowing when enough is enough—when to stop, rest, and give space for creativity, relationships, and personal growth to flourish. In this model, productivity is no longer the sole measure of value; rather, it is the quality of our engagement with the present moment that becomes the true measure of success.

Elegance in time is about learning to say no to excess, to focus on what truly matters, and to allow our time to be shaped by our values rather than the dictates of external pressures. It's about finding balance in a world that glorifies busyness. This shift from efficiency to elegance invites us to move away from the constant need to optimise and instead embrace a way of living that feels more fluid, more intentional, and more humane.

This concept is particularly relevant in today's world, where digital distractions and the ever-present pressure to "be more" often make it difficult to know when we've done enough. Elegance invites us to trust our instincts, to feel confident in our ability to prioritise what's important, and to resist the urge to fill every moment with "to-do" lists. It encourages a sense of grace in our time use—a recognition that we do not need to constantly strive for perfection, but instead, we can cultivate a life of sufficiency.

Slow is a Skill

One of the most valuable skills we can cultivate in today's world is the ability to slow down. Slowness is often perceived as a passive state—a form of inertia or resistance to progress. Yet, in reality, *slowness* is an active choice that requires discipline, mindfulness, and intentionality. It is the ability to move through life with presence, to resist the pressure to constantly rush from task to task, and to savour the moments that truly matter.

In a culture that glorifies speed, slowness has become a radical act. From the frenetic pace of modern work life to the constant stream of information, everything around us is designed to move faster, to get things done in less time, and to maximise every second. However, research in psychology and neuroscience suggests that when we rush, we miss out on the deeper, more meaningful aspects of life. Slowness, in contrast, allows us to be more present, more thoughtful, and more intentional in our actions.

Moreover, slowness is not just a luxury—it is a necessity for true creativity and reflection. As author Carl Honoré argues in his book *In Praise of Slow*, our fast-paced world often deprives us of the mental space needed for original thought and innovation. In fact, the most creative breakthroughs often come when we slow down and give our minds the time and space to wander, to reflect, and to make new connections. Slowness, therefore, is not just a response to an overstimulated world—it is a skill that allows us to engage more deeply with life and to find meaning in the moments that we would otherwise rush past.

In this chapter, we will explore how we can cultivate slowness as a learned skill, one that enhances our lives rather than detracts from them. We will examine the benefits of slowing down in both our personal and professional lives and offer practical ways to incorporate slowness into daily routines, decision-making processes, and creative endeavours. Slowness, it turns out, is not just a passive state—it is the key to living a more authentic, fulfilling life.

Deprogramming the Productivity Complex

In the end, deprogramming the productivity complex is about more than just rejecting the cult of efficiency—it is about reclaiming time as a space for self-care, reflection, and intentional living. It's about recognising that doing nothing does not make us worthless; that *elegance* in time use allows us to prioritise what truly matters; and that *slowness* is not a burden, but a skill that empowers us to engage more meaningfully with life.

As we move forward in the post-work world, where time becomes a more precious and flexible resource, the ability to manage our time with intention and grace will be one of the most important skills we can develop. This chapter offers not just a critique of the productivity complex, but a roadmap to a more fulfilling, mindful way of living—one that places value on presence, sufficiency, and the quiet power of slowness.

The Religion of Output

In the modern age, productivity has transcended its original role as a simple tool for getting work done. It has become, for many, a way of life—a quasi-religion where rituals, commandments, and promises of salvation shape our daily existence. This has been propelled by an insatiable culture of output that elevates efficiency to a form of spiritual devotion, one that offers the allure of success, fulfilment, and personal transcendence. We live in a world where our value is often measured by what we produce, not by who we are or the quality of our relationships. In this landscape, *wasting time* is not just a lapse; it is a sin, and *hustle culture* has become the path to salvation. The worship of output has become a new form of religion, one that demands constant sacrifice and delivers little in return, except exhaustion and burnout.

The parallels between modern productivity culture and religious devotion are striking. Just as religious followers adhere to prescribed rituals and practices, so too do the devotees of productivity engage in a relentless series of tasks and goals, driven by a deeply ingrained belief that the more they do, the more valuable they become. The pressure to be productive—24/7, without pause or reflection—creates a mindset where worth is tied to action, and inactivity is a moral failure. This is the religion of output: a system where *doing* becomes a moral imperative and *being* a secondary concern, if it is considered at all.

In this article, we will explore how productivity has become a religious-like phenomenon, complete with its rituals, its sins, and its promises of salvation. Drawing from philosophical, psychological, and cultural perspectives, we will analyse how the obsession with output has infiltrated our lives and how it has shaped both our personal and professional identities. By examining the ethical and emotional costs of this system, we will challenge the assumptions that underlie it and explore the possibility of a more balanced approach to work, time, and life.

The Rituals of Productivity

At the heart of productivity culture lies a series of rituals—routines, habits, and practices—that are designed to optimise our output. These rituals are not just about achieving efficiency; they have become rites of passage that mark the value of one's day, week, and year. The modern-day version of the "morning routine," for instance, is a perfect example. The formula is familiar: wake up early, engage in a series of disciplined actions—perhaps meditation, exercise, reading, and journaling—and then move seamlessly into a day filled with goal-setting, task management, and achievement. This routine, which promises productivity and personal growth, has become almost sacrosanct in modern culture. Those who follow it are seen as the enlightened few, the ones who have unlocked the secrets of success. For many, failing to adhere to this schedule is seen as a moral failing, a lapse into idleness or even self-sabotage.

The success of these rituals is not just about tangible outcomes—though those are certainly important—it's about their ability to create a sense of control. In a world that often feels chaotic and unpredictable, these rituals offer a form of structure and certainty. The rituals of productivity culture provide a sense of accomplishment, a belief that if we follow the right steps and maintain discipline, we will achieve our goals and live a meaningful life. In this way, the rituals themselves become a form of worship, as individuals devote time and energy to activities that promise the rewards of success, wealth, and happiness.

Yet, like any religious practice, these rituals often come with an unspoken cost. The pressure to keep up with the latest productivity trends, to optimise every waking hour, and to remain constantly "on" creates a paradox: while the rituals are designed to bring success and fulfilment, they often lead to burnout, stress, and a diminished sense of well-being. The constant quest for perfection, driven by the rituals of productivity, leaves little room for spontaneity, rest, or relaxation—things that are essential for genuine creativity and long-term mental health.

The Sin of Wasting Time

In the religion of output, one of the most egregious sins is *wasting time.* In a culture that constantly measures success by the quantity and quality of one's work, time spent away from productivity is often viewed as morally suspect. This belief runs deep in modern society: *time is money*, and time spent not producing is seen as lost. The shame associated with "wasting time" has become pervasive, and it extends to both our professional and personal lives. When we relax or take time off, we are not just resting; we are *wasting*—and this, in the eyes of many, is a grave offence.

The concept of "wasting time" is not just a societal construct; it is deeply embedded in our psychology. According to the work of sociologist Richard Sennett, modern capitalism has reshaped our relationship with time, turning it into a resource that must be maximised at all costs. The idea that any moment spent not working is wasted has become so ingrained that even moments of relaxation or leisure can trigger feelings of guilt or inadequacy. This cultural conditioning reinforces the belief that *doing nothing* is inherently wrong, even though rest and recovery are essential for maintaining long-term productivity and well-being.

This deep-seated shame around doing nothing also exacerbates the rise of burnout. In a society where "busy" is often equated with "important," those who are able to embrace leisure or unstructured time are often viewed with suspicion. We are taught to feel guilty for taking breaks, for stepping away from our desks, for engaging in activities that don't lead directly to productivity. This constant pressure to remain in a state of perpetual motion—physically, mentally, and emotionally—leads to exhaustion, disillusionment, and a growing sense of inadequacy.

To break free from the sin of wasting time, we must reframe our understanding of what constitutes valuable time. The belief that time is only valuable when it is used for productive output is deeply flawed. Time spent in leisure, in connection, in reflection, or in rest is not wasted. It is an investment in our long-term well-being, creativity, and personal fulfilment. Only by shedding the shame of inactivity can we reclaim a more balanced, humane approach to living and working.

Salvation Through Hustle Culture

At the centre of the religion of output is the promise of salvation through *hustle culture*. Hustle culture promises that by working harder, sacrificing more, and constantly striving for success, we will attain the rewards of wealth, recognition, and fulfilment. It is a culture built on the belief that there is no such thing as "enough" and that true success comes only through relentless effort and discipline. In many ways, hustle culture has become a form of salvation theology, where the ultimate goal is self-actualisation through work.

However, just as religious zeal can blind followers to the dangers of extremism, hustle culture's obsession with productivity can have destructive consequences. While the promise of salvation—greater wealth, recognition, and success—might seem appealing, the cost is often unsustainable. Studies on workaholism have shown that those who adhere to hustle culture are at increased risk for burnout, anxiety, and depression. The constant drive for more, the unrelenting pressure to produce, leaves little room for rest, reflection, or personal growth. In many ways, hustle culture is a modern form of asceticism, one that demands sacrifice without offering real rewards.

This idea of salvation through work is not just personal but societal. We are encouraged to view our worth through the lens of output, equating our value with our ability to produce. In this framework, success is a matter of *doing*, not *being*. But this leaves us with a question: *What happens when the hustle fails to deliver the promised rewards?* When success is tied solely to the ability to work without pause, we are left with lives that feel shallow, disconnected, and devoid of meaning. True salvation, then, must come not from more work, but from a reevaluation of what constitutes a fulfilling life.

Breaking the Cycle: Moving Beyond the Religion of Output

To move beyond the religion of output, we must first acknowledge the power that productivity culture holds over us. This culture is not just a set of behaviours; it is a deeply ingrained system of beliefs that shapes our identity, our relationships, and our sense of worth. To deprogram ourselves from this complex, we must challenge the belief that productivity is synonymous with value. We must also learn to embrace stillness and rest without guilt, recognising that these moments are essential to our long-term well-being and creativity.

One of the first steps in breaking free from hustle culture is to redefine what success looks like. True success is not about doing more, but about doing *what matters*—whether that's nurturing relationships, engaging in creative expression, or contributing to causes we care about. It's about recognising that a life filled with meaningful work, balanced with rest and play, is a life that is truly worth living. In this sense, salvation comes not through more work, but through a more integrated approach to life that values time as a resource for personal growth, connection, and purpose.

To reclaim our time and our lives from the grip of productivity culture, we must move from the cult of *hustle* to the art of *elegant sufficiency*—doing enough, with grace, and allowing ourselves the space to simply *be*. This shift is not only a personal transformation, but a societal one. It is an invitation to redefine what it means to live well, to break free from the constant worship of output, and to cultivate a more balanced, meaningful existence. In this new world, salvation lies not in doing more, but in being present, engaged, and authentic in each moment.

The Shame of Doing Nothing

In an age where productivity is relentlessly equated with personal worth, the idea of doing nothing has become one of modern society's greatest taboos. It is, in many ways, viewed as a moral failure—a lapse in both personal and societal duty. Our calendars are filled with meetings, deadlines, and tasks, all measured by an invisible standard that values constant action over presence. To be idle, to spend time without purpose, is often considered a shameful act. In fact, in today's productivity-obsessed world, the act of *doing nothing* can trigger a profound sense of shame—a visceral response that is both culturally constructed and deeply ingrained in our nervous systems.

This article explores the origins and implications of the shame surrounding unstructured time, delving into how this deep-rooted cultural programming affects our emotional well-being. By examining the psychological mechanisms that underpin our fear of doing nothing, we will uncover how this anxiety about idleness is not just a personal struggle, but a societal construct. More importantly, we will explore ways to recondition our nervous systems, helping us reclaim unstructured time without guilt, and ultimately fostering a more balanced, authentic approach to living.

The concept of *doing nothing* isn't new, yet its stigma has grown more potent in recent decades, fuelled by the pervasive narrative of hustle culture and the modern work ethic. There is, in fact, a moral and emotional cost to this shame—a cost that often goes unacknowledged. As we move further into an era where work is increasingly automated and productivity can be outsourced, the value of our unstructured time—the moments where we pause, reflect, or simply exist—should be reconsidered. This chapter aims to provide a framework for understanding the emotional weight of doing nothing and, crucially, how we can learn to embrace it as an essential part of living well.

The Historical Roots of the Productivity Complex

To fully understand why we experience such profound shame when faced with unstructured time, we must first recognise the historical roots of the productivity complex. This deep-seated belief that value is intrinsically tied to work and output is not an inherent part of the human condition, but a cultural construct that has evolved over centuries. In early agricultural societies, time was largely determined by natural cycles—seasonal changes, the rhythm of day and night, and the demands of planting and harvest. Work and rest were more clearly defined by the land's needs, and there was less of a notion that idleness was inherently immoral or unworthy.

However, with the rise of the Industrial Revolution, time began to be commodified. The workday became regimented by the clock, and the value of an individual was increasingly measured by the number of hours worked and the efficiency with which tasks were completed. The factory model, which demanded unwavering focus and productivity, was adopted across society. It was during this period that the Protestant work ethic gained prominence, reinforcing the idea that hard work was not only virtuous but a moral duty. This belief was soon internalised by millions, forming the foundation of what we now recognise as the modern productivity complex.

The shift from agrarian rhythms to industrial time management marked the beginning of a cultural paradigm where unstructured time became suspect. If one was not working, they were viewed as lazy, unproductive, or worse—*unworthy*. This cultural programming has since been amplified by the advent of technology and the increasing demands of the digital economy. Today, with the rise of remote work, gig economies, and the expectation of constant availability, the pressure to remain "on" at all times is pervasive, and the shame associated with inactivity has never been stronger.

The Psychology of Idleness: The Neural Mechanics of Shame

The shame of doing nothing is not merely a social construct; it is also a psychological phenomenon rooted in the way our brains respond to perceived failure. According to research in neuroscience, the human brain is hardwired to respond to perceived lapses in productivity with stress and anxiety. The brain's reward system is designed to release dopamine in response to actions that promote survival or success, such as completing a task or achieving a goal. This system reinforces the notion that *doing* equals value, and *doing nothing* equals a lack of worth.

When we engage in unstructured time, our brains do not receive the same positive feedback. The absence of productive activity leads to a withdrawal of dopamine, triggering feelings of unease or guilt. This biological response is compounded by the cultural programming that equates inactivity with laziness. Over time, these feelings become entrenched in our nervous systems, creating a conditioned response to downtime that feels uncomfortable and even shameful.

Moreover, the neurobiological effects of chronic stress, which is often linked to a productivity-driven lifestyle, can exacerbate this shame. The constant pressure to remain productive can lead to dysregulation of the autonomic nervous system, making it difficult for the body to relax and recover. As a result, the brain becomes conditioned to associate inactivity with discomfort, and we experience guilt or anxiety when we are not engaged in a task.

Reconditioning this response requires an intentional effort to retrain the nervous system. This process involves shifting our relationship with time, reinterpreting the role of rest, and understanding that stillness is not an absence of value, but a crucial component of a well-lived life. By breaking the cycle of guilt and anxiety that accompanies unstructured time, we can begin to embrace rest as an essential practice for mental and emotional well-being.

The Cultural Stigma of Doing Nothing

The social stigma surrounding doing nothing is reinforced by the dominant narratives in contemporary society. Social media, with its constant stream of productivity tips and success stories, perpetuates the belief that being busy is synonymous with being valuable. Influencers and entrepreneurs constantly showcase their packed schedules, positioning themselves as models of success who never stop moving. In this environment, taking a break or engaging in unstructured time can feel like an act of rebellion—or worse, an admission of failure.

This cultural pressure is particularly acute in professional settings, where employees are expected to demonstrate visible output at all times. In a society where the 40-hour workweek is often seen as a minimum, any deviation from this norm is interpreted as laziness. This is particularly true in industries driven by performance metrics, where employees are expected to constantly "produce" results, often at the expense of their mental and emotional health.

Moreover, the rise of the "entrepreneurial" mindset has created a culture that rewards those who are always hustling, striving, and working harder. The idea that *you are your work* is pervasive, and those who do not fit into this mould are often regarded as less ambitious, less driven, or less worthy of success. The underlying message is clear: doing nothing is not just a personal choice—it is a moral failing.

This stigma is not only harmful to individuals but also to society as a whole. The glorification of constant work leads to a cycle of burnout, stress, and disconnection. The inability to take time off or engage in unstructured activities impedes creativity, stifles innovation, and leaves little room for the kind of reflective thinking that drives personal and professional growth. The belief that rest is a luxury rather than a necessity is a deeply entrenched cultural issue that needs to be addressed if we are to foster healthier, more balanced societies.

Reconditioning Our Nervous Systems: Embracing Unstructured Time

Breaking free from the shame of doing nothing begins with a shift in perspective. The first step is recognising that unstructured time—whether spent resting, daydreaming, or simply being present in the moment—is not only valuable but essential. It is in these moments of stillness that we often find our greatest insights, our most creative ideas, and our deepest sense of connection with ourselves and others.

One way to recondition our nervous systems is through mindfulness practices. Meditation, breathing exercises, and mindful walking are all effective ways to help the brain enter a state of relaxation and ease. These practices encourage us to experience the present moment without judgment or expectation, fostering a sense of peace and acceptance. Over time, they help to recalibrate the body's stress response, allowing us to engage in unstructured time without the underlying guilt or anxiety that often accompanies it.

Another important practice is to consciously *prioritise* downtime. This can be achieved by scheduling rest as you would any important task or meeting. By making time for stillness an intentional part of your daily routine, you signal to your brain that rest is not something to be feared, but something to be embraced. This intentionality also helps to shift the cultural narrative that values constant work over rest. When we prioritise rest, we begin to challenge the deeply ingrained belief that only productivity has value.

Finally, cultivating *self-compassion* is key to overcoming the shame of doing nothing. This involves being kind to ourselves during moments of inactivity, recognising that rest is not an indulgence but a necessary component of a balanced life. Studies in positive psychology have shown that self-compassion is strongly correlated with well-being and emotional resilience. By practising self-compassion, we give ourselves permission to take breaks, to rest, and to engage in unstructured time without the weight of guilt.

Reclaiming the Power of Unstructured Time

Reclaiming unstructured time is not just a personal matter—it is a collective endeavour. If we are to create a society that values rest, creativity, and presence, we must begin by challenging the shame surrounding idleness and recognising the profound value of stillness. In doing so, we can recondition our nervous systems to embrace unstructured time as a vital part of a well-lived life.

By shifting the narrative away from constant productivity and embracing the power of doing nothing, we open ourselves to a life of greater balance, creativity, and authenticity. Doing nothing is not a sin. It is a necessary part of the human experience—a space where rest, renewal, and reflection can take place. Only when we shed the shame of inactivity can we begin to live more fully, with a deeper sense of meaning, purpose, and connection.

From Efficiency to Elegance

In an age defined by the ceaseless drive for efficiency, the idea that *just enough* could ever be a virtuous approach seems, to many, anathema to success. The dominant mantra of the modern world tells us that more is always better—that we must optimise every moment, every action, every decision to extract the highest possible return. The cult of efficiency has, for decades, permeated every aspect of life, from business to education, from personal development to societal expectations. We are constantly told to do more, faster, better, squeezing every last drop of productivity from our finite hours. But in this relentless pursuit, we may have lost something vital: the *art of elegant sufficiency*. The concept of doing just enough, with grace and space, is an antidote to the hyper-competitive, hyper-efficient world we have come to accept as the norm.

This shift—from efficiency to elegance—requires not merely a change in mindset, but a fundamental reimagining of how we approach time, value, and success. It challenges us to break free from the worship of perpetual busyness and instead embrace the idea that less, done thoughtfully and intentionally, can be far more fulfilling and effective than the endless grind. *Efficiency* tells us to aim for perfection, to optimise, and to achieve at all costs, but in doing so, we sacrifice depth, creativity, and presence. In contrast, *elegance* is about finding balance—doing what is necessary and important, with enough space for reflection, for enjoyment, and for rest.

This article will explore how we can move beyond the tyranny of efficiency and embrace the elegance of sufficiency in our professional and personal lives. We will delve into why the pursuit of maximum output often leaves us feeling drained and disconnected, and how by recalibrating our relationship with time and productivity, we can cultivate a life of greater meaning, creativity, and joy. Drawing on psychology, philosophy, and contemporary cultural insights, we will examine how to replace the demands of efficiency with the mindful, graceful approach of *doing just enough.*

The Rise of the Cult of Efficiency

The 20th and 21st centuries have been marked by an unprecedented obsession with efficiency. It began with the industrial revolution, where efficiency in manufacturing became a key driver of progress. As factories grew, productivity metrics were developed to ensure that every worker, every machine, every process was optimised for maximum output. *Time is money*, the maxim went, and any inefficiency was a wasted opportunity.

Over time, this principle of efficiency was extended far beyond the factory floor and became a societal norm. In the world of business, in education, and even in the realm of personal development, the language of optimisation, targets, and KPIs became the measure by which success was judged. From the spreadsheets that fill boardrooms to the apps on our phones that track our exercise, diets, and daily tasks, efficiency has woven itself into every fabric of modern life. It is no longer simply about completing a task—it is about completing it in the least amount of time, with the least amount of energy, and for the highest return.

Yet, as we strive for greater efficiency, we often overlook the cost: the human element. In our relentless quest for optimisation, we have reduced the value of work to a transactional model: effort equals reward. We view time through the lens of productivity rather than presence. And in doing so, we have sacrificed something deeper—our creativity, our well-being, and, most poignantly, our ability to enjoy the moment.

The modern efficiency paradigm demands that we constantly move faster and further. But in doing so, we often miss the subtle, meaningful moments that add richness to our lives. We rush through tasks, relationships, and experiences without allowing ourselves the time to reflect, to appreciate, or to simply be. This disconnect from the present is a by-product of an efficiency-driven mindset that values speed and quantity over depth and quality.

The Art of Elegant Sufficiency

What if the key to a fulfilling and sustainable life is not in doing more, but in doing less—*doing just enough*? This is the philosophy of elegant sufficiency, an antidote to the demands of productivity culture. Rather than striving for maximum output, elegant sufficiency invites us to focus on what is truly important and to approach it with intention and grace.

The idea behind elegant sufficiency is simple: rather than attempting to optimise every second, every decision, and every outcome, we focus on achieving what is necessary and meaningful. This does not mean abandoning ambition or effort—it means recognising that success does not always require maximum efficiency. Sometimes, the most meaningful outcomes come not from pushing ourselves to the limit but from allowing space for creativity, rest, and reflection.

Elegant sufficiency is about achieving balance. It is the art of finding the sweet spot between effort and ease, action and rest, productivity and relaxation. This is not a rejection of hard work, but a rejection of the *cult* of relentless efficiency, which tells us that only by constantly striving can we achieve value. Instead, it is about recognising that our most valuable moments and achievements often arise when we stop pushing and simply *are*—when we allow ourselves to breathe, to enjoy the process, and to make room for the unexpected.

Take, for example, the process of writing. In an efficiency-driven world, the focus is often on output—how many words can be written in an hour, how quickly can an article be completed, how fast can we reach the goal? But in an approach rooted in elegance, the emphasis shifts to the quality of the words, the depth of the thinking, and the experience of the writing itself. It is not about rushing to finish, but about enjoying the process of creation. The result is often more thoughtful, more creative, and more fulfilling than a piece that has been churned out in the name of efficiency.

The Power of Slowness: A Learned Skill

One of the cornerstones of elegant sufficiency is the ability to *slow down.* In a world that values speed and instant gratification, slowness has become a radical act. It is often perceived as a passive, unproductive state—an impediment to progress. However, in reality, slowness is a *learned skill*, one that allows us to engage with the world more fully and with greater intention.

In his groundbreaking work on *flow*, psychologist Mihaly Csikszentmihalyi demonstrates that deep engagement and true creativity often arise not from rushing through tasks, but from being fully present and absorbed in them. The ability to slow down, to focus on the task at hand, and to allow ourselves to become immersed in the process is what leads to the kind of results that are both deeply satisfying and highly creative. This contrasts with the quick-fix mentality that often prioritises speed over substance.

Slowness also allows for the space to reflect, to make better decisions, and to engage more meaningfully with the world around us. Whether it's taking time to truly listen to a colleague during a meeting, allowing space for creativity to flow in a personal project, or simply pausing to appreciate a moment in nature, slowness gives us the opportunity to engage in a deeper, more thoughtful way.

In fact, research has shown that cultivating the ability to slow down can lead to better mental health, greater creativity, and a more fulfilling life. In his book *In Praise of Slow*, Carl Honoré argues that the ability to slow down in certain areas of life is essential for overall well-being. Slowness is not about doing less—it's about doing what is needed with greater awareness, care, and attention to detail.

Reframing Success: Quality Over Quantity

Ultimately, the shift from efficiency to elegance requires a fundamental reframing of what success looks like. In a culture that prizes *doing more*—more work, more hours, more achievements—the focus often lies on quantity. But true success is not about how much we do, but about how well we do it. It is not about maximising every moment but about making each moment meaningful.

In this light, the elegance of sufficiency offers a more sustainable and fulfilling path. It invites us to consider the quality of our efforts rather than the sheer volume of them. This philosophy encourages us to focus on what truly matters: our relationships, our creativity, our health, and our sense of purpose. By aligning our actions with our values and embracing the idea of doing just enough, we create space for deeper engagement, richer experiences, and a more profound sense of fulfilment.

This approach doesn't diminish ambition—it transforms it. Instead of striving for unattainable perfection, we aim for *elegance*: a life that is sufficient in its fullness, where we do what is necessary with care, focus, and grace. It is a life where we work not to meet the arbitrary demands of productivity culture, but to achieve personal meaning and connection.

The Future of Time: Beyond the Cult of Efficiency

As we move into an era where automation, artificial intelligence, and shifting societal structures increasingly make traditional work models obsolete, the cult of efficiency may become even more entrenched. But it is also in this very disruption that we find the opportunity for transformation. As work becomes more flexible and less central to our sense of identity, we have the chance to rethink how we use our time.

Rather than continuing the race towards infinite productivity, we can embrace the elegance of sufficiency—doing enough, with grace, and creating space for life beyond work. This shift will require courage, for it challenges not only societal norms but also deeply ingrained personal habits. But by moving from efficiency to elegance, we can create a more balanced, meaningful existence—one that values presence over performance, quality over quantity, and sufficiency over surplus. In this way, elegance becomes the true path to a life well-lived.

Slow is a Skill

In a world that constantly prizes speed, efficiency, and instant gratification, *slowness* has become an almost revolutionary concept. We live in an era where emails are expected to be answered within minutes, meetings are crammed into tight schedules, and progress is often defined by how quickly results can be achieved. Yet, beneath this relentless pace lies a growing recognition that *slowness*—far from being a passive state of inertia—is a learned skill, one that holds the key to a more intentional, creative, and meaningful future. As we continue to grapple with the demands of an ever-accelerating world, the ability to slow down has become one of the most important soft skills for the 21st century.

The notion that slowness can be cultivated as a skill is both radical and essential. In the same way that physical fitness requires practice and discipline, so too does the ability to slow down in a world that conditions us to move ever faster. It is no longer enough to simply advocate for "work-life balance" or suggest that we "take a break" when feeling overwhelmed. The skill of slowness involves a deliberate shift in mindset, a recalibration of how we perceive time, and a commitment to engaging more deeply with the present moment. It requires not only resisting the urge to rush through life but embracing slowness as a way to foster creativity, enhance productivity, and cultivate well-being.

This article explores the concept of slowness as a learned skill, positioning it as one of the most vital competencies for individuals navigating the demands of the modern world. We will examine why slowness is increasingly being recognised as a strategic advantage, both in personal development and in the workplace, and how we can intentionally develop this skill. Drawing from psychological research, case studies of successful slow practices, and historical perspectives, we will demonstrate that slowness is not only a necessary counterbalance to the chaos of modern life but an essential ingredient for success in an ever-changing world.

The Pace of Progress: The Tyranny of Speed

To fully appreciate the value of slowness, we must first understand the cultural forces that have shaped our current obsession with speed. From the Industrial Revolution to the rise of digital technology, the pace of progress has been tied to the speed at which tasks can be completed. In the early days of industrialisation, efficiency was synonymous with time saved. The advent of the assembly line and mechanised production enabled businesses to increase output exponentially, and in doing so, reshaped societal norms around work. Time was no longer seen as a finite resource to be respected; it became something to be manipulated, stretched, and optimised.

This cultural shift towards speed has only accelerated with the advent of the digital age. The internet has created a world where information is available at the click of a button, communication happens in real-time, and expectations for quick responses are higher than ever. The rise of "hustle culture" reinforces this sense that to be successful, one must be in constant motion, always achieving, always progressing, always accelerating. The notion of slowness, by contrast, is often dismissed as inefficiency, laziness, or a lack of ambition. In this context, the idea of slowing down seems counterintuitive, even indulgent.

Yet, in the rush to achieve more and move faster, we often sacrifice something far more valuable: *depth.* We speed through tasks, meetings, and even conversations, prioritising productivity over presence. This constant acceleration leads to mental fatigue, burnout, and, ironically, diminished effectiveness. As the world grows faster, the need for slowness becomes more urgent. The ability to slow down—to pause, reflect, and engage with the world at a different pace—is no longer a luxury; it is a necessity for sustainable success, creativity, and well-being.

The Science of Slowness: Why It Matters

While slowness may be seen as a luxury or indulgence by some, research from psychology and neuroscience reveals that it is, in fact, a critical skill that enhances cognitive function, creativity, and emotional well-being. The human brain is not designed to function at a constant high speed. In fact, studies show that when we are under stress or constantly multitasking, our cognitive abilities are diminished, and our decision-making becomes less effective. *Cognitive overload*—a state where the brain is overwhelmed with too much information or too many tasks—leads to errors, poor memory retention, and burnout.

One of the most compelling arguments for slowness comes from the concept of *deep work*, as described by Cal Newport in his book *Deep Work: Rules for Focused Success in a Distracted World.* Newport argues that the ability to focus deeply on a single task without distraction is becoming increasingly rare but is also a crucial skill for success. Slowing down allows us to engage in deep work, where our cognitive resources are fully devoted to one activity, leading to higher levels of creativity and productivity. The result is not just faster output, but better output—more thoughtful, more innovative, and more valuable.

Moreover, the deliberate act of slowing down can have profound effects on our mental and emotional health. Mindfulness practices, which encourage a slower, more intentional way of engaging with the world, have been shown to reduce stress, improve focus, and enhance emotional regulation. By taking the time to slow down, we allow ourselves to be more present, which in turn improves our relationships, our work, and our overall sense of well-being.

Slowness as a Competitive Advantage

In a world that glorifies speed, the ability to slow down may seem counterproductive. However, the most successful individuals and organisations recognise that slowness can be a competitive advantage. Far from being a passive or unproductive state, slowness is an active choice that can enhance performance and innovation.

Take, for example, the practice of *deliberate practice* in fields like music, sports, and business. Experts in these fields often engage in slow, focused work to hone their skills. They don't rush through their practice sessions; instead, they slow down, paying attention to the smallest details, making adjustments, and allowing time for reflection. This approach to practice allows for deeper learning and mastery. Similarly, the most innovative companies, such as Apple and Google, are known for creating environments that encourage slow thinking, reflection, and deep focus—spaces where employees can step away from the constant rush of work and give themselves the time and mental space to think creatively.

In a business context, the ability to slow down also means taking time for strategic thinking and long-term planning, rather than focusing solely on short-term results. Fast-moving markets and fast-paced technologies can make it difficult to slow down, but companies that are able to take a step back, analyse trends, and make thoughtful, strategic decisions often emerge as leaders in their industries. By embracing slowness as a skill, businesses can differentiate themselves from competitors who are stuck in the rush to do more, faster.

Cultivating the Skill of Slowness

If slowness is indeed a skill, then how do we cultivate it? The first step is recognising that slowness is not an absence of action but a deliberate choice to engage with the world in a more intentional way. It involves training our minds and bodies to resist the constant urge to move quickly, to multitask, and to optimise every moment. Instead, it requires us to embrace *presence*—to slow down, focus on one thing at a time, and give ourselves permission to be less than perfectly efficient.

One practical approach to cultivating slowness is through mindfulness meditation. This practice trains the mind to focus on the present moment without judgment or distraction. Over time, mindfulness can help us become more aware of our thoughts, feelings, and physical sensations, allowing us to better regulate our response to stress and distractions. This heightened awareness helps us make more deliberate choices about how we spend our time and energy, ensuring that we prioritise what truly matters.

Another approach is to incorporate *slow time* into our daily routines. This could mean taking breaks throughout the day to step outside, go for a walk, or simply sit in silence. It could involve setting aside specific times for deep work or reflection, free from the constant demands of emails, meetings, and notifications. The key is to create spaces where we can slow down, recharge, and focus deeply on one task at a time.

Slowness as the Future's Most Needed Skill

As we look to the future, the skill of slowness will be one of the most important tools we can cultivate. In a world where technological advancements are accelerating, and the pace of work and life shows no signs of slowing down, the ability to pause, reflect, and engage deeply with the present moment will become increasingly rare—and increasingly valuable. Slowness, far from being a passive state, is an active choice that enhances creativity, productivity, and well-being. It is not about doing less, but about doing more with intention and presence.

In the coming decades, as automation and artificial intelligence take over more routine tasks, the human capacity for *slow, intentional thinking* will be the defining characteristic of those who excel. The ability to slow down and think deeply will be a rare skill, one that sets apart those who can innovate, strategise, and lead in a world that is increasingly overwhelmed by speed and distraction. In this sense, the future belongs to those who can master the skill of slowness—those who can choose to move at a pace that allows for depth, creativity, and human connection.

Conclusion: The Power of Slowness

In the fast-paced, efficiency-driven world we inhabit, the skill of slowness offers a powerful antidote. It allows us to engage more fully with our work, our relationships, and our lives. It invites us to do just enough, but with grace, presence, and intention. Far from being a passive state, slowness is an active, learned skill—one that holds the potential to transform our work, our creativity, and our well-being. By cultivating this skill, we can navigate the demands of the modern world with greater focus, clarity, and depth, making slowness not just a choice, but the most valuable skill of the future.

Chapter 5
Designing the Time-Rich Life

We find ourselves in a world governed by the relentless beat of the clock—a culture in which time is carved into units of productivity, tallied in tasks ticked off lists and goals frantically pursued. The rhetoric is everywhere: optimise your calendar, master your mornings, hack your habits. It's a drumbeat that insists we do more, be more, squeeze every drop from every hour. And yet, somewhere in that restless pursuit, something essential slips quietly through the cracks. Something spacious. Human. Irreplaceable. The texture of time, perhaps—its potential to soothe, to restore, to root us in what truly matters.

To live time-rich is not simply to have more of it. Nor is it about managing our minutes with greater ruthlessness. Rather, it invites a reorientation—a subtle but profound shift from wringing time dry to inhabiting it fully. It is a life not measured by how many hours we log, but by how we inhabit those hours. A time-rich existence asks not how efficiently we can perform, but how consciously we can live. Can we choose presence over haste? Depth over breadth? Joy—not merely function?

This chapter charts a path toward that more generous experience of time. Not through productivity hacks, but through practices that cultivate depth and connection. We will explore three foundational elements: the quiet anchoring power of ritual, the transformative space offered by sacred pauses, and the often-overlooked wisdom of embodied time awareness. These are not abstract ideals but lived, tangible shifts—simple, even—yet radical in a world obsessed with forward motion.

Let us begin with ritual. Unlike routine, which often carries the dry weight of obligation, ritual carries intention. It is less about what we do and more about how we do it. Lighting a candle before writing. Walking slowly at dusk. Brewing tea with care rather than haste. These seemingly small acts, when repeated with reverence, have the power to tether us to the present, to offer moments of sanctuary amidst the churn of daily demands. They speak not to efficiency, but to meaning.

Equally vital is the art of pausing—not in the dramatic, sabbatical sense, but in the gentle, ordinary way that carves out brief intervals of stillness within our days. A breath before speaking. A glance out the window. A refusal to rush from one obligation to the next. These sacred pauses, though fleeting, recalibrate our nervous systems. They stretch our sense of time, slow the heartbeat of the day, and remind us—if only for a moment—that we are not machines. We are human, and we need room to breathe.

Then there is the body—our most honest timekeeper. While the mind darts forward, tallying, planning, chasing the next thing, the body remains in the now. It holds a quieter, steadier rhythm, one shaped not by deadlines but by cycles, hunger, fatigue, sensation. Too often, we override these cues in favour of mental hustle. But when we learn to listen—truly listen—we begin to understand time differently. Not as a line to race along, but as a rhythm to move with. This embodied awareness invites us to align our choices with something deeper than the clock: our own inner tempo.

To craft a time-rich life, then, is not to escape the world but to move differently within it. It is to live as though time were not an adversary but a companion. A collaborator. A canvas. It asks that we look not to accumulation, but to integration—not how much we can fit in, but how fully we can be where we are.

What follows in this chapter is not a blueprint, but an invitation. To slow. To listen. To recalibrate your relationship with time so that it becomes something you inhabit, not something that hounds you. For in the end, richness is not found in the stretch of our calendars, but in the quality of our hours. Not in doing more, but in being here—wholly, deliberately, now.

Rituals Over Routines: The Soul of Time

The modern-day routine is often a march toward greater efficiency—checklists, calendars, apps, and systems designed to maximise every moment of the day. While routines undoubtedly have their place, they often become a mechanical way of filling time, leaving little room for creativity, reflection, or personal growth. Routines are external systems that organise our lives, but they often fail to nourish us on a deeper level. In contrast, rituals are the internal practices that connect us with our sense of meaning, our emotions, and our spirituality. Rituals provide a framework that transforms the ordinary into the sacred, turning simple tasks into moments of connection with ourselves and the world around us.

Rituals are deeply personal and can take many forms—morning meditations, a walk in nature, a family dinner, or even the act of lighting a candle before beginning a task. What makes these practices *rituals* is the intentionality with which we engage in them. Rituals provide us with a sense of grounding and presence, allowing us to pause and reflect before moving forward. They are often linked to something greater than the task at hand—whether it's a sense of connection with the divine, a commitment to personal growth, or a desire to strengthen relationships. These practices foster an awareness that we are not just moving through life passively but are actively shaping our experience of time in meaningful ways.

Unlike routines that can feel like obligations, rituals invite us to engage with time in a way that feels nourishing and restorative. They help us cultivate presence and mindfulness, offering a rich contrast to the pressures of productivity culture. By incorporating rituals into our daily lives, we can create pockets of time that are devoted not to tasks but to *being*—being present, being mindful, being connected. Over time, these rituals accumulate, offering us a profound sense of time richness, of a life that is lived with intention rather than simply passed through.

Sacred Pauses: Expanding Time Through Presence

In a world that urges us to keep moving, to keep doing, and to keep achieving, the concept of the pause has become radical. Yet it is in the pause—the sacred moment of stillness—that we often find clarity, creativity, and calm. Sacred pauses are micro-moments throughout the day where we intentionally stop, take a breath, and recalibrate. These pauses do not require long hours or special circumstances; they can happen in the midst of the busiest day, between meetings, during a commute, or before a meal.

The power of sacred pauses lies in their ability to expand our experience of time. When we are constantly moving from one task to the next, we experience time as fragmented and rushed. But when we pause, we give ourselves permission to step outside the flow of productivity and reconnect with the present moment. This shift in focus can help us reset our nervous systems, reduce stress, and enhance our capacity for focus and decision-making. A few seconds of mindful breathing, a quick stretch, or a moment of reflection can profoundly affect our emotional and physical well-being, helping us regain clarity and avoid burnout.

Sacred pauses are not simply breaks from work—they are opportunities to reconnect with our inner rhythms and the world around us. By incorporating intentional pauses into our day, we can cultivate a deeper relationship with time, allowing us to use it not just as a resource to be managed, but as a space to be truly present. These pauses, though small, have the potential to transform our days, enriching our experience of time and expanding its potential for creativity, reflection, and connection.

Embodied Time Awareness: The Body as the Keeper of Time

While the mind is often preoccupied with tasks, deadlines, and future plans, the body has a more immediate relationship with time. We feel time in our bodies—whether through the rhythm of our breath, the tension in our muscles, or the signals of fatigue or hunger. Yet, in our modern culture, we have become so focused on mental productivity that we often neglect the body's inherent wisdom. We push ourselves beyond our physical limits, ignoring the signals of exhaustion or discomfort, all in the name of efficiency and progress.

Embodied time awareness is the practice of tuning into our bodies and using them as a guide to align our actions with our physical rhythms. The body perceives time differently from the mind; it is more attuned to the cycles of rest, movement, and nourishment. By learning to listen to these somatic cues, we can design a lifestyle that honours both the mental and physical aspects of time. This means recognising when we need rest, when we need to move, and when we need to slow down or speed up.

For example, many of us experience the "afternoon slump" when our energy levels dip and we feel less focused or productive. By attuning ourselves to these bodily rhythms, we can design our days around these natural ebbs and flows. Instead of pushing through fatigue, we might take a short nap, stretch, or engage in a walk to revitalise ourselves. Embodied time awareness also involves recognising when we are working too hard and when we need to pause to nourish ourselves physically and emotionally. By aligning our mental and physical rhythms, we can work more efficiently, experience less burnout, and cultivate a greater sense of presence and satisfaction in our lives.

Conclusion: Time as a Source of Richness

Designing a time-rich life is not about finding more hours in the day; it is about consciously choosing how we spend the time we already have. By prioritising rituals over routines, embracing sacred pauses, and cultivating embodied time awareness, we can create lives that are not just productive but deeply fulfilling. These practices allow us to engage with time in a way that nourishes our minds, bodies, and spirits, helping us lead more meaningful and balanced lives. As we move forward, the question is no longer how to make the most of our time, but how to make *time* itself a source of richness and connection.

The Architecture of a Free Day

In the hyper-productive world we inhabit, a "free day" is often seen as a rare luxury—something to be filled with catch-up work, errands, or the nagging tasks we've put off. The idea of a true *free* day, one that is not bound by obligations, calendars, or productivity metrics, seems almost foreign to many. But what if, instead of viewing a day without obligations as a gap or a void, we saw it as an opportunity—a blank canvas where time could be designed, not as an extension of work or duty, but as a reflection of our values, needs, and rhythms? What if a free day, rather than being empty, could be one of the richest, most fulfilling days of our week?

The concept of designing a free day is a deliberate act of self-care, a conscious choice to disconnect from the pressure to *do* and instead focus on *being*. It is a chance to create a day that is aligned not with external demands or societal expectations, but with our internal rhythms and core values. In this chapter, we will explore how to architect a day from first principles—by understanding the energy dynamics of our bodies, the importance of rest, and the need for activities that nourish the mind, body, and spirit. This approach doesn't just make a day free—it transforms it into a day of intentionality, creativity, and presence.

The idea of a free day designed by values and energy rhythms isn't just a theoretical concept. In fact, research from the fields of psychology, neuroscience, and time management all point to the fact that structured rest and mindful engagement with time contribute to better decision-making, increased creativity, and more fulfilling lives. This chapter will guide you through a practical framework for creating a free day that not only supports your well-being but also enhances your ability to return to your responsibilities with renewed energy and clarity.

From Obligation to Intention: Designing a Day Based on Values

At its core, the architecture of a free day begins with a deep reflection on *what truly matters*—not just what needs to be done, but what brings us joy, nourishment, and meaning. Too often, our days are shaped by obligations: work tasks, social expectations, family duties. These external pressures create a sense of *urgency* that often overrides our internal needs. A free day, however, is an opportunity to step out of the cycle of obligation and into a space where time is shaped by intention, not obligation.

Designing a free day from the ground up begins by defining your values. What do you hold most dear in your life? For some, it may be creativity—time to write, paint, or explore new ideas. For others, it might be connection—spending time with loved ones or engaging with the community. And for many, it could be self-care, the simple act of giving oneself the time to rest, relax, and recharge. This step requires a moment of reflection: How do you want to feel at the end of this free day? Fulfilled, inspired, peaceful, or maybe energised? Once you've clarified your values, it becomes easier to choose activities that resonate with those values, making the day feel genuinely free, rather than merely free from external obligations.

A well-designed free day isn't about cramming in every possible "restorative" activity you can think of; it's about intentionality. If creativity is your focus, maybe your day includes time spent reading, drawing, or journaling. If connection matters most, you might choose to spend the day with friends or family, engaging in deep conversations or sharing an experience together. When the choices made align with what you value most, the day becomes rich and fulfilling, not just in terms of its activities but in its ability to affirm your sense of self.

Energy Rhythms: The Science of Time and Rest

While many people think of time in linear terms—past, present, future—our relationship with time is also deeply influenced by the natural rhythms of our bodies. As much as we strive to manage time, our energy is a far more powerful determinant of how we experience a day. Understanding how our bodies move through different energy phases throughout the day is key to designing a free day that is not only relaxing but also restorative.

Research on chronobiology, the study of biological rhythms, shows that our bodies operate on an internal clock, often referred to as the *circadian rhythm*. This rhythm influences everything from our sleep-wake cycles to our peak energy levels, alertness, and cognitive function. By understanding these natural fluctuations in energy, we can align our day to honour these rhythms, rather than fight against them.

For example, many people experience a natural energy dip in the afternoon—a phenomenon known as the "afternoon slump." Instead of powering through this dip, a well-architected free day might include a break during this time, a moment of relaxation or reflection, rather than forcing productivity. In contrast, the morning hours may be when we feel most energized and focused. A free day can then be designed to start with activities that require creativity or deep focus, such as writing, problem-solving, or working on a personal project, and followed by activities that engage our social or physical energy, such as walking or spending time with others.

This alignment of activities with energy rhythms is not just about being productive or efficient—it's about being more *present* with the time we have. When we listen to our bodies and engage with time in ways that support our natural rhythms, we expand our ability to be fully immersed in each moment, allowing us to savour and enjoy the activities we've chosen to include in our free day. The benefit is that we not only feel more engaged but also more *restored*, carrying that energy into the days that follow.

Rituals and Rest: The Sacred Art of Pauses

In a society that constantly pushes for more—more output, more connections, more activity—the importance of *pausing* is often overlooked. Yet, rest is not the opposite of productivity; it is an essential component of sustainable productivity. A free day designed around rituals and rest acknowledges the value of pauses—those moments of intentional stillness that allow us to recharge and renew our energy.

Pauses can take many forms: a five-minute break between tasks, a quiet moment of reflection before starting a new activity, or even a day-long retreat into nature. The key is to integrate rest into the fabric of the day—not as an afterthought but as a *ritual* in itself. Rituals have been shown to be powerful tools for establishing grounding and balance in our lives. Whether it's a morning meditation, a mid-day tea ritual, or an evening walk, rituals create a sense of sacredness in time—reminding us that time is not just a resource to be consumed but a space to be experienced fully and intentionally.

Sacred pauses offer a profound opportunity to reconnect with ourselves. In a culture that glorifies busyness, taking a break becomes an act of rebellion, a choice to reclaim time for the most important aspects of our being. Rather than rushing from one task to the next, the ritual of pause invites us to *be*, to reflect, and to simply exist without expectation. By giving ourselves permission to pause throughout the day, we acknowledge the importance of rest as an essential part of living well.

The Embodied Experience of Time

While much of our modern world is driven by the intellectual demands of time—deadlines, schedules, and appointments—our relationship with time is also deeply rooted in the body. Time is not only a mental construct; it is felt, experienced, and processed physically. Yet, in our fast-paced world, we often neglect the embodied experience of time, ignoring the cues our bodies give us about how much energy we have left or when we need to slow down.

The practice of *embodied time awareness* involves tuning in to the sensations, rhythms, and signals of the body as a way of navigating time. This means listening to the signals that indicate when we need to rest, when we need to move, and when we need to reconnect with our surroundings. Embodied time awareness asks us to move away from a purely cognitive approach to time management and instead incorporate *somatic* cues into our understanding of how to design our days. It's a practice that honours our physical needs and emotional state, helping us craft a free day that supports both our mental and physical health.

For example, if you feel physically drained after a few hours of intense activity, an embodied approach to your free day might suggest slowing down or incorporating movement, like a gentle stretch or a brief walk. If you're mentally tired, it might be time to switch gears to something that feels restorative—whether that's a creative activity, journaling, or time spent in nature. Listening to the body is not about being passive; it's about recognising that our bodies hold valuable insights into how we experience time. By honouring these cues, we can design a day that isn't just free of obligations but deeply nourishing and rejuvenating.

The Architecture of a Free Day: Designing Your Time

Designing a free day is about reclaiming time as a source of richness rather than simply filling it with distractions or obligations. It requires intention, awareness of your body's rhythms, and a commitment to rest. Rather than seeing a free day as empty or unproductive, we can view it as a day for full engagement with the present moment—where activities are chosen not out of obligation but because they align with our values and needs.

In creating a free day, we move from the tyranny of the to-do list to the freedom of intention. By focusing on rituals over routines, incorporating sacred pauses, and tuning in to the body's rhythms, we create time that nourishes and revitalises us. This kind of free day is not a rare luxury but a regular practice, one that can be designed to enrich our lives and restore our energy. The result is not just more time, but *better* time—a time that aligns with who we truly are and supports the well-being we deserve.

Rituals Over Routines

In our relentless pursuit of productivity, we have come to fetishise *routines*. We are encouraged, at every turn, to optimise our days, streamline our actions, and organise our lives into neatly categorised chunks, all in the name of doing more and achieving more. Morning routines, work routines, self-care routines: the world is flooded with advice on how to create the perfect system for efficiency and success. Yet, in this pursuit of maximised output, we often miss the profound power that lies in something deeper: *rituals*. Rituals are not just actions performed regularly—they are intentional, soul-anchoring practices that nourish the mind-body system. Unlike routines, which can often feel like mechanical tasks or obligations, rituals invite us into a space of sacredness, presence, and deep connection with ourselves and the world around us.

This shift from routine to ritual is more than just semantics; it represents a fundamental change in how we engage with time, activity, and our inner selves. Routines are often about control, predictability, and external expectations—tasks to be completed with a focus on efficiency. Rituals, on the other hand, are about connection, mindfulness, and presence. They honour the emotional, psychological, and spiritual dimensions of our lives. Rituals engage us holistically, inviting us to integrate body, mind, and spirit in ways that routine-based productivity cannot achieve.

In this article, we will explore the distinction between routines and rituals, highlighting how the shift towards ritual can bring more meaning, purpose, and nourishment to our days. By delving into the psychological and cultural significance of rituals, we will uncover why they are essential in a world where busyness is often mistaken for worthiness. This is not an argument against routines—there is certainly a place for structured activities in our lives—but a call to elevate those activities into rituals that feed our souls rather than merely ticking boxes.

Routines vs. Rituals: The Difference That Matters

At first glance, routines and rituals may appear similar: both involve repetition, both help structure our days, and both create a sense of order. However, the key difference lies in *intentionality*. A routine can be a series of tasks—waking up, brushing teeth, checking emails, exercising, making breakfast—all of which can be performed automatically, often without much thought. They may be the actions of a busy life, but they lack a deeper emotional or spiritual connection.

Rituals, by contrast, carry with them intention, mindfulness, and a sense of reverence. Rituals can be simple acts—such as lighting a candle before a meal, taking a moment of silence before starting work, or engaging in a mindful stretch—but they are done with *awareness* and a connection to something larger than the task itself. Rituals are often associated with religious or spiritual practices, but their power extends far beyond these contexts. A ritual can be anything that *creates a sacred space* in our lives, no matter how mundane the task might appear.

For example, many of us have a morning routine that includes making coffee. But what if that act became a ritual? What if, instead of simply preparing a cup to fuel the day ahead, we took the time to notice the aroma of the beans, the warmth of the cup in our hands, the quiet of the morning, and the simple gift of the present moment? Suddenly, the act of making coffee becomes more than just a routine—it becomes a ritual that nourishes us emotionally, spiritually, and mentally.

This shift from routine to ritual helps to combat the sense of disconnection that often accompanies the modern, productivity-driven lifestyle. When we turn ordinary activities into rituals, we cultivate a sense of mindfulness that can ground us in the present, allowing us to savour the small moments that make up our day. Rituals do not rush us; they invite us to slow down, to feel, and to be. And this slowing down is essential in a world that values speed over depth.

The Psychological Power of Rituals

Why do rituals have this profound effect on us? The answer lies in their psychological impact. Rituals are powerful because they create *meaning* and *order* in our lives, offering a counterbalance to the chaos and unpredictability of daily existence. Psychologists have long studied the role of rituals in human behaviour, particularly in the context of religious or cultural practices, and have found that they serve several important functions.

First, rituals help to reduce anxiety and provide a sense of control. In a world that is often unpredictable and outside of our control, rituals create a structure that brings comfort and stability. They provide us with a way to ground ourselves, particularly in times of stress. For example, a calming bedtime ritual might include reading, drinking tea, or performing a brief meditation. The act of engaging in these behaviours consistently signals to the brain that it is time to wind down, preparing us for rest. This is especially significant in an age where many of us are bombarded by overstimulation from work, technology, and the demands of daily life.

Secondly, rituals foster a sense of *connection*—both with ourselves and with the wider world. When we engage in rituals that are meaningful to us, we tap into a deeper sense of purpose. This could be as simple as a gratitude ritual before bed, where we reflect on the things we are thankful for, or a creative ritual that allows us to express ourselves artistically. By connecting with our inner selves through these rituals, we are able to align our daily actions with our values, creating a sense of fulfilment and purpose.

Moreover, rituals act as an anchor. When the world feels overwhelming or we feel disconnected from our sense of self, rituals can bring us back to centre. They allow us to reclaim a sense of agency and presence, even in the most mundane of circumstances. In doing so, rituals help us stay grounded and present in the moment, rather than feeling lost in the constant push for productivity.

Rituals in the Modern World: Cultural Significance

The role of rituals extends beyond individual psychology; they are deeply embedded in culture, society, and tradition. Throughout history, rituals have been used to mark significant transitions in life—births, marriages, deaths, and everything in between. These rituals serve as communal markers, creating a sense of shared meaning and belonging. They also help individuals navigate the complexities of life's transitions, providing a framework for understanding and processing emotions during significant life events.

In modern times, however, many of these traditional rituals have been lost or diluted. The fast-paced, globalised nature of contemporary life has led to the erosion of many communal rituals, leaving individuals to fend for themselves in creating meaningful, intentional practices. This disconnection from cultural rituals is partly responsible for the rise of feelings of isolation, anxiety, and disorientation in modern life. Without shared rituals that provide context, meaning, and community, individuals can feel adrift, as if they are merely going through the motions without truly engaging with the world around them.

As a result, there is a growing movement to *reclaim* rituals—not only for spiritual or religious reasons but as a means of reconnecting with our deepest needs as human beings. In a culture obsessed with efficiency, we are now rediscovering the power of rituals to slow us down, help us reflect, and ground us in the present moment. The rise of mindfulness practices, for example, is a direct response to the alienation and stress of modern life. These practices, which often include ritualistic elements such as meditation, journaling, and mindful eating, offer a space for personal connection and reflection.

In this sense, rituals are not only personal practices but also social and cultural acts of resistance. They are a way of reclaiming time, of rejecting the commodification of every moment, and of insisting that we deserve time to slow down, reflect, and truly *be*.

Creating Your Own Rituals: A Practical Guide

The beauty of rituals is that they can be tailored to fit your individual needs, values, and circumstances. While it is tempting to replicate the rituals of others, true rituals arise from an understanding of what personally resonates with you. Designing your own rituals involves paying attention to what brings you peace, joy, and a sense of purpose. It might involve activities that promote creativity, connection, or self-care—things that nourish you, rather than things you feel obligated to do.

A practical approach to creating rituals begins by identifying what you need most. Are you craving rest? Connection? Creativity? Once you've identified your needs, you can begin to shape rituals around them. Perhaps you create a morning ritual that involves stretching, breathing, and reflection—activities that set the tone for the rest of the day. Or, maybe you incorporate a ritual into your workday that involves pausing for a few minutes to reflect or meditate, grounding yourself before diving into the next task.

The key is to make these rituals something you look forward to, rather than tasks you must perform. Rituals should be infused with meaning, not obligation. They can be simple or elaborate, quiet or expressive, but the common thread is that they allow you to reconnect with yourself and the world around you.

The Nourishing Power of Rituals

By prioritising rituals over routines, we reclaim our time from the tyranny of productivity. Rituals are not about doing more—they are about creating space for presence, for self-reflection, and for deep connection. They are about nourishing the mind-body system rather than merely filling the hours of the day. In a world that constantly demands more of us, rituals offer us the opportunity to step back and remember what truly matters. They remind us that time is not just a commodity to be managed but a sacred gift to be lived.

Sacred Pauses: Expanding Time Through Presence

In the race against the clock, time often feels like a scarce resource—an ever-decreasing commodity to be spent, wasted, or invested. From the moment we wake up to the moment we collapse into bed, our lives are filled with an almost constant flow of activity. We rush through the day, marking off our tasks, adhering to routines, and checking off items on endless to-do lists. But what if the way we experience time is not solely determined by the quantity of hours or tasks completed, but by how *present* we are within those hours? What if the most transformative way to expand our experience of time is by learning to pause—not just in moments of rest, but throughout the day, in the midst of our busiest, most demanding activities?

The concept of a "pause" may seem counterintuitive in a world that idolises productivity and constant movement. Yet, it is precisely these pauses—what I call *sacred pauses*—that have the potential to enrich our lives by expanding our sense of time. Sacred pauses are micro-moments of stillness, attention, and intentionality, woven throughout the day. They serve as an antidote to the urgency and stress that often characterise modern life, offering us a moment to step out of the frenzy and into the present. These pauses are not just breaks from work—they are practices that ground us, allow us to reconnect with our bodies and minds, and open up space for clarity, creativity, and true rest.

In this article, we will explore the power of sacred pauses, their psychological and physiological benefits, and how to integrate them into your daily life. We will draw upon scientific research, philosophical reflections, and real-world examples to show that the practice of pausing, far from being a waste of time, is a profound tool for expanding our experience of it.

The Psychology of Sacred Pauses

Our relationship with time has been shaped by centuries of social conditioning, technological innovation, and the demands of industrialisation. In the past, time was a more communal, cyclical concept, often tied to natural rhythms and collective practices. But with the rise of modernity, time became something to be controlled, manipulated, and maximised. The advent of clocks, calendars, and the 9-to-5 workday set the stage for our current obsession with efficiency and productivity. In such a world, we often view pauses as a form of inefficiency, an interruption to our productivity rather than a means of enhancing it.

This cultural tendency to view pauses as wasteful or unproductive has significant psychological consequences. Research in psychology suggests that constant busyness and a lack of downtime can lead to burnout, anxiety, and a diminished sense of well-being. The absence of intentional pauses leaves us feeling scattered, overstimulated, and disconnected from our bodies and the present moment. In fact, studies show that when we are not given time to pause and reflect, our cognitive and emotional capacities are compromised. We are less able to focus, less able to engage creatively, and more likely to experience stress and fatigue.

Sacred pauses offer a remedy to this constant state of "doing." They provide opportunities to recalibrate, reset, and reconnect with our inner selves. Taking a moment to stop, breathe, and reflect activates the parasympathetic nervous system—the body's natural relaxation response. This not only helps reduce stress but also enhances cognitive function, emotional regulation, and creativity. By pausing regularly throughout the day, we allow ourselves to step out of the cycle of overwhelm and into a space of presence, where we can access a deeper sense of clarity, intuition, and calm.

The Physiology of Pausing: A Breath for the Body

The benefits of sacred pauses are not just psychological but also physiological. As mentioned, pausing triggers the parasympathetic nervous system, which counters the "fight-or-flight" response activated by stress. When we pause and breathe consciously, we signal to our bodies that it is safe to relax, to release tension, and to enter a state of restoration.

But this is more than just a momentary relief. Regular pauses throughout the day can have a profound impact on our long-term health. Chronic stress is a leading cause of many physical health issues, including cardiovascular disease, digestive problems, and weakened immune function. By introducing small moments of stillness—whether through deep breathing, stretching, or mindful awareness—we can interrupt the cycle of stress and restore balance to our bodies. This is not just about avoiding burnout; it is about promoting sustained health and vitality. The more we practice these sacred pauses, the more we learn to regulate our nervous systems, ensuring that we are better equipped to handle the challenges of daily life.

Furthermore, pausing allows us to listen to our bodies in a way that continuous activity cannot. In the rush of constant doing, we often miss the subtle signals our bodies are sending—signals of tiredness, hunger, discomfort, or tension. Sacred pauses create a space where we can check in with ourselves, honour these signals, and respond accordingly. This might mean taking a short walk to stretch our legs, sipping water to hydrate, or simply closing our eyes for a few moments to reset our mental focus. In this way, pauses not only enhance our productivity but also contribute to our long-term physical and emotional health.

The Sacredness of Pausing: A Philosophical Exploration

The concept of the sacred pause is deeply rooted in philosophical and spiritual traditions. Across cultures and religious practices, pauses have been used as a way of creating space for reflection, gratitude, and connection with something greater than oneself. In the Christian tradition, for example, moments of prayer and contemplation serve as a means of connecting with the divine and seeking guidance. In Buddhist and Hindu practices, meditation and mindfulness offer opportunities to cultivate inner peace and transcend the distractions of the material world. These pauses are not seen as interruptions, but as essential components of spiritual growth, grounding, and self-awareness.

The sacred pause invites us to step outside the relentless flow of activity and reconnect with the deeper aspects of our lives. Whether through prayer, meditation, or simple mindfulness, pausing offers a chance to reflect on our values, our purpose, and our place in the world. It is a practice that transcends the busy-ness of life, allowing us to find meaning and connection in the present moment. In this sense, sacred pauses are not just about relaxation—they are about cultivating *presence*—the ability to be fully alive and engaged in the here and now.

In a world that often prioritises external achievement and material success, sacred pauses serve as a reminder that true fulfilment comes not from doing more, but from being more. They offer a radical redefinition of productivity, one that is rooted in mindfulness, self-awareness, and connection with the present moment. Sacred pauses teach us that we do not need to be constantly doing in order to be valuable or worthy. We are worthy in our stillness, in our presence, and in our ability to honour the time we have.

Practical Tips for Incorporating Sacred Pauses into Your Day

While the concept of sacred pauses may sound abstract, they can be easily integrated into even the busiest of days. Here are some practical ways to incorporate micro-pauses into your daily routine:

1. **Mindful Breathing:** Take a few moments each hour to pause and focus on your breath. Inhale slowly for a count of four, hold for four, and exhale for a count of four. This simple exercise can help reset your nervous system and bring you back into the present moment.

2. **Mini-Meditations:** Set aside five minutes during the day to sit quietly and meditate. Even a short session can help reduce stress, improve focus, and increase your sense of well-being.

3. **Body Awareness:** Throughout the day, check in with your body. Are you tense or fatigued? Take a moment to stretch, adjust your posture, or move around to release any physical discomfort.

4. **Gratitude Pauses:** Pause for a few moments to reflect on the things you are grateful for. This practice helps shift your focus from what you need to do next to what is already good in your life.

5. **Scheduled Breaks:** Schedule short breaks throughout your day to step away from your work and do something restorative—whether it's a walk, a cup of tea, or simply sitting in silence. These intentional breaks can help you recharge and maintain your focus throughout the day.

The Art of Expanding Time

The practice of sacred pauses is not just about "taking a break"; it is about cultivating presence and mindfulness in the midst of our busy lives. These micro-pauses offer a powerful way to expand our experience of time—not by filling it with more activity, but by being more present within it. Sacred pauses help us slow down, reconnect with ourselves, and create space for creativity, reflection, and self-care. In a world that often seems overwhelmed by the demands of productivity, these pauses remind us that true success lies not in doing more, but in being more—being fully engaged, fully present, and fully alive in each moment.

Embodied Time Awareness: Aligning Body, Mind, and Time

Time is often viewed through the lens of the mind—an intellectual construct shaped by schedules, deadlines, and the incessant ticking of clocks. But what if the way we experience time is not solely a product of our thoughts and external obligations? What if our bodies, too, have their own perception of time—a perception that is deeply tied to how we move, feel, and exist in the world? This is the central premise of embodied time awareness: the practice of tuning into the body's rhythms, cues, and sensations as a means of understanding and managing our relationship with time.

While modern society has conditioned us to perceive time as a linear, quantifiable resource, the body offers a different, more fluid and intuitive way of experiencing it. Our physical state, emotions, and energy levels shape how we navigate time—whether we feel rushed, energised, fatigued, or present. By learning to recognise and interpret these bodily signals, we can better align ourselves with the rhythms of our own time, rather than being slaves to externally imposed deadlines or the constant pressure of productivity.

In this article, we will explore the concept of embodied time awareness, its importance in maintaining a healthy, balanced life, and how you can cultivate this practice to enrich your daily experience of time. Drawing on scientific research, psychological insights, and practical examples, we will examine how tuning into the body's time cues can lead to greater clarity, focus, and well-being. We will also discuss how to cultivate somatic awareness through mindful practices, so you can reclaim agency over your time and achieve a more harmonious existence.

The Body's Timekeeper: How the Body Perceives Time Differently from the Mind

We are often taught to think of time as something external—an abstract force measured in hours, minutes, and seconds. But this intellectual understanding of time is only part of the picture. The body has its own time system, which is less concerned with clocks and more attuned to rhythms, cycles, and sensations. This is particularly evident when we consider the ways in which our bodies respond to the passage of time.

One of the most significant ways in which the body perceives time differently from the mind is through *biological rhythms*—the inherent cycles that govern many of our physiological processes. The most obvious example of this is the circadian rhythm, the body's natural 24-hour cycle that governs sleep, wakefulness, and energy levels. The circadian rhythm is a deeply ingrained biological process that influences how alert we feel at different times of day, how we experience fatigue, and even how our bodies respond to external stimuli. Understanding our circadian rhythm is crucial for aligning our time with our body's natural patterns, rather than trying to force ourselves into artificial schedules.

In addition to the circadian rhythm, our bodies also have other internal clocks that regulate processes such as digestion, heart rate, and hormone production. These rhythms are interconnected and can influence how we experience time. For example, if we try to push through a workday when our body is signalling fatigue—say, in the afternoon slump—we may feel rushed, irritable, and mentally foggy, even if we're "working" the same number of hours. Alternatively, if we align our tasks with our body's natural cycles—working on high-focus tasks when we are most alert and taking breaks when we feel tired—we are more likely to feel in tune with our time, rather than overwhelmed by it.

The body also communicates its experience of time through physical sensations. When we are stressed, we may feel a tightness in our chest or a knot in our stomach. When we are engaged in something meaningful, we might experience a sense of flow, where time seems to expand and contract based on our level of immersion. These bodily cues are not just random; they are indicative of how the body is processing time and energy. By learning to tune in to these signals, we can develop a deeper understanding of how our body and mind interact with time.

The Psychology of Embodied Time Awareness: Stress, Flow, and Energy

Understanding embodied time awareness is also a matter of psychology. The mind and body are intimately connected, and the way we perceive time can have a profound impact on our emotional and mental well-being. When we ignore our bodies' natural rhythms and push ourselves too hard, we often experience stress, burnout, and fatigue. This is particularly true in today's fast-paced, work-driven culture, where long hours, constant multitasking, and the relentless pursuit of productivity are the norm. When we push ourselves to the limits of our energy, we disrupt our body's natural time cycles, which can lead to both physical and mental exhaustion.

Research in the field of *positive psychology* has shown that stress, particularly chronic stress, can distort our perception of time. When we are stressed, we tend to view time as something scarce—something to be managed, rationed, and maximised. We feel as if we are running out of time, and this sense of urgency can create a feedback loop of anxiety and overwhelm. In contrast, when we are relaxed and present, our experience of time tends to expand. We are able to savour the moment, and time feels more abundant and expansive.

The concept of *flow*—the state of deep concentration and immersion in an activity—provides a powerful example of how embodied time awareness can enrich our experience of time. When we are in flow, we are completely absorbed in what we are doing, and time seems to lose its usual constraints. This is not just a subjective feeling; it is backed by scientific research that shows how the brain operates differently during flow states, with increased levels of dopamine and reduced activity in areas of the brain responsible for self-awareness and time perception. Flow states often occur when we are engaging in activities that align with our strengths and passions, and when we are fully immersed in the present moment.

By practising embodied time awareness, we can increase our ability to enter flow states more frequently, allowing us to engage with time in a more fluid and rewarding way. We can also reduce the negative effects of stress by learning to tune in to our body's signals and recognise when we need to rest, recharge, or take a break. This alignment between body, mind, and time creates a sense of balance and harmony, where time is no longer something to be conquered but something to be experienced with mindfulness and presence.

Practical Steps to Cultivate Embodied Time Awareness

Cultivating embodied time awareness involves both mindful attention to the body's signals and practical strategies to align our activities with our natural rhythms. Here are some key practices to help you develop a more embodied approach to time:

1. **Tune In to Your Body's Energy Levels:** Throughout the day, take moments to check in with how you're feeling physically. Are you feeling energetic, or are you starting to experience signs of fatigue? Adjust your activities accordingly. For example, if you feel alert in the morning, you might choose to tackle high-priority tasks or engage in creative work. If you feel tired in the afternoon, it might be time for a break or a more restorative activity.

2. **Practice Mindful Breathing:** Deep, mindful breathing can help you ground yourself in the present moment and reset your nervous system. Practice deep breathing exercises several times throughout the day, especially when you feel stressed or overwhelmed. This simple practice can help you expand your sense of time and bring you back to the present moment.

3. **Engage in Body-Focused Activities:** Incorporate activities that connect you with your body, such as yoga, stretching, walking, or dancing. These practices help you develop a greater awareness of your body's time cues and promote relaxation and focus.

4. **Pay Attention to Physical Sensations:** Notice how your body responds to different activities. When you're engaged in something meaningful or enjoyable, do you feel a sense of flow or energy? When you're stressed or fatigued, do you feel tightness or discomfort? Paying attention to these sensations can help you understand how your body experiences time.

5. **Create Space for Rest and Reflection:** Regular pauses throughout the day, as we discussed in the previous chapter, are essential for maintaining embodied time awareness. Allow yourself time to rest, reflect, and recalibrate—whether through meditation, journaling, or simply sitting in silence. These breaks allow you to reconnect with your body and return to your natural rhythms.

6. **Synchronise with Your Circadian Rhythms:** Try to align your daily activities with your body's natural circadian rhythms. This might mean adjusting your sleep schedule, taking breaks at certain times of the day, or scheduling high-focus tasks when you feel most alert. Honour your body's time to maximise your energy and productivity.

The Benefits of Embodied Time Awareness: A New Relationship with Time

By cultivating embodied time awareness, we are not simply managing time more effectively; we are redefining our relationship with it. Time becomes less of a commodity to be controlled or consumed, and more of a space to be lived in—a space where we can engage fully with the present moment, listen to our bodies, and move in alignment with our natural rhythms. This approach to time allows us to experience greater fulfilment, well-being, and clarity, rather than feeling constantly pressured or out of sync.

In a world that values doing over being, embodied time awareness offers a path to reconnect with the present, to reclaim our time as a source of nourishment rather than a source of stress. By embracing the wisdom of the body, we can create a life where time is no longer something to be conquered, but something to be lived with intention, presence, and alignment.

Chapter 6
The Philosophy of Enough

In today's world, the drumbeat of "more" is nearly impossible to ignore. From the steam and soot of the Industrial Revolution to the always-on, data-saturated culture we now inhabit, the notion that more equates to better has entrenched itself into our very way of life. More money. More recognition. More stimulation. More boxes ticked and horizons expanded. And yet—if we are honest—there's often a faint discomfort beneath it all. A question we rarely voice: What if we've already crossed the line where "more" begins to erode rather than enrich?

This chapter, *The Philosophy of Enough*, proposes a different lens—one that calls into question the taken-for-granted virtue of accumulation. It introduces the quietly radical idea of *enoughness*, a principle that suggests the good life might lie not at the farthest edge of ambition, but somewhere nearer—a place where contentment, clarity, and coherence begin to take precedence over expansion for its own sake. Enough, in this view, is neither lack nor limit. It's not about scraping by or settling. Rather, it's about reaching that precise, intuitive point where continuing to add only subtracts.

We start with the notion of the "enough point"—a threshold that will look different for everyone, yet carries a universal resonance. It's the moment when chasing more becomes not only futile, but draining. The crucial question becomes: Can we recognise that moment? And more importantly, will we honour it when we do? This is not about anti-ambition. It's about recalibrating our compass so that it points to what truly sustains rather than what merely stimulates.

From there, we enter the curious, liberating terrain of the *Joy of Missing Out*. Yes—*joy*, not guilt, not shame. In a culture that lionises presence and participation, that floods our feeds with curated lives and endless possibility, there is something quietly defiant, even noble, about opting out. Choosing stillness over spectacle, solitude over saturation. JOMO is not about withdrawal—it's about re-engagement on your own terms. It's not indifference; it's discernment. And in a world drunk on options, it might be one of the most courageous decisions we can make.

Finally, we'll revisit the ever-slippery concept of ambition. For many, ambition has long been tethered to a model of ceaseless striving—of climbing, accumulating, outperforming. But what if we redefined it? What if ambition were not about more, but about deeper? What if its true expression lay in alignment—when what we do, why we do it, and who we become in the process all begin to harmonise? In such a frame, ambition doesn't evaporate; it evolves. It becomes sustainable, generous, even restorative.

The philosophy of enough does not call for us to abandon desire, or retreat from excellence. Rather, it invites a more mature, more human approach to living—a kind of conscious sufficiency. It asks us to resist the pull of endlessness and instead trace a line, gently but firmly, around what nourishes us. That line is not rigid. It flexes with our seasons, our needs, our deeper knowing. But it is a line nonetheless—a boundary not of limitation, but of liberation.

In what follows, we will explore how living from a place of enough can unburden our time, recalibrate our ambitions, and bring us back into right relationship with our lives. Not by doing less, necessarily, but by needing less—and in so doing, finding far more than we ever expected.

The Enough Point: Defining Your Threshold of Sufficiency

In a world that glorifies the hustle, the notion of *enough* can feel like an anomaly. After all, aren't we always told that we need to keep striving, to push harder, to reach for the next rung on the ladder of success? The prevailing ethos of modern life dictates that success is measured by how much we can achieve, how much we can accumulate, and how many goals we can tick off. But this narrow definition of success overlooks a fundamental truth: More isn't always better. In fact, more can sometimes be detrimental. It can lead to burnout, dissatisfaction, and a chronic sense of unfulfillment.

The concept of the *enough point* is the realisation that there is a point at which our basic needs and desires are met, and beyond that point, additional pursuit—whether of wealth, achievement, or experience—ceases to contribute to our happiness or sense of purpose. For some, this point may come in the form of financial sufficiency; for others, it may be a sense of emotional or intellectual fulfillment. This threshold is deeply personal and shaped by our values, goals, and life experiences. But the essential idea is that there exists a point where continuing to accumulate, to strive, or to achieve no longer adds value to our lives. Instead, it may even begin to detract from it.

Understanding your own *enough point* requires introspection and mindfulness. It asks you to consider what truly matters in your life and to draw a clear boundary around the things that bring genuine meaning. For example, a person may reach the conclusion that accumulating wealth beyond a certain level brings little additional joy and may, in fact, complicate their relationships or detract from their time. Another person might recognise that professional success has already provided them with enough recognition and stability, and further advancement will only add stress without increasing their sense of fulfilment. By defining this threshold, you free yourself from the tyranny of "more" and begin to make choices based on sufficiency rather than scarcity.

The *enough point* can also extend to how we allocate our time. In today's world, we often over-extend ourselves, saying "yes" to every commitment and opportunity that comes our way. However, recognising when enough is enough—when our time and energy have been sufficiently dedicated to our passions, relationships, and growth—helps prevent the depletion that comes from spreading ourselves too thin. When we define our enough point, we start prioritising quality over quantity in every aspect of our lives, creating space for what matters most.

The Joy of Missing Out: Liberating Ourselves from the 'Everything, Everywhere' Trap

The pervasive culture of FOMO (Fear of Missing Out) has taken root in the collective psyche, driven by social media, peer pressure, and the constant bombardment of information. We are led to believe that in order to be happy, successful, or fulfilled, we must always be in motion, always participating, and always experiencing more. The relentless pursuit of *everything* leads to an exhaustion of self, where even moments of joy become tinged with anxiety about what we might be missing elsewhere.

However, the antidote to this compulsive need to "do it all" is the concept of *JOMO*—the *Joy of Missing Out*. JOMO is the deliberate choice to disengage from the constant noise and demands of modern life in order to reconnect with what is truly meaningful. Instead of feeling regretful for what you are not experiencing, JOMO invites you to feel a sense of liberation in choosing to *miss out* on what doesn't serve you. It is a rejection of the pressure to participate in every social event, consume every bit of information, or chase every fleeting trend. JOMO is about embracing silence, solitude, and stillness, and finding joy in being fully present in what matters, without the distraction of constant comparison or external validation.

The power of JOMO lies in its ability to free us from the constraints of external expectations. It allows us to reclaim our time, our attention, and our energy. JOMO doesn't mean disengaging from life—it means engaging more deeply with life on our terms. By consciously choosing where we direct our attention, we can create more space for meaningful connections, personal growth, and rest.

JOMO, then, is not about renunciation or isolation—it is about prioritising presence over participation and depth over breadth.

Anti-Ambition as Wisdom: Redefining Ambition for a Sustainable Life

Ambition has long been considered a virtue in the modern world—a driving force that propels individuals to climb the ladder of success, accumulate wealth, and achieve status. However, the relentless pursuit of ambition can often lead to exhaustion, burnout, and a sense of emptiness. This is particularly true when ambition is driven solely by external markers of success rather than an internal compass of meaning.

In this chapter, we propose a redefinition of ambition—not as an unrelenting drive for more, but as the *alignment* of one's energy and efforts with personal values and meaningful contribution. True ambition, in this sense, is not about striving for the sake of achieving more; it is about striving for purpose. It is about using our talents and resources to contribute to something larger than ourselves, whether that be through our work, our relationships, or our community involvement. This type of ambition is deeply rooted in self-awareness and sustainability, recognising that burnout and disconnection from our true selves are not the by-products of ambition, but its antithesis.

By embracing anti-ambition, we invite a wisdom that balances striving with rest, achievement with reflection, and success with fulfilment. We begin to prioritise quality of life over quantity of success, recognising that the true measure of a life well-lived is not in how much we acquire, but in how deeply we engage with the people and pursuits that align with our authentic selves.

Living with Enough: A Radical Shift in Perspective

The philosophy of enough is a radical shift in perspective. It challenges the dominant cultural narratives of endless growth and accumulation, and instead invites us to slow down and assess what truly matters. It encourages us to define our *enough point*, reclaim the joy of missing out, and reframe ambition as the alignment of effort with purpose. By doing so, we liberate ourselves from the tyranny of more, creating space for deeper connections, greater satisfaction, and a life of sustained well-being. This chapter will help you navigate this shift, offering tools, reflections, and practices to help you live a life that is not driven by external measures of success, but by an internal sense of sufficiency, balance, and meaning.

Minimalism Beyond Materialism: Cultivating Cognitive and Temporal Clarity

When most people hear the term "minimalism," they immediately think of physical spaces—clean, decluttered homes, with only the bare essentials carefully curated. The image of stark white walls, sleek furniture, and a sparse, tidy environment often comes to mind. Yet, the true essence of minimalism stretches far beyond the objects we own. In fact, it is not simply about shedding possessions; it is about shedding the mental, emotional, and temporal clutter that weighs down our lives. Real minimalism is about cultivating clarity—*cognitive clarity* and *temporal clarity*—and learning to focus on what truly matters in a world that constantly demands our attention.

In today's fast-paced, hyper-connected world, the pressure to constantly do more, be more, and have more is overwhelming. We are bombarded with information, deadlines, social media updates, and a never-ending stream of distractions that pull us in countless directions. This state of perpetual busyness, combined with the clutter of material possessions, has resulted in a society that is simultaneously overwhelmed and disconnected. Yet, the pursuit of *enough*—a life defined by intentionality rather than accumulation—offers a path to liberation. True minimalism is not about deprivation, but about fostering an environment—both mentally and physically—that supports our deepest needs and most meaningful goals.

In this article, we will explore how minimalism extends beyond material possessions to include our cognitive and temporal spaces. We will examine how decluttering our minds can lead to greater mental clarity, improved focus, and enhanced emotional well-being. Similarly, we will explore how cultivating temporal clarity—by rethinking how we use our time and intentionally choosing where to invest our energy—can help us live more purposefully and authentically. Through this exploration, you will learn how to create a life that prioritises what matters most and lets go of what no longer serves you.

Cognitive Clarity: Decluttering the Mind

Much like physical clutter, mental clutter can stifle our ability to think clearly and act with intention. The modern mind, conditioned by the incessant demands of daily life, is constantly juggling multiple tasks, worries, and distractions. Whether it's the pressure of work deadlines, the never-ending to-do lists, or the constant barrage of notifications from our phones, our mental space often feels like a chaotic, cluttered room in need of a good clean-up. The effects of this mental clutter are profound: research in psychology and neuroscience has shown that cognitive overload impairs decision-making, reduces creativity, and increases stress. When we are constantly preoccupied with a multitude of thoughts and concerns, we become less capable of focusing on the present moment and engaging in meaningful, productive work.

The first step towards cultivating cognitive clarity is to create space in the mind. This can be achieved through practices such as mindfulness meditation, journaling, and intentional reflection. Mindfulness, in particular, is a powerful tool for decluttering the mind. By training ourselves to be present with our thoughts and emotions, we can start to identify and release the mental clutter that no longer serves us. This may involve letting go of excessive worrying about the future, ruminating on past mistakes, or obsessing over unimportant details. By reducing this mental noise, we open ourselves to deeper focus, creativity, and insight. Cognitive clarity also enables us to discern between what truly matters and what is merely a distraction, allowing us to direct our attention and energy where it can have the greatest impact.

Another key aspect of cognitive clarity is the ability to simplify decision-making. The more options we have, the more our minds become bogged down by choice fatigue. In fact, studies have shown that when we are faced with too many decisions, we are more likely to procrastinate or make poor choices. Minimalism offers a solution to this dilemma by encouraging us to make fewer decisions, but with more intention. This might mean eliminating unnecessary choices from our daily routines—such as simplifying our wardrobe or automating our finances—to free up mental energy for more important decisions. It also means learning to say no to commitments or distractions that detract from our true priorities. When we simplify our mental landscape in this way, we create space for greater mental clarity and a more focused, purposeful life.

Temporal Clarity: Rethinking Time as a Resource

Just as the mind can become cluttered, so too can our time. Time, much like material possessions, is a finite resource—yet we often treat it as if it is limitless. We overschedule ourselves, saying yes to too many commitments, and end up spreading ourselves too thin. The relentless pace of modern life, with its constant demands for attention, leaves little room for rest, reflection, or meaningful engagement with the people and activities that matter most. In this state of busyness, time becomes a commodity to be consumed, rather than a resource to be savoured.

True minimalism, however, encourages us to rethink our relationship with time. It asks us to become more intentional with how we use our time, and to focus on what is truly valuable. Temporal clarity is the practice of recognising and aligning your time with your values, goals, and deepest needs. This requires evaluating how we spend our time and making conscious choices about where to invest it. It also involves learning to recognise when we are spending time on things that drain us, rather than replenish us.

One of the most important aspects of cultivating temporal clarity is learning how to say no. In our culture of productivity and achievement, there is often pressure to take on more—more projects, more commitments, more activities. However, true minimalism teaches us that saying no is an essential act of self-care. By setting boundaries and eliminating tasks that don't align with our priorities, we create more space for the things that truly matter. This may mean turning down social invitations that drain our energy, delegating tasks that don't require our personal involvement, or letting go of work that doesn't align with our values. By being selective with how we spend our time, we begin to reclaim our schedules and redirect our energy towards what brings us the most fulfilment.

It is also important to recognise the role of rest and recovery in cultivating temporal clarity. In a culture that celebrates overwork, rest is often seen as a luxury, rather than a necessity. However, research in cognitive science has shown that rest is essential for maintaining productivity, creativity, and overall well-being. Minimalism encourages us to build periods of rest and reflection into our schedules—whether through regular breaks, vacations, or simply carving out time for stillness and quiet. By valuing rest as much as we value work, we not only rejuvenate our minds and bodies, but we also allow ourselves to experience time more fully, without the constant pressure to do more.

Minimalism as Cognitive and Temporal Liberation

True minimalism is not about living with less for the sake of deprivation. Rather, it is about freeing ourselves from the constraints of excess—whether in material possessions, mental clutter, or time-consuming obligations—so that we can focus on what truly matters. It is a philosophy that invites us to embrace simplicity, intentionality, and mindfulness in every aspect of our lives. By cultivating cognitive clarity and temporal clarity, we gain the freedom to direct our time, attention, and energy towards the things that nourish us and contribute to our long-term well-being.

In practice, this means cultivating an awareness of how our time is spent and learning to simplify our choices and commitments. It means reducing mental noise through practices like mindfulness and reflection, and creating more space for creativity, focus, and rest. It means recognising our *enough point*—the moment when we have what we need, and any further accumulation or striving will only detract from our peace of mind. It is about being intentional with our resources—our time, our energy, and our attention—and choosing only those pursuits that align with our values and bring us lasting fulfilment.

In a world that constantly demands more, minimalism offers a radical and liberating alternative. By focusing on cognitive and temporal clarity, we free ourselves from the pressures of excess and discover a deeper, more meaningful way to engage with life. Through this lens, minimalism becomes not just an aesthetic or lifestyle choice, but a philosophy for living a more intentional, fulfilled, and authentic life.

The Enough Point: Defining Your Personal Threshold of Sufficiency

In a world where excess is often celebrated and more is almost always considered better, the concept of "enough" seems almost foreign. We are constantly told that the pursuit of more—whether in terms of money, status, achievements, or experiences—is the key to happiness and fulfilment. The idea that we could ever have *enough* runs counter to the narrative that defines success by accumulation, progress, and the relentless drive for bigger and better. Yet, what if the pursuit of more is not the answer, but the problem itself? What if true contentment and purpose lie not in striving for more, but in recognising and embracing the sufficiency of what we already have?

This is where the concept of the *enough point* comes into play. The enough point is the threshold at which additional effort, achievement, or material wealth no longer brings increasing returns in terms of happiness, satisfaction, or fulfilment. It is the point where we recognise that what we have—whether in terms of financial resources, relationships, or time—is sufficient for our needs, and that further accumulation or striving would not add meaning or value to our lives. Defining your enough point is one of the most powerful tools for reclaiming your time, energy, and mental well-being. It allows you to break free from the ever-present pressures of consumerism and competition, and instead focus on what genuinely brings joy and meaning.

This article will delve into the concept of the enough point, exploring how to define your own personal threshold of sufficiency, and how recognising this point can free you from the endless pursuit of more. We will examine why it is crucial to identify your enough point in order to live a life that aligns with your values and prioritises quality over quantity. Drawing on insights from philosophy, psychology, and modern cultural analysis, we will explore how the pursuit of *enough* is not a step backwards, but a path toward greater freedom, contentment, and self-actualisation.

The Enough Point: Understanding the Threshold of Sufficiency

The concept of sufficiency, or the enough point, is grounded in the idea that well-being and contentment are not derived from an ever-expanding list of possessions, achievements, or experiences, but from recognising when we have attained what we truly need. In the context of our material world, the enough point represents the realisation that the constant accumulation of goods, wealth, or success does not correlate with an increase in happiness. Indeed, research in positive psychology suggests that once we have met our basic needs—such as those for security, comfort, and connection—

the pursuit of additional wealth or status does little to enhance our long-term well-being.

A seminal study by the psychologist Daniel Kahneman, for example, demonstrated that while increased income may correlate with greater happiness up to a certain point, beyond a threshold of approximately $75,000 per year, additional income has little to no effect on a person's subjective well-being. This threshold varies for each person, depending on their values, priorities, and context. For some, it might be financial security, for others it might be professional achievement or social recognition. But the key insight remains: at some point, more of what we want does not equate to more happiness.

The enough point also applies to time. We often find ourselves overwhelmed by the constant demands on our time—work obligations, social commitments, and the pressure to be constantly busy. Yet, in our quest to achieve, we overlook the reality that *doing more* does not always lead to greater fulfilment. In fact, it can often detract from the quality of our lives. At some point, our need for more time becomes a need for more *meaningful* time. The enough point in the realm of time, therefore, is the recognition that we have enough space to live fully, and that striving for more commitments or experiences can actually dilute the quality of the moments we already have.

To define your own enough point, you must first reflect on what truly matters to you. What brings you lasting satisfaction, joy, and purpose? What are the things you truly need in order to feel fulfilled? Identifying these core needs and values is the first step toward recognising your own personal threshold. This requires a deep, honest examination of your life and priorities—one that challenges the conventional narrative of *more* and encourages you to question what is genuinely enriching, rather than what is simply expected or culturally rewarded.

The Pressure of More: The Cultural Conditioning of the 'Always More' Mentality

In a society that celebrates excess and measures success by quantity—more money, more success, more recognition—the idea of *enough* can feel countercultural, even radical. The constant messages we receive through advertising, media, and social platforms tell us that to be happy, we must always strive for more. More followers, more likes, more accomplishments, more possessions. These external pressures push us to continuously seek validation, whether through material wealth or social approval. This relentless drive for more is often described as the "tyranny of more" because it traps us in a never-ending cycle of dissatisfaction.

Psychologically, the pursuit of more is driven by a concept known as the *hedonic treadmill*, a theory in psychology that suggests that as we acquire more—whether in terms of wealth, status, or possessions—we quickly adapt to these gains and return to our baseline level of happiness. While the initial excitement of achieving a goal or acquiring a new possession may provide a temporary boost in happiness, it is short-lived, and we soon find ourselves yearning for the next achievement or acquisition. This cycle perpetuates the belief that happiness can be found in the acquisition of more, leading to an endless chase for what is ultimately an elusive prize.

However, when we recognise the concept of the enough point, we begin to question this narrative. Instead of chasing after external markers of success, we focus on what we already have, appreciating it for its intrinsic value rather than its potential to increase our status or possessions. This shift in perspective allows us to move away from the hedonistic treadmill and embrace a more sustainable, fulfilling approach to life.

The Liberating Power of Enough: Freedom from the Tyranny of More

Recognising your enough point offers a profound sense of liberation. When you accept that you have enough, you free yourself from the pressures of comparison and competition. You stop measuring your worth by how much you have or how much you achieve, and instead measure it by the depth of your experiences and the richness of your relationships. You can begin to enjoy the present moment more fully, without the constant desire for future achievements or possessions.

This freedom also extends to your relationship with time. The more you recognise the point at which you have enough time—enough space for rest, creativity, relationships, and reflection—the less you feel the need to fill every minute with activity or obligation. You can start saying no to commitments that drain your energy and yes to the things that nourish you. In doing so, you reclaim your time and begin to live with intention, purpose, and authenticity.

Moreover, the philosophy of enough fosters greater contentment and gratitude. When you recognise that you already have enough, you shift your focus from what is lacking to what is abundant in your life. This mindset of sufficiency allows you to experience greater peace and joy in the present moment, without the constant anxiety of striving for more. It also encourages you to focus on what you can give rather than what you can acquire, fostering a sense of contribution and connection to others.

Practical Steps to Discover Your Enough Point

Defining your enough point requires both reflection and action. It is not a one-time exercise, but an ongoing process of tuning in to your inner needs, values, and desires. Here are some practical steps to help you identify and embrace your enough point:

1. **Assess Your Priorities**: Reflect on what truly matters to you. What are your core values? What do you need in order to feel fulfilled? Identify the areas of your life where you feel most at peace and recognise when further striving will not add value.

2. **Simplify Your Commitments**: Evaluate how you are spending your time. Are there commitments or obligations that no longer align with your values or that are draining your energy? Saying no to these can help you create more space for what truly matters.

3. **Practice Gratitude**: Regularly take stock of what you already have—whether in terms of material possessions, relationships, or experiences—and cultivate a sense of gratitude for it. This can help shift your focus from scarcity to abundance.

4. **Set Boundaries**: Establish clear boundaries around what is enough in terms of work, social obligations, and material possessions. This will help prevent burnout and allow you to focus on quality over quantity.

5. **Evaluate Your Relationship with Money**: Consider how much money you truly need to feel secure and fulfilled. Once you reach this threshold, recognise that further accumulation will likely not bring you greater happiness or peace.

The Path to True Fulfilment: Embracing the Enough Point

In a world that is obsessed with growth, more, and accumulation, the concept of enough offers a radically different path—one rooted in contentment, sufficiency, and mindful living. Defining your enough point allows you to free yourself from the tyranny of more and cultivate a life that is aligned with your deepest values. By recognising when you have enough, you create the space to focus on what truly matters and begin living with greater intention and joy. Ultimately, the enough point is not about doing less, but about doing what truly enriches your life, and doing it with greater clarity, purpose, and fulfilment.

The Joy of Missing Out: Reclaiming FOMO Through Intentional Disengagement

We live in an era that glorifies busyness, connectivity, and the constant accumulation of experiences. The pressures of social media, the demands of professional life, and the constant bombardment of information leave us feeling like we must always be *doing*—attending events, consuming content, and keeping up with trends. The fear of missing out, or FOMO, is pervasive, constantly lurking in our minds as we scroll through social feeds filled with curated snapshots of what others are experiencing. The result is a culture of perpetual engagement, where rest, reflection, and disconnection are undervalued.

But what if the secret to true contentment lies not in the pressure to be everywhere and experience everything, but in the *freedom* to step away from the noise and intentionally disengage? What if, instead of feeling anxious about what we're missing, we could embrace the liberating power of missing out, and use that space to nurture what truly matters? In this article, we explore the concept of the Joy of Missing Out (JOMO), a philosophy that flips FOMO on its head by celebrating the power of intentional disengagement, mindfulness, and presence.

By diving into JOMO, we can reclaim our time, our attention, and our mental well-being. We will look at why disengagement is not a retreat from life, but an active, empowering choice to focus on what *we* truly value. From this perspective, missing out is not a loss; it is a means of aligning our time with our deepest priorities, cultivating a sense of freedom and fulfilment in a world that constantly demands more.

The Tyranny of FOMO: How Constant Connectivity Drives Anxiety

FOMO, or the fear of missing out, has become a defining feature of modern life. With the advent of social media, our awareness of what others are doing—where they are, who they are with, what experiences they are having—is constantly heightened. Through Instagram, Facebook, Twitter, and other platforms, we are flooded with curated snapshots of people's lives, creating an illusion of omnipresence. It seems that there is always something happening somewhere, always something more to experience, always something more to *have.*

For many, this constant exposure to what others are doing can lead to a pervasive sense of inadequacy or anxiety. We start to feel as though we are not living fully unless we are part of every event, every conversation, every trend. There is a sense that to opt out, to step away, is to somehow be less than, or to miss out on the opportunity to live a *complete* life.

Psychologically, the effects of FOMO can be detrimental. Studies have shown that constant exposure to social media and the fear of missing out can lead to increased feelings of loneliness, envy, and dissatisfaction. This anxiety is compounded by what psychologists call *social comparison theory*—the tendency to compare ourselves to others, often unfavourably. As we look at the seemingly perfect lives of others, we begin to measure our worth based on what we have—or don't have—compared to theirs. The result is a cycle of anxiety and discontent, driven by the belief that our lives will be better if only we could keep up with everything.

But in truth, this cycle of comparison and striving only serves to dilute the richness of our experiences. The more we chase external validation, the less we are able to connect with our own authentic desires and needs. The constant rush to experience more often leads to overwhelm, burnout, and a lack of true fulfilment.

JOMO: The Liberating Power of Missing Out

In contrast to FOMO, the Joy of Missing Out (JOMO) offers a refreshing antidote. JOMO is not about disengagement for its own sake—it is about choosing to disconnect from the overwhelming demands of modern life so that we can reconnect with ourselves and our true priorities. It is about recognising that our time, attention, and energy are finite resources, and that we must be discerning about where and how we invest them.

At its core, JOMO is about intentionality. It is about making conscious choices to opt out of experiences, commitments, or distractions that do not align with our deepest values or bring us true joy. Instead of rushing to join every event, social gathering, or digital conversation, JOMO encourages us to *choose* where we direct our attention, to focus on the activities that nurture us—whether that means spending quality time with loved ones, dedicating time to creative pursuits, or simply resting and recharging.

One of the most powerful aspects of JOMO is the way it shifts our perspective on time. In a society that often equates busyness with worth, we begin to recognise that doing less can be far more fulfilling than doing more. By intentionally disengaging from the noise and chaos of modern life, we create the space to cultivate meaningful experiences, build deeper connections, and live with greater presence. In this space of disengagement, we begin to understand that true joy comes not from *more* but from *enough*—from the richness of the moments we choose to embrace, and from the clarity that comes with focusing on what truly matters.

The Mindfulness of Disconnection: How JOMO Improves Well-Being

The practice of JOMO invites us to embrace *mindful disconnection*—the deliberate act of stepping away from distractions in order to reconnect with ourselves and our present reality. Mindfulness, as a practice, encourages us to be fully present in each moment, to observe our thoughts and feelings without judgment, and to cultivate a deeper awareness of our inner world. JOMO, in this sense, is a natural extension of mindfulness. It is not merely about disengaging from external distractions, but about using that space to engage more fully with our own thoughts, feelings, and desires.

Research has shown that mindfulness and intentional disengagement have numerous mental and physical health benefits. Regular practices of mindfulness can reduce stress, improve emotional regulation, and enhance cognitive focus. By practising JOMO, we give ourselves permission to step back, breathe, and reflect, allowing us to restore our mental and emotional balance. This sense of spaciousness—of having enough time, space, and energy to focus on what we truly value—is one of the key elements of well-being. It is in this space that we reconnect with our sense of purpose, creativity, and peace.

Intentional disengagement also has important social benefits. In a culture of constant connectivity, the pressure to be "always available" or "always on" can erode the quality of our relationships. By embracing JOMO, we create space for more authentic interactions, free from the distractions of notifications and social media updates. We are able to engage with those around us with more presence, empathy, and attention. This leads to deeper, more meaningful relationships, and helps foster a sense of community and belonging.

Practical Ways to Embrace JOMO in Daily Life

Embracing JOMO requires a shift in mindset and a conscious effort to prioritise what matters most. Here are some practical steps you can take to cultivate the joy of missing out:

1. **Limit Digital Distractions**: Set boundaries around your use of social media and digital devices. Consider designating specific times for checking emails or browsing social feeds, and allow yourself time to be offline. This creates space for more mindful engagement with the world around you.

2. **Say No More Often**: Practice the art of saying no to commitments or invitations that do not align with your values or bring you joy. Recognise that saying no is a powerful form of self-care, and that your time is a finite resource.

3. **Cultivate Meaningful Hobbies**: Engage in activities that nourish your soul—whether that's reading, writing, painting, gardening, or spending time with loved ones. Prioritise these activities over those that feel obligatory or superficial.

4. **Schedule Downtime**: Allow yourself time to rest and recharge. This may mean scheduling "do nothing" days or intentional breaks throughout your week. Use this time to reconnect with yourself and experience the present moment without external distractions.

5. **Be Present in the Now**: Practice mindfulness in your everyday interactions. Rather than looking ahead to the next task or event, focus on being fully present in the moment, appreciating the richness of the experience.

JOMO as a Path to a More Fulfilling Life

The Joy of Missing Out offers a refreshing alternative to the culture of constant striving, accumulation, and comparison that defines much of modern life. By intentionally disengaging from the pressures of FOMO, we open ourselves to a life of greater purpose, contentment, and peace. We shift our focus from external validation to internal fulfilment, recognising that true joy comes not from doing more, but from embracing what is truly meaningful. In embracing JOMO, we create space for the things that truly matter: meaningful relationships, personal growth, creativity, and rest. Ultimately, the joy of missing out is not about deprivation, but about embracing the richness of a life lived with intention, presence, and authenticity.

Anti-Ambition as Wisdom: Redefining Ambition as Meaningful Contribution Without Burnout

In the modern world, ambition is often celebrated as the ultimate driving force behind success. It's synonymous with achievement, status, and personal fulfilment. From a young age, we are taught to strive, to push for more, and to never stop until we reach the top.

The conventional narrative of ambition—one of relentless striving, competition, and external validation—has become ingrained in our cultural psyche. It is as if ambition, in its most aggressive form, is the only path to success. The unspoken message is clear: the more you strive, the more you achieve; the more you achieve, the greater your worth.

But what if this notion of ambition, so deeply entrenched in our society, is fundamentally flawed? What if ambition, as we traditionally understand it, is not a virtue but a trap? A trap that leads not to fulfilment, but to burnout, stress, and a constant sense of inadequacy. The idea of "anti-ambition" may sound contradictory, yet it is increasingly being recognised as a necessary antidote to the unsustainable hustle culture that pervades our lives.

In this article, we will explore how *anti-ambition*—not the rejection of ambition entirely, but the redefinition of ambition—can be a source of wisdom. This shift in perspective allows us to reframe our drive for success, placing meaning and personal fulfilment at the heart of our efforts, rather than the relentless pursuit of external rewards. We will challenge the traditional understanding of ambition, shifting it from a narrow focus on material success to a broader, more holistic vision of contributing meaningfully to the world without sacrificing our health or happiness. Anti-ambition is not about settling for less; it is about aligning ambition with inner values and living a life that honours our well-being.

The Strain of Conventional Ambition: A Cycle of Stress and Burnout

Traditional ambition, driven by external measures of success, has led to what many now recognise as an epidemic of stress, burnout, and existential dissatisfaction. The modern workplace, in particular, often demands that we sacrifice our personal lives, our mental health, and our relationships in the name of achievement. Long hours, constant deadlines, and an ever-expanding list of tasks have become the norm, leading many to feel overwhelmed, disconnected, and drained. The more we accomplish, the more we are expected to do. And this cycle continues, with little room for reflection or rest.

This type of ambition, grounded in the idea of perpetual striving, encourages individuals to measure their worth by external accomplishments—how much money they make, how many followers they have, how many awards they collect. Yet, despite the outward success, many ambitious individuals find themselves spiritually impoverished, emotionally exhausted, and searching for meaning. This is the paradox of traditional ambition: it promises fulfilment but often delivers exhaustion and disillusionment.

From a psychological perspective, the constant pressure to strive for more can lead to feelings of anxiety, inadequacy, and a lack of intrinsic satisfaction. Research into motivation suggests that individuals driven by *extrinsic* goals (such as fame, wealth, or social status) are less likely to experience long-term well-being than those driven by *intrinsic* values—those that come from within, such as personal growth, creativity, and meaningful connection. Yet, in a society that values external markers of success, it becomes difficult to pursue the deeper, intrinsic motivations that are key to genuine happiness.

Anti-Ambition: A Redefinition of Success

Anti-ambition is not the rejection of all ambition, but rather the rejection of the narrow, external markers of success that so often define our lives. It is a shift from striving endlessly for more, to focusing on what *is enough*—a conscious choice to pursue goals that align with our core values and contribute meaningfully to the world without the need for validation from others.

At its core, anti-ambition invites us to reframe our understanding of success. Instead of measuring success by the number of accolades, material possessions, or social recognition we accumulate, we are encouraged to measure it by the impact we have on others, the integrity with which we live our lives, and the sense of fulfilment we derive from the work we do. In this sense, anti-ambition is about aligning our ambitions with purpose rather than external validation. It is about recognising that true success comes not from striving harder, but from striving more *wisely*—choosing to focus on meaningful contributions rather than superficial achievements.

This redefinition of ambition also brings with it a recognition of the importance of balance and well-being. The modern obsession with success often overlooks the fundamental need for rest, reflection, and self-care. Anti-ambition, therefore, challenges us to reject the glorification of overwork and instead embrace a more balanced, sustainable approach to life. It calls for a shift from productivity-driven living to a more mindful approach, where our energy is spent on pursuits that nourish us emotionally, physically, and spiritually.

The Wisdom of Anti-Ambition: Contributing Meaningfully Without Burnout

One of the most profound aspects of anti-ambition is that it allows us to contribute meaningfully to society without sacrificing our well-being. When we focus on intrinsic goals—such as nurturing relationships, contributing to our communities, or creating art—we are often more engaged and fulfilled than when we are driven solely by external rewards. Research in positive psychology has shown that people who engage in meaningful work—work that aligns with their values—are not only happier but also experience less stress and greater life satisfaction.

Anti-ambition also allows us to cultivate a deeper sense of wisdom. By rejecting the constant pressure to "do more" and instead focusing on what is *enough*, we learn to make more thoughtful, deliberate choices about how we invest our time and energy. We begin to understand that life is not a race, and that meaningful success comes from living authentically, not from ticking off achievements on a checklist.

Furthermore, anti-ambition promotes a healthier relationship with failure. In a society that equates ambition with success and failure with inadequacy, the fear of failure often prevents people from pursuing what they truly care about. By embracing anti-ambition, we acknowledge that failure is an inevitable part of growth, and that it does not diminish our worth or undermine our ability to contribute meaningfully. This shift in perspective frees us from the paralyzing fear of failure and allows us to take more risks, embrace new challenges, and pursue projects that bring us joy, regardless of the external outcomes.

Practical Steps to Cultivate Anti-Ambition

Embracing anti-ambition requires a conscious shift in mindset and a willingness to reject the external pressures that often dictate our lives. Here are some practical steps you can take to cultivate anti-ambition and align your goals with meaning and purpose:

1. **Redefine Success**: Take a step back and reflect on what success truly means to you. What are the values, relationships, and contributions that matter most? Shift your focus from external recognition to internal fulfilment.

2. **Set Meaningful Goals**: Rather than setting goals based on external rewards, set goals that align with your values and passions. Focus on the impact you want to have in the world, rather than the recognition you seek to receive.

3. **Prioritise Well-Being**: Create space in your life for rest, reflection, and self-care. Recognise that achieving balance and maintaining mental, emotional, and physical health are essential for long-term success.

4. **Embrace Failure**: Reframe your relationship with failure. See it as an opportunity for growth rather than a reflection of your inadequacy. Failure is a necessary part of the creative and learning process.

5. **Be Present**: Practice mindfulness and presence in your daily life. By focusing on the present moment and cultivating gratitude for what you have, you can begin to disconnect from the pressure to constantly strive for more.

Anti-Ambition: A Path to True Fulfilment

Anti-ambition does not reject the idea of ambition entirely; rather, it redefines it as a means of aligning our energy with what truly matters. By focusing on meaningful contributions, nurturing our well-being, and living authentically, we can achieve a more profound sense of success and satisfaction than the traditional, external markers of achievement ever could. Anti-ambition invites us to let go of the pressure to strive endlessly for more and instead embrace the wisdom of *enough*. In doing so, we free ourselves from burnout, create space for deeper fulfilment, and contribute to the world in ways that are aligned with our true purpose.

Chapter 7
The Emotional Aftermath of Liberation

In a culture that has, for generations, bound personal worth to productivity, to busyness, to the relentless cadence of output, stepping away from the grind can feel like both an escape and a rupture. It's tempting to imagine that leaving behind the hustle will bring instant calm—but for many who have long been tethered to achievement as a measure of identity, what follows is not immediate serenity, but a strange, uncharted quiet. And in that stillness? A host of questions we may not be prepared to answer.

For those who've spent years, even decades, sprinting toward milestones—promotions, accolades, the constant hum of doing—it is no small thing to find oneself suddenly in possession of unscheduled time. At first, there might be a breath of relief. A sense that something long clenched has begun, at last, to loosen. But then comes the disorientation. Without the usual scaffolding—titles, routines, performance metrics—many are left wondering: who am I, when I'm no longer achieving?

This chapter delves into that uneasy in-between—the emotional terrain we seldom prepare for when we speak of "breaking free" from hustle culture. It's not just a shift in pace. It's a profound and often jarring psychological metamorphosis. One that calls into question not only how we spend our time, but who we believe ourselves to be beneath the roles we've played.

The truth is, the aftermath of liberation is not always a glide into tranquillity. More often, it's a reckoning. There is grief, surprisingly—not because we mourn the hustle itself, but because we must part ways with the version of ourselves who thrived in it. Or at the very least, survived by it. We begin to peel back layers—expectations inherited, personas constructed for the applause of others—and what emerges isn't always immediately clear. It may feel like a void. And it is tempting to fill that space with yet another project, another metric, another mission.

But if we resist that impulse—if we allow the stillness to linger—a new relationship with time and self begins to take root. Yes, there may be guilt: the nagging sense that one ought to be doing something, anything, to justify existence. There may be anxiety, too, as we lose the sharp outlines of the old self and step uncertainly into the undefined. Yet this discomfort is not a sign that something is wrong. It is, in fact, evidence that something deep is shifting.

Over time, as the dust of urgency settles, what often arises is not emptiness, but clarity. The joy that comes is quieter than what we're used to—it doesn't clamor for recognition. It simply *is*. And with it, a sense of groundedness begins to emerge. A reorientation, not around what we do, but who we are when we're no longer trying so hard to be someone else.

This chapter invites you to sit with that process—not to rush it, not to mask it with new ambitions, but to witness it fully. Liberation, it turns out, is not only an act of escape. It is a tender, sometimes turbulent act of becoming.

Grieving the Old Self: Letting Go of the Hustle

For many, the idea of liberation is intertwined with the act of letting go—letting go of the constant striving, the endless to-do lists, the perpetual quest for validation. It requires us to mourn the version of ourselves that was defined by external measures of success. This grieving process can be disorienting, especially when we've built much of our identity around the grind and the hustle. We may question: Who am I if I'm not busy? What happens if I'm no longer defined by my work?

The first step in this emotional transformation is recognising that the identities we have clung to are often artificial constructs. We may have learned, either from societal expectations or from our own internalised beliefs, that our worth is tied to our productivity and busyness. In this framework, the act of slowing down or doing "nothing" is seen as a failure, a sign of weakness or laziness. However, this view overlooks the essential truth: rest is not a luxury, but a necessity for mental, emotional, and physical well-being.

Letting go of the hustle identity is not an overnight process. It involves untangling the belief systems that have shaped our understanding of self-worth. This can be deeply uncomfortable—like losing a part of ourselves that we've spent years cultivating. But as we gradually release these old narratives, we create space for something far more authentic. The grieving of the old self is an opportunity to reconnect with the parts of us that may have been buried under the weight of constant striving. It is a chance to embrace a deeper, more expansive sense of self that is not tethered to the idea of perpetual doing.

The Stillness Spiral: From Anxiety to Ecstasy

One of the most powerful aspects of liberation from the hustle is the psychological transition from anxiety to ecstasy. Initially, freedom from the pressure to constantly achieve can evoke feelings of discomfort and disquiet. Without the familiar structure of work, deadlines, and external demands, many people feel adrift. The absence of a rigid framework can trigger anxiety, as we question whether we are "doing enough" or "wasting time."

This period of adjustment can feel like a downward spiral—where the mind constantly battles with the lack of structure, and the ego struggles to reconcile the new reality. However, just as with any profound transformation, this spiral is not an end but a process. In the early stages, it may feel like we are spiralling into unproductive voids. But over time, if we allow ourselves to surrender to the process and trust in the transition, we begin to experience a shift.

As we adjust to a life with more space, we learn to reclaim our time and energy—not as a commodity to be hoarded or "spent," but as an opportunity to engage with life in a more intentional way. The stillness that once felt unsettling becomes a sanctuary, a space where creativity, clarity, and presence can thrive. Over time, anxiety begins to dissolve, and we move into a state of ecstasy—the exhilarating joy that comes from simply being, without the constant pressure to prove our worth through external achievement.

This transition is not linear, nor is it easy. There will be moments of doubt and fear, particularly as we confront the ingrained habits of hustle and achievement. But with each passing day, as we embrace stillness, the spiral begins to turn upwards. We begin to experience the deep satisfaction that comes from living in alignment with our true values, with the freedom to act from a place of deep inner peace rather than external validation.

Learning to Receive Time: The Liberation of Idleness

A key part of the emotional aftermath of liberation is learning how to *receive* time, rather than always striving to *fill* it. Many of us have been conditioned to believe that time is something to be managed, maximised, and "spent" wisely. Our culture prizes efficiency and productivity above all else, and the idea of idle time is often viewed with suspicion. This mindset has led to an overwhelming sense of scarcity—not only in terms of time, but in terms of our ability to enjoy life without guilt.

To liberate ourselves from this scarcity mindset, we must learn to receive time as a gift. This means allowing ourselves to experience joy, idleness, and inspiration without the need to justify them. Time, in this context, is not a resource to be "used up," but an expansive space to be enjoyed. Learning to receive time requires us to challenge the deeply ingrained belief that we must always be doing something in order to be worthy.

The act of receiving time with joy requires us to unlearn the notion that we must constantly strive or justify our existence through productivity. It is about allowing ourselves to rest, to be still, and to engage in activities that nourish our bodies, minds, and spirits without guilt. Whether it's enjoying a leisurely walk in nature, spending time with loved ones, or engaging in a creative pursuit, the practice of receiving time allows us to fully inhabit the present moment without the weight of future goals or past regrets.

This process of receiving time is intimately connected with the larger journey of emotional healing and liberation. When we learn to embrace the fullness of time without needing to earn it or justify it, we cultivate a deeper sense of self-worth and presence. We become more attuned to our bodies, our emotions, and our needs. We learn to move through life not with urgency, but with intentionality, aligning our actions with our inner truth rather than external pressures.

The Emotional Aftermath: Embracing a New Way of Being

The emotional aftermath of liberation is not simply a transitional phase, but a profound shift in the way we relate to ourselves, our time, and the world around us. As we grieve the loss of our old identity, adapt to the rhythms of stillness, and learn to receive time with joy, we create space for a more authentic, balanced, and fulfilling life.

This process requires patience, self-compassion, and an unwavering commitment to living in alignment with our values. It may not always be easy, and it may involve moments of discomfort and uncertainty. But it is through this discomfort that we make room for growth, healing, and transformation. The emotional aftermath of liberation is not the end of a journey, but the beginning of a new way of being—one that honours both the stillness and the vitality within us, and that allows us to live with greater clarity, joy, and purpose.

The Anxiety of Unstructured Time: Unlearning Decades of Time-Discipline

Time has long been a commodity to be controlled, managed, and shaped by rigid schedules and the relentless tick of the clock. For decades, we've been conditioned to structure every moment of our day, filling it with tasks and responsibilities that demand our attention, our energy, and, often, our identity. The rise of the productivity culture, which prizes efficiency and output, has led many of us to become increasingly dependent on a time-discipline framework that tells us when to rise, when to work, when to rest, and when to engage. But in a world that increasingly offers opportunities for unstructured time—time free from the demands of schedules, deadlines, and external expectations—the psychological effects of this newfound freedom can be profoundly unsettling.

This shift away from time-discipline is not just an adjustment of our daily routines; it can feel like an unraveling of the very fabric of our sense of self. The liberation from the grind and the tyranny of productivity can trigger deep-rooted anxiety, confusion, and emotional dissonance. For those accustomed to the structured life, unstructured time may feel like a vacuum—an empty space that demands to be filled, a void that calls up unresolved emotional issues long buried under the weight of busyness. The very absence of structure, while liberating in theory, can provoke feelings of purposelessness, discomfort, and existential doubt. How does one fill the expansive, unmarked hours? What does it mean to *be* when there is nothing to "do"?

This chapter delves into the emotional and psychological impact of unstructured time, exploring how the process of unlearning decades of time-discipline can bring up unresolved emotional voids. We will examine the reasons why the freedom of unstructured time can be so difficult to embrace, and we will offer insights on how to navigate this transition from anxiety to clarity. More importantly, we will explore how, by confronting these fears and emotions, we can reclaim time as an authentic, enriching part of our lives—one that is defined not by external demands but by our own values, presence, and joy.

The Psychological Toll of Time-Discipline

The pressure to be perpetually "on" and engaged with the demands of work, family, social expectations, and the digital world has created a cultural norm of ceaseless busyness. This relentless cycle of doing has become so ingrained in our psyche that the mere idea of unstructured time can feel like an affront to our sense of purpose. For years, we have been conditioned to equate worth with output. Time is seen as a scarce resource, one that must be spent efficiently, invested in tasks that yield measurable results. We become accustomed to living in response to external prompts—email notifications, project deadlines, social engagements—schedules that govern every moment of our day.

When we suddenly find ourselves with unstructured time, free from the constant demands of the clock, it can feel unsettling. The familiar rhythm of productivity gives way to the unknown, and with it comes a sense of anxiety. Without external structure, the mind begins to question its place. How do we define ourselves when we are no longer defined by what we do? The fear of waste—of "doing nothing"—can seep in, evoking feelings of inadequacy, guilt, or shame. These feelings often arise not because the time is being wasted, but because we have been conditioned to believe that time must be "used" in specific, productive ways.

Psychologically, the shift from structured time to unstructured time is akin to the process of uncoupling a deeply embedded habit. When we've spent years operating under a time-discipline regime, our nervous systems become wired for efficiency and task completion. The sudden loss of this structure can create a cognitive dissonance, where the mind searches for something to "do" even when there is nothing required. This manifests as anxiety, unease, or even a sense of emptiness, as we struggle to reconcile the idea of time being "unfilled" with our internalised sense of purpose.

The Fear of Idleness: A Cultural Condition

The fear of idleness is not simply a personal struggle—it is a societal construct. In the Western world, particularly, productivity has been idealised as a measure of individual worth. From the earliest stages of education through to our professional careers, we are taught to optimise our time, avoid procrastination, and remain busy. The very idea of rest, of simply being present without doing, has become a luxury—or worse, a moral failing. This fear of idleness runs deep, and when faced with the possibility of unstructured time, it often triggers an emotional and existential crisis.

Idleness, in this context, is not just seen as a lack of activity but as a void—an absence of value. The idea that "time off" or "doing nothing" is not productive feeds directly into feelings of guilt. Why? Because, in a culture that values productivity above all, if we are not actively doing something, we are not contributing. And if we are not contributing, we fear we are losing our value.

But this is where the emotional work comes in. We must unlearn this conditioning. We must recognise that time, in its unstructured state, is not an empty space to be feared but a fertile ground for growth, creativity, and self-discovery. Unstructured time is the canvas on which we can create meaning—not based on external validation or the completion of tasks, but based on our own innate sense of fulfilment, joy, and connection.

Confronting the Void: From Anxiety to Acceptance

The process of confronting the anxiety of unstructured time is a journey—a path that moves from discomfort and restlessness towards acceptance and clarity. The first step is to acknowledge that these feelings of unease are normal. Transitioning from a life of constant busyness to one of time freedom is not an immediate or easy process. It takes patience, self-compassion, and a willingness to sit with discomfort.

As we begin to allow ourselves more unstructured time, it is helpful to create space for mindfulness practices, reflective journaling, or simple moments of stillness. These practices can act as anchors, helping us navigate the uncertainty that comes with freedom. Through meditation or mindfulness, we learn to let go of the constant pressure to do, to produce, and to perform. We allow ourselves to experience the present moment without judgment or the need for justification.

In time, as we practice embracing unstructured time without the pressure of filling it, the anxiety begins to dissolve. We move from a mindset of "doing" to one of "being," where the value of time is not determined by what we accomplish but by how we engage with it. The feelings of emptiness transform into a sense of spaciousness—of opportunity. We begin to realise that time is not a finite resource to be spent but an expansive space in which we can fully experience life.

Learning to Receive Time: Redefining Our Relationship with the Clock

One of the most liberating aspects of unstructured time is the opportunity it provides to *receive* time, rather than merely manage it. The concept of receiving time is a radical departure from our traditional view of time as a taskmaster. It invites us to see time as a gift, a resource that does not need to be earned or justified but can be simply lived.

Learning to receive time means embracing moments of idleness, joy, and inspiration without the need for productivity. It is the recognition that our worth is not defined by how much we accomplish, but by how fully we engage with the present moment. This shift in perspective can be deeply freeing. It allows us to feel the full richness of life without the underlying anxiety that often accompanies the clock's relentless ticking.

Conclusion: Embracing Unstructured Time as a Path to Growth

The anxiety of unstructured time is not a barrier to be overcome, but an invitation to reimagine how we engage with life. It is a call to unlearn the ingrained habits of time-discipline and to embrace the space that is available when we stop rushing, stop striving, and simply *be*. As we release the fears and conditioning that tie us to external measures of productivity, we open ourselves to a new, more enriching relationship with time—one that allows us to receive its gifts with gratitude, presence, and joy.

This chapter invites you to explore this emotional terrain, to face the discomfort of unstructured time head-on, and to ultimately experience the profound freedom that comes when we stop measuring our worth by the clock and begin to truly *live* within it.

Grieving the Old Self: Letting Go of Identities Built Around Hustle, Workaholism, and Urgency

In a world where productivity reigns as the ultimate virtue and the constant hum of urgency fills every waking moment, the idea of stepping away from the hustle can feel unsettling, even unnatural. We are conditioned from an early age to define ourselves by what we do—to derive our worth from the work we accomplish and the roles we play. Our jobs, titles, and to-do lists have become the primary markers of identity. But when the pursuit of success, status, and constant doing starts to take its toll, when we begin to question the cost of living in perpetual motion, we face an unsettling truth: *who are we without all of that?*

This chapter explores the emotional journey of letting go of the identities built around hustle, workaholism, and urgency. As we begin to question the systems that have defined us for so long, we must also confront the grieving process that comes with shedding these old selves. For many, this can feel like the loss of a familiar companion—the very essence of their identity. But this grief is not a mark of failure; it is a necessary step toward true liberation and personal transformation. The process of unlearning the deeply ingrained patterns of striving and achievement allows space for new, more aligned identities to emerge—ones that are based not on external markers of success, but on inner fulfilment and authenticity.

The Cult of Productivity: The Identity Built on Doing

To understand the emotional toll of letting go of work-centric identities, it's essential to first explore the nature of these identities. For decades, many of us have been raised in a culture that glorifies productivity, equating our value with the amount of work we do and the speed at which we do it. From an early age, we are encouraged to pursue career ambitions, accumulate achievements, and check off endless lists of tasks. The idea of "busyness" has been elevated to a badge of honour, with societal praise often reserved for those who manage to balance multiple roles while maintaining the appearance of effortless success.

This conditioning is so pervasive that, for many, our very sense of self becomes tied to our work. We find it difficult to separate who we are from what we do. Job titles, promotions, and external validation become the building blocks of self-worth. The fear of not achieving, not progressing, or—perhaps worst of all—not *doing* anything, leads to anxiety and guilt. Over time, we internalise these pressures, and our identities become conflated with our ability to produce, achieve, and perform.

However, this way of living is unsustainable. The weight of these expectations creates a system of burnout, exhaustion, and emotional disconnection. It's no surprise that so many people experience feelings of emptiness when they slow down or find themselves without a structured sense of purpose. We have trained ourselves to keep moving forward, not because we need to, but because we fear what happens when we stop. The fear of failure becomes inextricably linked to our inability to remain busy, and as such, we constantly strive to fill our schedules to stave off the quiet discomfort of stillness.

The Emotional Cost of Hustle Culture

The culture of hustle and urgency takes a toll that is often invisible until it becomes overwhelming. Beneath the facade of constant activity, there is a growing sense of emotional depletion. The idea that we must always be striving to achieve more leads to a pattern of relentless doing, which can leave little room for self-reflection, relaxation, or even true joy. Workaholism—defined by the compulsive need to work excessively and often at the expense of one's health or relationships—can feel like a security blanket. It shields us from confronting deeper fears: the fear of inadequacy, the fear of being unworthy, and the fear of living a life without tangible achievements.

But as we begin to take steps away from this frantic pace, we are confronted with an unexpected and often uncomfortable reality: the grief of letting go of the familiar. For many, this grief may manifest as a sense of loss. The absence of structure or a clearly defined role creates a void that feels disorienting. We may struggle to answer questions like, *Who am I without my work?* or *What value do I bring if I am not constantly doing?* These questions can trigger profound emotional responses—anxiety, confusion, sadness, or even anger—as we wrestle with the discomfort of no longer being defined by external markers of success.

The grief process can feel like mourning the death of a version of ourselves. But rather than being a destructive force, this grief is part of the healing and reinvention process. It is an invitation to let go of outdated identities and embrace new, more sustainable ways of living that are aligned with our deeper values. Letting go of the "hustle" doesn't mean abandoning ambition or productivity; it means redefining them on our own terms, in a way that nourishes rather than depletes us.

The Stillness Spiral: From Anxiety to Ecstasy

When we finally allow ourselves to pause and release the incessant drive to work, we enter what can be described as a "stillness spiral." At first, this shift may feel jarring, unsettling, and perhaps even undesirable. The initial phase of this transition is often marked by anxiety, as we confront the discomfort of having no agenda, no to-do list, and no immediate sense of purpose. Our minds, trained to be in constant motion, may struggle to adapt to this slower pace. The anxiety can be overwhelming, and we may find ourselves seeking distractions in an attempt to alleviate the discomfort of this newfound stillness.

However, with time, the stillness begins to transform. As we embrace the freedom that comes with unstructured time, we discover new depths of clarity, creativity, and presence. The initial anxiety gives way to a sense of peace and joy that is deeply rooted in the present moment. The stillness becomes a fertile ground for reflection, for reconnecting with our inner selves, and for nurturing the relationships that matter most to us. Over time, we begin to realise that true productivity is not about the quantity of work completed, but about the quality of our time and energy. By embracing stillness, we make space for deeper fulfilment and more meaningful contributions to the world.

Learning to Receive Time: The Liberation of Letting Go

One of the most profound lessons that come with shedding the identity of workaholism is the ability to *receive* time. We live in a culture that teaches us to earn everything, including our moments of rest. However, the concept of receiving time invites us to shift from the mindset of scarcity to one of abundance. It encourages us to let go of the need to justify our time off, to stop measuring our worth based on productivity, and to begin fully experiencing the gift of simply *being*.

Learning to receive time means allowing ourselves to be present without needing to earn the right to relax or take a break. It means embracing joy, inspiration, and rest as essential components of a balanced life. When we learn to receive time, we find that we don't have to strive constantly to prove our value; instead, we can allow time to unfold naturally, rich with potential and possibilities for growth.

Embracing the Transformation: A New Identity Beyond Hustle

Letting go of the identities built around hustle and urgency is not a process of loss, but one of transformation. As we grieve the old self—the self that defined worth through doing—we make space for the emergence of a new self, one that is more aligned with our deeper needs and values. This new self is not defined by the work we do or the tasks we complete, but by the quality of our presence, the depth of our relationships, and the clarity of our vision for the future. This new self is free from the constraints of hustle culture, allowing us to live a life that is more intentional, more fulfilling, and more meaningful.

By embracing this transformation, we can cultivate a life that prioritises health, well-being, and joy, without sacrificing productivity or ambition. The grief we experience in letting go of the old self is a sign that we are evolving into something more authentic and sustainable. And in this process, we reclaim not just our time, but our sense of self, free from the need to hustle, to burn out, and to prove our worth.

This chapter is an invitation to reflect on the identities we've built around work, to grieve the loss of the self that no longer serves us, and to embrace the profound freedom that comes with letting go of the need to constantly strive. It is a call to move towards a life that is more balanced, more meaningful, and ultimately more *whole*.

The Stillness Spiral: Phases of Psychological Adaptation from Anxiety to Ecstasy in the Age of Time Freedom

In a world that thrives on hustle culture, the very idea of having time to do nothing seems anathema to success. We live in an era of perpetual motion, where productivity is equated with worth, and busyness is viewed as the pinnacle of achievement. Yet, in a surprising paradox, the pursuit of time freedom—a life where one can slow down, rest, and embrace stillness—can initially evoke feelings of discomfort, even anxiety. When one finally has the luxury of unstructured time, the psychological shift can be both profound and disorienting.

This process, though, is not one of static peace but a dynamic transformation—a journey that moves from anxiety and self-doubt to the euphoric freedom of genuine presence. This "Stillness Spiral" describes the phases through which an individual passes as they adjust to a life no longer governed by the tyranny of clocks and deadlines. Far from being a linear experience, the journey involves a series of emotional and psychological adaptations, where old fears give way to new forms of connection and meaning.

This chapter explores the psychological stages of this spiral, tracing the evolution of the individual's relationship with time—from the anxiety of unstructured moments to the liberation that comes with a deep, embodied sense of presence. Understanding these phases not only clarifies why the transition to a slower pace is so challenging but also why it is ultimately one of the most profound and rewarding shifts a person can make.

The Initial Jolt: Anxiety and Restlessness

When we first step into time freedom, the initial experience is often less liberating and more anxiety-inducing. The sudden absence of an imposed schedule—no deadlines, no meetings, no urgent tasks—can feel like a void. For many, this absence quickly becomes uncomfortable. The sense of productivity that once provided structure and purpose is lost, and with it, the external markers of success.

At first, we may feel a sense of restlessness. This isn't a case of boredom, necessarily. Rather, it's the unsettling realisation that we've become so accustomed to being in motion, both physically and mentally, that stillness itself becomes an unfamiliar space. We may feel a heightened sense of vulnerability: "What should I be doing? How can I fill this time? Am I wasting it?" This stage often brings with it the intrusive thoughts of self-doubt, guilt, or even fear of falling behind. The constant drive for productivity is not easily silenced, and in the absence of it, anxiety can rise.

What we are experiencing in these early moments is a clash between our ingrained identity as a "doer" and the new reality of being without the need to constantly do. It's crucial to acknowledge that these feelings are entirely normal—and even essential—parts of the process. They represent a shedding of old habits and beliefs about what makes us worthy, productive, or valuable. The anxiety we feel is not just a response to empty time; it is the anxiety of confronting a life we've been conditioned to fear—one that values presence over accomplishment.

The Confrontation with Identity: The Old Self Fights Back

As we move beyond the initial shock of stillness, the next phase of the Stillness Spiral involves an internal confrontation. In this stage, we are forced to face the question: "Who am I without the work?" For many, this is the hardest part of the transition. Our identities have long been tied to our roles, our productivity, and the external validation that comes from being "busy" and "successful."

Without work or a clear purpose to define us, we may feel lost. In this phase, individuals often experience what might be called an identity crisis. The labels we've worn—worker, provider, achiever, creator—begin to feel hollow, and we are left wondering whether we are enough without them. We may grieve the loss of our former self, or more accurately, the loss of the version of ourselves that was rooted in constant doing.

This phase of confrontation can be painful, as we reckon with deep-rooted beliefs about self-worth and value. The hustle culture has taught us to measure our worth by our output, and now, in the absence of that output, we must redefine what it means to be worthy, to be valuable, and to be alive. For many, this can be an uncomfortable reckoning—one that shakes the very foundation of who we believe we are. Yet, this phase is crucial. It is in these moments of discomfort that we begin to realise that our identity does not have to be rooted in productivity. We are allowed to *be*, not just to *do*.

Finding the Flow: Acceptance and Relief

After the initial struggles with anxiety and identity, the next phase of the Stillness Spiral involves finding a new flow. At this stage, the intensity of the initial anxiety starts to diminish. We have begun to accept the unstructured time, even if it is still not entirely comfortable. It is during this phase that we start to cultivate a new relationship with time—one where we begin to enjoy the freedom that it offers, without feeling the need to justify or prove its worth.

The notion of "doing nothing" slowly shifts from a source of anxiety to a source of creativity, joy, and clarity. In this phase, we discover the deep sense of peace that comes with simply being present, without the pressure to fill every moment. It is here that we may experience moments of profound joy—whether it's a walk in nature, a quiet moment of reflection, or simply sitting with our own thoughts.

In many ways, this phase mirrors the practice of mindfulness: being fully present in the moment without judgment or expectation. The stillness no longer feels like a void but a rich space for introspection, creativity, and connection with our true selves. As we accept that time is not something to be filled or controlled, we begin to find satisfaction in simply existing in the present.

Ecstasy of Freedom: The Joy of Time without Urgency

As we progress through the Stillness Spiral, we move into what could be described as a state of ecstasy—a state of complete liberation from the need to strive. At this stage, we have fully integrated the concept of time freedom into our lives. We have made peace with the absence of structure and urgency, and as a result, we feel more connected to ourselves, our relationships, and the world around us.

This phase represents the ultimate freedom: the ability to experience life without the pressure of achieving, performing, or measuring success. It's here that we begin to see time not as a resource to be spent or invested, but as a gift to be savoured. We can now enjoy time for its own sake, appreciating the beauty of simply being present. This ecstasy is not about hedonistic indulgence or constant pleasure—it is the joy of living in alignment with our values, of choosing how we spend our time based on what truly nourishes us.

The Stillness Spiral as a Pathway to Authentic Living

The journey from anxiety to ecstasy in the Stillness Spiral is not just about the passing of time; it is about a deeper transformation of how we relate to time itself. It is an invitation to embrace life on our own terms, to step away from the relentless pressure of productivity, and to live in alignment with our true selves. The anxiety and discomfort we feel in the early stages of the Stillness Spiral are merely signs of old patterns breaking down—patterns that were never truly serving us.

As we move through the spiral, we emerge with a new understanding of what it means to live well. We discover that stillness, far from being an empty or wasted state, is a fertile ground for creativity, joy, and connection. We reclaim our time, not as a commodity to be maximised, but as a space in which we can truly live, fully and authentically. In doing so, we step into a new way of being, one where time is no longer a source of stress, but a source of freedom and fulfilment.

In this phase of ecstasy, we begin to experience what it means to live a truly time-rich life, where every moment is imbued with meaning, presence, and the joy of simply being. The Stillness Spiral, though challenging, leads us to a deeper, more fulfilling way of being, one that is not defined by what we do, but by how fully we experience the moments of our lives.

Learning to Receive Time: Embracing Joy, Idleness, and Inspiration Without Justification

In a society where time is relentlessly commodified, the very idea of simply receiving time—of allowing ourselves to enjoy it without the need for validation or justification—can feel almost foreign. We are taught from an early age that time must be earned, that its value lies in productivity and outcomes. We are trained to justify every minute spent, to feel the weight of guilt when we indulge in rest or leisure. The pressure to always be doing something, to constantly achieve, is so ingrained in our cultural psyche that we rarely pause to question it.

Yet, what if the true value of time lies not in how much we can accomplish within it, but in how fully we allow ourselves to experience it? What if joy, inspiration, and even idleness could be received without needing to earn them first? The concept of "learning to receive time" is a revolutionary one—a call to reclaim time as a gift, not a currency. It challenges the deeply embedded notion that our worth is tied to how much we produce and proposes an alternative vision where time becomes a space for nourishment, creativity, and presence.

This article explores the profound shift that occurs when we stop viewing time through the lens of productivity and start experiencing it as a resource that can be savoured. It looks at the psychological, cultural, and emotional barriers that prevent us from receiving time freely and offers practical insights into how we can retrain ourselves to embrace joy, rest, and inspiration without the need for justification. Learning to receive time is not about laziness or escapism; it is about reconnecting with our inherent worth and allowing ourselves the grace to simply be, without the pressure to do.

The Culture of Time as a Transaction

In many ways, the culture we live in today reinforces the idea that time must be justified. From the moment we enter the workforce, we are conditioned to see time as something that must be "spent" in order to gain something in return. Time is a finite resource, and the more efficiently it is used, the more productive—and by extension, valuable—we become. This transactional view of time has led to the rise of time-management systems, productivity hacks, and a constant drive to "get more done" in less time.

This ideology creates an insidious cycle. We measure our days by how much we can cross off our to-do lists, how many hours we spend working or being busy, and how much we produce. The pressure to be constantly "doing" becomes internalised, and the very idea of taking time to rest, reflect, or enjoy life seems wasteful. We feel as though we must earn the right to be present, to relax, or to do something just for the sake of joy.

Yet, research in fields such as positive psychology and neuroscience shows that overworking, constantly striving for external validation, and ignoring the need for rest have detrimental effects on both our mental and physical health. Burnout, anxiety, depression, and chronic stress are all by-products of a culture that insists on constant productivity. The key to reversing this trend is not just about managing time more efficiently but learning to break free from the compulsion to justify every moment.

The Shame of Idleness and the Path to Permission

One of the key barriers to receiving time without justification is the deeply ingrained sense of shame associated with idleness. In many cultures, doing nothing is seen as morally wrong. From a young age, we are taught to fill every moment of the day with activity, with work, with study, with productivity. The idea of simply being, of doing nothing "productive," triggers feelings of guilt for many people.

This shame of idleness is compounded by the rise of "hustle culture," where not constantly striving for success is seen as a sign of failure. The message is clear: if you are not actively achieving something, you are wasting time. This ideology reinforces the notion that time must be filled with measurable outputs in order to be considered valuable.

To receive time freely, we must begin by giving ourselves permission to exist without always needing to justify our existence through our actions. This requires an internal shift in perspective: recognising that our worth is not determined by how much we produce, but by who we are in our entirety. It means letting go of the shame we feel when we take time for ourselves, and instead, embracing the idea that rest, joy, and inspiration are not luxuries, but necessities for our overall well-being.

Embracing Joy Without Justification

One of the most profound aspects of learning to receive time is embracing joy without the need to earn it. In the productivity-driven culture we inhabit, joy is often viewed as a reward for hard work—a kind of bonus that comes after we have met certain milestones or achieved specific goals. This transactional approach to happiness results in fleeting moments of pleasure, quickly followed by the anxiety of what's next on the to-do list.

But what if we could experience joy in its purest form—without strings attached, without conditions, and without needing to prove ourselves worthy of it? Learning to receive time involves giving ourselves the freedom to enjoy life simply because we are alive, without needing to justify it through achievements or external validation. This might look like taking an afternoon off to walk in nature, allowing yourself a long conversation with a friend without rushing to get back to work, or taking the time to engage in a hobby that fills your soul.

When we stop viewing joy as something we have to "earn" through hard work, we begin to experience a deeper, more sustainable form of happiness. Joy becomes a natural consequence of living in alignment with our values, not a fleeting reward for completing a task. In this way, learning to receive time means making space for joy and inspiration as essential elements of a fulfilling life.

The Role of Rest and Idleness in Creativity

A critical component of receiving time is allowing ourselves the space to rest and be idle. In the absence of external pressure, rest becomes a fertile ground for creativity, reflection, and self-discovery. Far from being a waste of time, rest is a necessary condition for the kind of deep thinking, innovation, and personal growth that cannot be forced or rushed.

Many of the most significant breakthroughs in history have come during periods of rest, when the mind is allowed to wander and explore without constraints. Think of the moments of inspiration that come while taking a walk, meditating, or even while in the shower. These moments of stillness allow our minds to process information in new ways, leading to greater insight and creativity.

In learning to receive time, we begin to recognise the value of these "unproductive" moments. Instead of feeling guilty for taking time to rest or reflect, we understand that these moments are integral to our overall well-being and success. Creativity flourishes when we stop forcing it and allow it to emerge naturally.

Time as a Gift, Not a Resource to Be Maximised

Perhaps the most radical shift that occurs when we learn to receive time is our perception of time itself. Rather than seeing time as a finite resource to be managed and maximised, we begin to view it as a gift—a gift that can be savoured, experienced, and cherished. This shift in perspective allows us to stop rushing through life, to slow down, and to be more present in each moment.

When we stop viewing time through the lens of productivity, we open ourselves up to a deeper, more meaningful experience of life. Time becomes less about how much we can "do" and more about how fully we can "be." Learning to receive time means giving ourselves permission to experience life in its fullness—without the need to justify every moment, without the constant pressure to do more, and without the burden of guilt when we rest.

This mindset shift requires practice, patience, and self-compassion. It involves unlearning years of conditioning around time and productivity and embracing a new way of living. But when we begin to receive time as a gift, we realise that it is not something we need to control, manage, or optimise—it is something to be cherished, something that allows us to experience the beauty of the present moment.

Conclusion: The Freedom of Time Unencumbered

Learning to receive time is not just about taking time off or disengaging from responsibilities. It is about recognising that time, in its truest form, is not a resource to be spent, but a gift to be enjoyed. By releasing the need to justify our moments of rest, reflection, and joy, we begin to reclaim our time and our lives. Time is not something to be constantly maximised; it is something to be fully inhabited.

In learning to receive time, we discover that our worth is not tied to what we do with it but to how fully we engage with it. When we allow ourselves to rest, reflect, and enjoy life without the need for justification, we experience a freedom that is both liberating and transformative. Time becomes a space for creativity, connection, and joy—essential elements of a life well-lived.

Chapter 8
Collective Rhythms and Time Justice

In an age increasingly obsessed with output and acceleration, time has been reduced to a commodity—measured, managed, sliced into tasks and squeezed for yield. We are urged to spend it wisely, save it when possible, and never, heaven forbid, waste it. But beneath this relentless drive lies a troubling assumption: that time exists to be harnessed rather than honoured, that our lives must always be calibrated toward doing. And in that unspoken calculus, we risk forgetting something vital—that time, in its most elemental form, may not be a tool at all, but a birthright.

This chapter invites a radical shift in perspective. What if time isn't merely the backdrop to productivity, but a shared inheritance—something every person deserves access to, irrespective of their economic utility? To suggest that time is a human right might sound idealistic, even naïve, in a world governed by output and urgency. And yet, consider what is lost when rest becomes a privilege, when reflection is relegated to the margins of life, and when merely existing without doing is seen as idleness rather than dignity.

We are not speaking here of time management—those tidy hacks and routines marketed as salvation—but of time justice. Of the belief that time, like shelter or clean water, is essential to human dignity. When time is monopolised by systems that reward constant activity and penalise stillness, the result isn't merely burnout; it is a quiet erosion of our collective well-being. The capacity to pause, to dream, to simply be—these are not indulgences for the few, but rights owed to all.

If we are to take this idea seriously, then the conversation must move beyond the individual. It is not enough to advise people to "make time" for themselves, as though this were simply a matter of willpower. The conditions under which time is stolen from people—through overwork, precarity, systemic inequality—must be brought into full view. After all, who has the luxury to meditate when rent is due? Who can afford leisure when survival takes precedence?

This is not to deny personal agency, but to highlight that real time freedom requires structural support. If the rhythms of life are to slow, or at least soften, it cannot be on the shoulders of individuals alone. We must look to the systems—economic, political, cultural—that dictate how time is distributed and who gets to claim it.

This chapter, then, is not a plea for better time management. It is a call to reclaim what has always been ours: the right to live lives not dictated solely by productivity, but shaped by presence, meaning, and connection. To treat time not as a resource to be optimised, but as a space in which we remember our shared humanity. And perhaps, in doing so, we might begin to restore not just ourselves, but something far larger.

Time as a Human Right

What would a world look like where time is considered a universal human right? For far too long, we have equated time with money, and in doing so, we have made it something to be bought, sold, and rationed. The concept of "time poverty" is real—many people spend the majority of their waking hours in service to a system that offers little in return for their well-being. The idea that time is ours to manage and use freely is a distant dream for the majority of the global population, especially in cultures that prioritise work above all else.

Reframing time as a human right challenges these assumptions. It proposes that rest, creativity, and reflection are not earned privileges, but innate human needs that must be recognised by society. Just as we have fought for equal access to food, education, and healthcare, so too must we fight for the right to time. A time-rich society would not place the highest value on how much we produce or how quickly we can deliver results but on the quality of life we can experience together—unencumbered by anxiety, hustle, or the crushing weight of obligation.

By framing time as a basic human right, we invite a larger conversation about the structures that deny us access to it: long working hours, the cult of productivity, and the myth that success is achieved only through relentless work. What would it take for these deeply ingrained structures to be challenged? How do we shift from a model that measures worth in terms of output to one that nurtures the human spirit through time well spent?

Communal Slowness

The concept of time as a collective experience is one that has been all but lost in our hyper-connected, fast-paced world. Yet, history offers rich examples of how shared experiences of slow time—whether through festivals, sabbaths, or communal siestas—have restored societal harmony and collective well-being. These rituals of collective slowness were not just about individual rest; they were about coming together as a community to recharge, reflect, and connect on a deeper level.

In many cultures, the tradition of shared time can be traced back to religious practices, societal celebrations, and simple, intentional breaks from the demands of everyday life. When communities take the time to slow down together, they restore a sense of connection and shared purpose. This sense of belonging and mutual care is foundational to a thriving society.

We can see these communal rhythms in action today in various forms—shared public holidays, cultural rituals, and even new movements like "slow cities" that prioritise quality of life over speed and efficiency. Festivals that celebrate rest, such as the siesta tradition in Spain or the Sabbath observed in Jewish cultures, stand in stark contrast to the endless hustle culture that drives modern capitalism. These communal practices are powerful tools for reconnecting with each other and with ourselves, offering both respite and meaning in a world that often feels overwhelming and fragmented.

By reintroducing communal slow time, we would not only be giving people the opportunity to rest but also nurturing the collective bonds that are essential for social cohesion. Communities that embrace slowness together are stronger, more resilient, and more capable of facing the challenges that arise in a complex world.

The Rhythm Revolution

At the heart of this chapter lies a vision of a "rhythm revolution"—a societal shift that embraces bio-diverse temporalities rather than imposing a one-size-fits-all approach to time. In many societies today, time is designed around the needs of the economy, where efficiency and productivity are the ultimate goals. Work hours, school schedules, and even social expectations are shaped by a model that prizes uniformity and constant activity. Yet, this system fails to account for the natural rhythms of individuals or communities—what it means to live in alignment with one's biological clock, creative flow, and emotional needs.

The concept of bio-diverse temporalities calls for a radical rethinking of how we structure time—not as something to be divided into rigid, cookie-cutter blocks but as something that should adapt to the rhythms of individual and collective well-being. Just as biodiversity is essential for the health of the planet, so too is temporal diversity essential for the health of societies. This could mean more flexible working hours, greater respect for personal time, or even reimagining the workweek entirely to allow for more balanced, creative, and fulfilling lives.

In practice, the rhythm revolution might look like this: shorter workdays, longer vacations, and more time dedicated to creativity, leisure, and community building. It could involve encouraging people to slow down, reconnect with their environment, and re-evaluate the things they value most. The rhythm revolution challenges the idea that more time spent working equals more success. Instead, it invites us to consider that the true measure of a thriving society is its ability to balance work with rest, creativity with routine, and individual time with collective time.

A Vision for Time Justice

The call for time justice is not just about individual well-being; it's about ensuring that everyone has access to the time they need to live meaningful, healthy lives. This involves recognising that the pressures of time inequality are disproportionately felt by those at the bottom of the social ladder—those who must work multiple jobs, who cannot afford time off, or who are denied the opportunity to rest because of economic necessity. Time justice is about recognising that no one should be denied their right to rest, to create, to reflect, or to connect because of their socio-economic status, race, or gender.

By advocating for time as a human right, communal slowness, and bio-diverse temporalities, we are moving towards a world that values people, not just productivity. It's a world where the collective rhythms of society are in harmony with the needs of the individual and where time is shared as a common resource rather than hoarded as a commodity. A society that honours time justice is one that honours the inherent dignity of all its members, ensuring that everyone has the space and freedom to live fully—not just to work tirelessly for an economic machine that has no regard for human flourishing.

This chapter presents a vision of time that transcends the rigid, productivity-driven models of the past, offering instead a holistic, equitable approach to how we engage with time in our personal and collective lives. It challenges us to rethink the very nature of time and to imagine a world where time is not something we struggle against, but something we learn to share, celebrate, and honour.

Temporal Inequality: How the Poor Rent Their Time and the Wealthy Buy It Back

The vast chasm between rich and poor has been well documented through disparities in wealth, access to resources, and life opportunities. Yet, perhaps the most insidious form of inequality is not one of material wealth or possessions but of time—the most finite and universal resource of all. In a society driven by productivity and efficiency, time is a currency, but it is not equally distributed. The wealthy buy back their time, outsourcing labour and responsibility, while the poor continue to rent theirs out, locked in an unrelenting cycle of work with little reprieve. This inequity, which may appear abstract at first glance, carries with it profound implications for personal well-being, social mobility, and the fabric of society itself. The concept of temporal inequality not only raises questions about how time is distributed but also highlights a deeper moral issue: how we value people based on the time they are allowed—or denied—to spend living.

The underlying premise of temporal inequality is deceptively simple: the rich, having accumulated sufficient wealth, are able to free themselves from the constraints of time. They pay for convenience, delegate tasks, and access the luxuries of leisure and rest. On the other hand, the poor often have no choice but to sell their time, sacrificing their hours for wages that do little to lift them out of poverty or provide meaningful opportunities for relaxation or creative fulfilment. This article explores the dynamics of temporal inequality, its manifestations in contemporary society, and the necessary shifts in policy and social structures that could begin to address this growing divide.

The Temporal Divide: Rich vs. Poor

At the most basic level, temporal inequality is a direct result of economic inequality. The wealthiest individuals, with access to significant financial resources, can afford to delegate tasks that consume time—whether it's hiring a cleaner, an assistant, or simply outsourcing mundane household responsibilities to services. This allows them to spend their time on higher-value activities, such as networking, pursuing personal interests, or simply resting. In doing so, they are able to 'buy back' their time—an increasingly desirable commodity in a world that values efficiency above all else.

For the average worker, however, time is not something to be bought. It is something to be exchanged, bartered, or sold. The impoverished, or those living paycheck to paycheck, are often caught in a cycle of labour, where every hour of the day is accounted for, and free time is a rare luxury. Even basic self-care, let alone leisure or personal growth, becomes difficult to prioritise. With bills, rent, and family responsibilities consuming their time, there is little space for creative expression or reflective thought.

This disparity in how time is spent—between the wealthy who buy back their time and the poor who rent it—is a reflection of the broader economic and social structures that favour those who already possess capital. The system is built around a work-based economy that values labour for profit, rather than the intrinsic value of time as a resource for human flourishing. Thus, while wealth is a marker of financial capital, time becomes the hidden currency that separates the classes.

Time as a Commodity

The commodification of time has accelerated with the rise of capitalism, where economic systems have become increasingly centred around profit maximisation, productivity, and the relentless pursuit of efficiency. Time is no longer simply a way to measure human existence—it is a resource that can be leveraged for maximum output. This view, deeply embedded in many modern cultures, operates on the assumption that more is better: more work, more productivity, more consumption. The mantra of "time is money" encapsulates the notion that the value of time lies solely in its utility for economic gain.

The wealthy, in particular, have perfected this commodification. They may buy time in the form of labour—employing others to do the tasks they deem unimportant—or by purchasing products and services that allow them to escape the mundane aspects of daily life. They can afford to outsource their care work, pay for convenience, and take time for personal pursuits such as travel, education, or leisure. For them, time is a luxury to be curated, spent, and enjoyed on their terms.

However, for the working class, time is both a burden and a necessity. With long working hours, low wages, and limited opportunities for advancement, their time becomes stretched thin. Work takes up the majority of their waking hours, and what little remains is often consumed by the pressures of daily life. Instead of time being a resource to enjoy or savour, it becomes a commodity to be traded for survival.

This reality creates a fundamental imbalance—one that perpetuates the cycle of inequality. The rich may hoard time while the poor struggle to retain even a sliver of it. The result is a widening gap not only in wealth but in opportunity and quality of life.

The Psychological Toll of Temporal Inequality

Beyond the economic ramifications, temporal inequality has profound psychological effects. For those who must constantly trade their time for survival, there is a loss of autonomy and agency. Work becomes a necessity, rather than a choice, and the prospect of relaxation or self-fulfillment fades into the background. In a culture that prizes constant productivity, the poor are often left feeling like their time is worthless, as if their value is measured only in terms of how much labour they can provide.

The psychological toll can manifest in numerous ways: stress, burnout, anxiety, and depression are all symptoms of a life spent in a state of perpetual motion. The inability to "stop" or take a break creates a constant sense of urgency and a lack of control. For many, the pursuit of basic survival becomes an all-consuming task, leaving little room for joy, inspiration, or personal growth.

On the other hand, the wealthy, with their ability to buy back their time, are often shielded from these burdens. They have the luxury to take time off, to invest in hobbies, to meditate, or simply to rest. In doing so, they gain not only physical rest but also psychological and emotional renewal. The ability to create space for creativity, reflection, and meaningful human connection becomes one of the greatest benefits of wealth—one that is not always fully appreciated by those who live in the fast lane of hustle culture.

A Call for Temporal Justice

To address temporal inequality, we must rethink the very structures that perpetuate the disparity between those who rent their time and those who buy it back. In the long term, this requires a fundamental shift in how we understand time as a resource and its role in human flourishing. Policies such as shorter work weeks, a living wage, paid family leave, and access to affordable services would go a long way toward reducing the time burden on the poor.

Furthermore, we must challenge the ingrained cultural belief that time must always be productive. By valuing rest, reflection, and creativity, we can begin to shift the narrative about time from one of constant labour to one of human well-being. Time, after all, is not only a commodity for consumption or a currency for productivity; it is an essential part of the human experience—one that must be shared equitably.

The fight for temporal justice is not just about improving the quality of life for those who are time-poor; it is about building a more just and compassionate society where time is valued as much as money, and where everyone has the opportunity to live a full, rich life—on their own terms. As we consider the ways in which time is distributed and utilised, we must ask ourselves: What would it take for all of us to have the time to live?

Time as a Human Right: Rethinking the Foundations of Freedom and Dignity

In a world that values productivity, progress, and relentless activity, time often emerges as an invisible yet highly coveted resource. Yet, the paradox is striking: while the wealthy can buy time—outsourcing chores, automating tasks, and enjoying leisure without guilt—the working class is left to sell it, bound by the rhythm of economic demands. Amidst this, the concept of time as a human right has remained largely unexplored. This chapter proposes a radical redefinition of human rights, calling for the inclusion of the right to rest, create, reflect, and connect as fundamental entitlements for all.

In modern society, time is increasingly regarded as a commodity. It is monetised, commodified, and consumed. We measure our worth through the lens of time—how efficiently we spend it, how much we can optimise it, and how much of it we can reclaim from obligations. Yet, when we reduce human value to time-bound productivity, we risk overlooking the most essential and human aspects of time: the ability to rest, to think, to dream, and to connect deeply with others. This chapter explores the moral, philosophical, and practical implications of reimagining time as a basic human right, accessible to all, regardless of economic status.

The Right to Rest: A Fundamental Human Need

At the heart of the proposed redefinition of human rights is the notion that rest is not a luxury but a necessity. In today's fast-paced world, the idea of a mandatory right to rest may sound controversial—especially in societies that emphasise workaholism and unyielding productivity. However, the scientific evidence supporting the importance of rest for mental and physical health is overwhelming. Studies show that sleep, relaxation, and unstructured downtime are vital for cognitive function, emotional regulation, and overall well-being.

In the 21st century, where burnout, anxiety, and depression are increasingly prevalent, the lack of time for genuine rest is a serious problem. The modern workplace, for example, often celebrates overwork, with employees expected to answer emails during off-hours, attend weekend meetings, and be available at all times. For many workers, especially those in low-wage and gig economy jobs, rest becomes a rare commodity, something to be squeezed in between shifts or sacrificed altogether.

The right to rest would not only alleviate the physical and emotional toll of overwork but would also recognise the inherent value of human beings beyond their capacity to produce. It would signal a cultural shift towards valuing people as whole individuals, rather than merely economic units. Rest is foundational to dignity, and just as we enshrine rights like freedom of speech or access to education, the right to rest and recharge should be embedded within the social contract.

The Right to Create and Reflect

In addition to rest, the right to create and reflect must also be regarded as essential for human flourishing. In a world that often measures success by tangible outputs—profits, productivity, and efficiency—the act of creation is frequently undervalued. Yet, creativity lies at the heart of personal expression, innovation, and societal progress. Whether through art, invention, or intellectual exploration, the ability to create is what allows humans to transcend the confines of survival and engage with the world in meaningful ways.

The right to create involves more than just freedom to make art or innovate; it is about having the time and space to think critically, reflect deeply, and explore new ideas. When society fails to grant individuals the time and resources to engage in creative endeavours, it denies them the opportunity to contribute to culture, knowledge, and societal development. Furthermore, reflection—the ability to step back from the demands of daily life and evaluate one's values, beliefs, and goals—is critical for personal growth and well-being.

By embracing the idea that time for reflection and creation is a human right, we acknowledge the deep connection between time and meaning. When people are deprived of time to reflect on their lives, to consider their place in the world, or to express themselves creatively, they are deprived of a fundamental human experience. It is in this time—outside the structures of work, obligation, and survival—that people can uncover their potential, connect with others, and live authentically.

The Right to Connect

In the digital age, where social media and virtual communication dominate, genuine human connection has never been more necessary—and, paradoxically, more elusive. The concept of time as a human right also includes the right to meaningful connection: with family, friends, and community. Social isolation and the erosion of face-to-face interactions are key issues in modern society, contributing to rising rates of loneliness, depression, and mental health challenges.

The right to connect means creating space for relationships that nourish us—not simply transactional or superficial interactions, but deep, authentic connections that foster empathy, understanding, and mutual support. This right encompasses not only our personal relationships but also our connection to the wider world and to society at large.

Time spent in connection is not time wasted. It is time invested in the social fabric that sustains us. Yet, too often, work and obligations pull people away from their relationships, leaving them with little time for meaningful social engagement. By prioritising the right to connect, we elevate the importance of human bonds and the emotional and psychological well-being they bring.

Shifting the Narrative: Time as a Social Right

The notion of time as a human right also invites a broader societal shift—one that moves beyond the relentless pursuit of productivity and towards a more humane, sustainable way of living. If we were to reframe time as a collective resource, one that is available for everyone to use freely, it would fundamentally alter our approach to work, leisure, and social justice.

At the societal level, this shift would require systemic changes, such as guaranteeing paid leave, reducing working hours, and ensuring access to affordable healthcare and child care. It would mean advocating for policies that promote work-life balance, protect workers from exploitation, and prioritise well-being over corporate profits. For instance, countries like Denmark and Sweden have pioneered progressive labour policies, such as paid parental leave and flexible working hours, which enable citizens to lead more balanced lives and invest in personal well-being without compromising their economic stability.

Importantly, time justice would also involve addressing the inequalities that exist in how time is distributed. In a world where some can afford to outsource their time, while others must work multiple jobs to survive, time justice demands that we close the gap between those who own time and those who rent it. Ensuring that all individuals have the time and opportunity to rest, reflect, create, and connect is an essential step towards a fairer, more just society.

A Vision for the Future

Imagine a world where rest is as valued as work, where time for creative expression is a social entitlement, and where human connection is prioritised over constant hustle. This is not a utopian dream; it is a vision that can be realised through the recognition of time as a fundamental human right.

Such a shift would require a radical rethinking of our values and structures—one that places people and their well-being at the centre, rather than efficiency, profit, and output. By enshrining the right to rest, creation, reflection, and connection, we not only affirm the worth of each individual but also nurture a society that is healthier, more empathetic, and more creative.

The time for this conversation is now. In a world where the boundaries between work and personal life are increasingly blurred, we must ensure that time becomes a shared resource—one that is free, accessible, and abundant for all.

Communal Slowness: The Restorative Power of Shared, Slow Time

In an increasingly fast-paced, productivity-driven world, the concept of slowness is often relegated to the margins of our consciousness. It is perceived as a luxury for the idle or the lazy—something to be indulged in only when there is no pressing deadline or work commitment. However, this perception is not only outdated but also dangerous. Time, when experienced at a communal, deliberate pace, has the power to restore, rejuvenate, and reconnect us on a deeper level than we could ever experience in isolation. **Communal slowness**—those collective rituals of shared, slow experiences such as festivals, siestas, and sabbaths—holds the potential to heal fractured communities and counterbalance the pervasive sense of burnout and isolation caused by modern living. This chapter delves into the power of communal slowness, exploring its ability to restore collective well-being and foster stronger human connections.

At its heart, communal slowness is about shared time—a slowing down that is not solitary but collective, where the rhythms of one person's day align with another's. It is the experience of existing together in time, where pauses and breaths are taken collectively, not in frantic isolation. While the idea of "slow" may evoke a sense of laziness or inefficiency in many cultures, there is a growing recognition that slowing down is essential for human well-being. The key here is that slowing down doesn't mean doing nothing; rather, it involves doing things with more presence, meaning, and connection.

The Case for Communal Slowness

The concept of time—what we do with it, how we spend it, and the speed at which it is consumed—has evolved dramatically over the centuries. From the agricultural cycle that governed pre-industrial societies to the relentless ticking of the digital clock in the modern age, time has been inexorably tied to productivity and efficiency. In many cultures today, time is seen not as something to be savoured, but as a limited resource to be maximised. The productivity myth, bolstered by advances in technology and the culture of constant connectivity, has resulted in an environment where rest and leisure are seen as frivolous pursuits. This cultural pressure to be constantly busy has led to stress, burnout, and a pervasive sense of disconnection.

However, an antidote to this culture of hyper-efficiency lies in the communal, shared practice of slowness. Festivals, siestas, and sabbaths—rituals that bring people together in stillness—serve as a means of slowing down in community. These practices are far from idle; they are deeply nourishing to the mind, body, and spirit. These collective experiences allow for the restoration of balance, a moment of reprieve from the pressures of modern life, and a reconnection with the human need for togetherness.

The positive impact of communal slowness on well-being is not merely theoretical. Across various cultures, there are examples of how these shared practices create deeper bonds and improve overall happiness. From the Mediterranean cultures that observe regular afternoon naps, to Jewish and Christian sabbaths which dedicate time for reflection and rest, these communal rituals have existed for centuries because of their power to restore harmony and meaning to everyday life. They are living proof that slowing down, when done collectively, can be not only restorative but transformational.

The Psychological Benefits of Shared Slowness

Slowness, as a psychological concept, is often perceived through the lens of "being idle" or "doing nothing." Yet, this couldn't be further from the truth. Slowness, when intentional and shared, is deeply aligned with restorative practices that bring both cognitive and emotional benefits. The experience of slowness allows individuals to recalibrate their nervous systems, find a sense of peace, and reconnect with their internal rhythms.

For those who are accustomed to high-paced, goal-oriented environments, the concept of slowing down with others may seem uncomfortable at first. In a society that values immediate returns, collective slowness challenges the norms of instant gratification and results. However, research in psychology suggests that participating in slow, collective experiences can bring about profound shifts in mental and emotional health. The communal aspect of these rituals provides a sense of belonging, an antidote to the loneliness and disconnection that often accompany modern living. Being with others in a shared, slow moment allows individuals to feel grounded, less anxious, and more present.

In fact, studies on mindfulness and meditation support the idea that slowing down in a community setting can help regulate emotional states, lower levels of stress, and enhance feelings of empathy. The act of sharing time, of collectively choosing to pause, allows individuals to reflect, process, and rejuvenate without the pressure of productivity or external expectations. The psychological effects are clear: reduced anxiety, increased feelings of joy and connection, and an improved sense of well-being.

Festivals and Rituals: Slow Time in Practice

Nowhere is the power of communal slowness more evident than in cultural festivals and collective rituals. These events, which are intentionally designed to slow down the pace of life, provide an opportunity for deep cultural connection, reflection, and shared joy. The practices themselves may vary, but the core principle remains the same: by pausing as a community, we open ourselves up to renewal and transformation.

Take the example of the *siesta* tradition in Spain and many Latin American countries. Originally intended as a break to rest during the hottest part of the day, the siesta has become a symbol of the region's slower, more intentional approach to life. While this practice is often under threat in modern urban settings, many individuals and communities still uphold the importance of a midday break. This collective slowing down is not merely about napping—it is about cultivating a rhythm of life that values rest, relationships, and moments of pause.

Similarly, Jewish and Christian sabbaths, where entire communities disengage from work to observe rest and reflection, serve as a reminder of the power of communal time. These practices, rooted in religious traditions, provide a designated time each week for individuals to focus on spiritual growth, family connections, and relaxation. These slow, collective practices stand as examples of how shared rest can benefit individual well-being and, in turn, strengthen societal bonds.

Likewise, communal festivals—whether celebrating the changing of seasons, a harvest, or a national holiday—serve as powerful moments of shared slowness. These events allow communities to come together, slow their pace, and engage in traditions that reflect cultural heritage, values, and unity. During these festivals, time is intentionally expanded, as people set aside their usual tasks and obligations to experience the present moment together.

The Call for a Rhythm Revolution

While festivals and rituals provide meaningful examples of communal slowness, there is an urgent need for a more systemic shift—one that acknowledges the importance of collective, slow time in modern life. Today's societal structures are still largely built on a model of constant productivity, which leaves little room for intentional rest or community-building. The solution, then, lies in a revolution of rhythms—a shift from the fast-paced, efficiency-driven approach to time to one that supports diverse and more human-centered temporalities.

A **Rhythm Revolution** would prioritise collective well-being, encouraging individuals and communities to embrace slower rhythms as a means of rejuvenation and connection. This revolution would not only reframe how we think about time, but it would also foster spaces for shared relaxation, creativity, and community engagement. We would begin to value not only what we produce but also the quality of our connections, our moments of rest, and our capacity for shared joy.

This would mean creating policies and spaces that nurture communal slowness. Urban planning could incorporate spaces for rest and gathering, workplaces could embrace more flexible hours and mandatory breaks, and schools could prioritise social-emotional learning alongside academic achievement. This revolution would celebrate time that is slow and spacious, not time that is filled and busy.

Conclusion: The Future of Collective Slowness

As we increasingly confront the emotional, psychological, and social toll of modern life, it is time to reclaim the value of communal slowness. By integrating shared rituals, festivals, and slow moments into our daily lives, we not only restore balance to individuals but also rebuild the fabric of our communities. These collective experiences remind us that time is not only a commodity to be spent and consumed but a gift to be shared and savoured. To embrace communal slowness is to embrace a future where well-being, connection, and joy are given the space to thrive.

The Rhythm Revolution: Embracing Bio-Diverse Temporalities for a More Humane Society

In the modern world, time is often viewed as an impersonal, uniform resource—one that should be maximised and used efficiently to generate more profit, more productivity, and, by extension, more success. The ubiquitous 9-to-5 workday, with its emphasis on punctuality, deadlines, and relentless efficiency, remains the cornerstone of societal organisation. Yet, beneath this uniform, rigid structure, there lies a profound truth: not all human beings experience time in the same way. Our personal rhythms, rooted in biology, culture, and circumstance, create a need for a broader understanding of time—a time that acknowledges difference, nuance, and, above all, the richness of slowing down.

This chapter is an invitation to imagine a **Rhythm Revolution**—a world where societal structures no longer enforce a singular, efficiency-driven tempo, but rather support a **bio-diverse approach to time**. In such a world, the diversity of human experience would be celebrated, and our shared rhythm would no longer be a mandate to conform to the ticking clock, but a flexible and empowering reflection of the way we naturally move through life. This vision requires a shift from the entrenched assumptions of productivity to a model that values well-being, creativity, and connection just as much as output.

The Tyranny of Uniformity

In most societies, the relentless drive for productivity shapes how time is structured. Our lives are often defined by externally imposed schedules that dictate how and when we are expected to work, rest, and socialise. From the corporate boardroom to the classroom, there is a near-universal expectation that time is a scarce commodity to be optimised. This model of time—as a finite resource to be worked into tight, prescriptive blocks—ignores the natural rhythms of the human body, the complexity of individual lives, and the need for different kinds of temporal engagement.

For instance, the 9-to-5 workday, which has its origins in the industrial revolution, is rooted in an outdated idea of human labour. This model assumes a one-size-fits-all approach to productivity, where all workers are expected to function at the same level of efficiency at the same time. Yet, studies have shown that our cognitive and physical abilities fluctuate throughout the day. Some people are morning people, others are night owls. Some thrive in bursts of activity, while others work best in steady, uninterrupted rhythms. These variations are not only natural but also biologically ingrained.

The **overemphasis on uniform time structures** has real consequences for our well-being. It leads to stress, burnout, and a general disconnection from the natural ebb and flow of our lives. We have internalised the idea that rest, leisure, and reflection are rewards, to be earned only after the completion of a day's work. As a result, we have become divorced from the more holistic, human experience of time, which involves space for contemplation, creativity, and genuine connection.

The Case for Bio-Diverse Temporalities

Bio-diverse temporalities refer to the natural, individual rhythms and cycles that vary from person to person, and even from one biological system to another. These rhythms reflect not only individual preferences but also deep-rooted biological processes—sleep cycles, circadian rhythms, hormonal fluctuations, and energy levels throughout the day. Acknowledging this diversity allows us to see time as something more than a uniform grid of hours and minutes.

In a society that embraces bio-diverse temporalities, the rigid uniformity of work hours would be replaced by a more flexible, human-centred approach to time. This would mean acknowledging the peak hours of productivity for different individuals, allowing for the kind of temporal flexibility that could transform how people work, rest, and live. For instance, the traditional workday could be reimagined as a flexible block, where individuals can choose their hours based on their natural rhythms, rather than adhering to the same rigid schedule set by external forces.

One example of this is the growing recognition of **flexible working hours** in response to the global pandemic. Companies that have embraced remote working have noticed the positive impact of allowing workers to choose their own hours. Many employees report greater productivity and a better work-life balance. The rhythm of working when it feels most natural has allowed for more creativity, less stress, and a renewed sense of autonomy.

Another example lies in the **siesta**—the midday rest that many Mediterranean cultures have long embraced. While the siesta has largely fallen out of favour in urbanised areas, it is beginning to see a resurgence as people reconsider how best to balance work with rest. In countries like Spain and Mexico, where the afternoon heat can make work difficult, the siesta provides a natural rhythm of slowing down, offering an intentional pause in the day. This period of rest allows workers to return to their tasks with renewed energy and focus, which could ultimately increase productivity.

By embracing bio-diverse temporalities, we can foster a society where time is not just a commodity, but a **living, breathing entity** that adapts to our needs. This doesn't mean eliminating productivity or deadlines, but rather finding a balance between work and rest that honours the natural cycles of human life.

The Rhythm Revolution: A New Vision for Time

At the heart of the Rhythm Revolution is the belief that society must reimagine its relationship with time. This reimagining involves breaking free from the **myth of productivity**, which has dominated our understanding of time for centuries, and instead embracing a world that is **attuned to human needs**. This vision calls for societal structures that allow for **flexible rhythms**—that is, schedules that take into account both the biological rhythms of the individual and the collective rhythms of society.

A **Rhythm Revolution** would require a complete rethinking of many aspects of life. From **education systems** that could incorporate more flexible learning times based on students' natural rhythms, to **workplaces** that support a range of schedules to match different types of workers, to **urban planning** that provides spaces for communal pauses and reflection. It would involve moving away from a culture of overwork and towards one that prioritises **holistic well-being**. The revolution would also challenge the current economic system, which often places profit over people's health and happiness, and demand policies that **recognise the right to rest** and time for creativity, reflection, and human connection.

As **bio-diverse temporalities** are recognised and celebrated, we could begin to see a society where **time justice** prevails. This would be a world where the right to **rest** is seen as fundamental as the right to work; where the **right to reflection** is valued as much as the right to succeed; where **communal time** is not just for leisure, but for collective rejuvenation and empowerment.

Time for a New Normal

To make the Rhythm Revolution a reality, we need to begin by changing the way we think about time. We need to acknowledge that not all people experience time the same way and that forcing individuals to fit into one narrow model of productivity does them—and society—a disservice. It is time to question the assumptions that have long governed our lives and embrace the possibility of a future where **diverse rhythms** are not only accepted but celebrated.

In practical terms, this might look like:

Policies that ensure workers have time to **recharge** without fear of penalisation.

Schools that allow students to engage with the curriculum at their own pace, recognising that each child has different needs.

Communities that celebrate collective rest, taking intentional pauses together through rituals, festivals, or simply time spent in nature.

A **restructuring of urban environments** to accommodate not just work but spaces for reflection, play, and interaction that nurture human flourishing.

This **Rhythm Revolution** would mark a pivotal moment in human history, where society moves away from uniform productivity towards a more holistic, compassionate understanding of time—one that values not only what we do, but who we are when we're not doing. In doing so, it opens the door to a future where time is experienced as a shared, regenerative force for personal, communal, and societal well-being.

Chapter 9
The Future Isn't Hustling—It's Harmonising

In an era enamoured with expansion, where success is too often measured by upward curves and widening margins, a seductive belief continues to shape how we build, create, and live: the myth of infinite scale. It is a story told in boardrooms and co-working spaces alike, whispered in investor pitch decks and echoed across entrepreneurial manifestos—the idea that growth, especially exponential growth, is both inevitable and inherently good.

We've come to venerate the hustle: the startup that scales overnight, the side project that morphs into an empire, the personal brand that never sleeps. But beneath this breathless chase lies a quieter reality—one we're often too busy to confront. There are limits. Natural, human, ecological. And when we ignore these limits in pursuit of ever more, the consequences don't merely accumulate—they compound.

So here is a question worth asking, perhaps even lingering over: what if the goal was never scale for its own sake? What if sustainability—not the buzzword, but the actual practice of honouring boundaries—were seen not as a constraint but as wisdom? Might we find, buried beneath the dogma of endless growth, a different kind of richness?

This chapter offers not a rejection of ambition, but a reimagining of what ambition might look like when rooted in sufficiency rather than scarcity. It asks us to consider the power of creating from a place of overflow—from presence, clarity, and integrity—rather than desperation or depletion. Not everything needs to scale. Some things are most potent when held small, when tended with care rather than pushed to perform.

There's a different rhythm here. One that doesn't worship velocity or volume, but values depth, nuance, and sustainability. Imagine systems—of work, of creativity, of collaboration—that are consciously designed with time at their centre. Not merely efficient, but humane. Not built to extract, but to nourish.

To work this way is to resist the dominant tempo of modern life. It's to accept that thresholds exist—not as barriers, but as guides. Every organism in nature respects them. Trees don't grow into the sky forever. Rivers don't run endlessly in flood. Why, then, should we?

Let this be an invitation: not to do less for the sake of it, but to do differently. To build not with the brittle ambition of infinite scale, but with the quiet courage of enough.

The Myth of Infinite Scale

The narrative of unlimited growth has been deeply embedded in the global consciousness for centuries, particularly within the capitalist framework. From the rise of Silicon Valley to the explosion of the gig economy, the mantra of "scale fast or fail" has governed how businesses grow, expand, and compete. In this world, success is measured by how much you can grow—how quickly you can increase your market share, customer base, or bottom line.

Yet, this obsession with infinite scale is increasingly showing its limits. The idea that businesses—or even individuals—can continually grow without ever reaching a plateau is not only unsustainable but also harmful. **The myth of infinite scale** fails to account for the environmental and emotional costs of such rapid expansion, or the diminishing returns that inevitably come with growth. As companies grow larger, they often become less agile, more bureaucratic, and less human-centred. Likewise, the individual experience of "scaling up" often leads to burnout, stress, and a fractured sense of purpose. Rather than chasing ever-larger targets, we must recognise that there are inherent **limits to growth**—limits that, when respected, can lead to greater sustainability, happiness, and creativity.

The notion of growth for the sake of growth itself must be challenged. **The wisdom of thresholds**—acknowledging when enough is enough and when to pause—offers a healthier, more sustainable model of success. This shift in perspective is particularly vital in an age where environmental crises, economic inequality, and mental health challenges are becoming increasingly pervasive.

Creating from Overflow, Not Lack

A culture that thrives on scarcity cannot foster true creativity. The dominant narrative of hustle—of working until exhaustion, of squeezing every ounce of potential out of people and resources—assumes that we must constantly be striving, that the value of our work is defined by how much we can produce. This belief, rooted in scarcity, holds that only under pressure, tension, and urgency can creativity truly emerge. Yet, this assumption is not only untrue; it is damaging. Creativity, true creativity, cannot thrive under duress.

Instead, **creating from overflow**—not lack—represents a more holistic approach to work and innovation. When we allow ourselves space, time, and rest, we are able to cultivate a surplus of energy, ideas, and inspiration. In this surplus, creativity flourishes. Rest, reflection, and balance become the fertile ground from which new ideas grow.

This concept is rooted in several philosophical and psychological frameworks. For example, the **psychology of flow**, as coined by Mihaly Csikszentmihalyi, demonstrates that optimal creativity and productivity occur when individuals are fully immersed in an activity that is challenging yet not overwhelming. This sense of balance—between challenge and ability—can only be achieved when we have the space and time to approach our work with clarity and purpose, not under the duress of a never-ending to-do list. Moreover,

positive psychology teaches us that our most innovative ideas often come not from frantic efforts, but from moments of relaxation, boredom, and even idle daydreaming.

The question, then, is not how to work harder, but how to create the conditions for true creativity. By **scheduling in rest, reflection, and leisure**, we allow our minds and bodies to recharge and return to our work with renewed vigour. Creativity doesn't thrive in the rush of deadlines or the clutter of over-commitment—it flourishes when we make space for it.

Designing Time-Conscious Systems

As we begin to rethink what productivity and success mean, we must also reimagine the systems that shape our work, communities, and culture. **Time-conscious systems** are those that respect human limits and encourage sustainable rhythms. These systems are not driven solely by profit or efficiency but by the well-being of individuals and the community as a whole.

Businesses, for example, can be designed to respect employees' time and mental health rather than extract every ounce of productivity from them. This could involve **flexible working hours**, **results-based performance metrics** rather than hours worked, and an organisational culture that values rest as much as effort. Companies like **Basecamp** and **Buffer** have pioneered such models, with Basecamp famously adopting a four-day workweek and Buffer embracing transparency and flexibility in its work culture. The result is not just happier employees, but also more engaged and creative teams.

Similarly, in communities, the principles of time-conscious systems can be applied to public spaces, social programmes, and cultural initiatives. **Urban planning** can prioritise the rhythms of nature, incorporating green spaces that invite people to slow down, relax, and reconnect. **Cultural festivals**, community events, and sabbaticals can also serve to create shared experiences of slow time, helping to restore balance in a society that often moves too fast.

Even technology can be designed to align with bio-rhythms and support well-being. Instead of building apps that constantly demand attention or gamify productivity, we can create software that supports **deep work**, promotes mindfulness, and encourages intentional disengagement from the digital world. **Tech companies** like **Apple** have started introducing features like "Screen Time" to track and limit screen usage, while meditation apps like **Headspace** encourage users to slow down and focus on the present moment.

The **future of business, technology, and communities** must be time-conscious, fostering environments where individuals can work and rest at their natural pace. This vision doesn't call for the elimination of work or productivity, but for the creation of systems that respect the **human experience of time**—systems that prioritise balance over hustle and well-being over profit.

A Future Beyond Hustle

The future of work, creativity, and well-being is not about scaling endlessly. It is about harmonising with the natural rhythms of life. It's about recognising that creativity thrives in spaces of overflow, not scarcity, and that true success lies not in doing more, but in doing what truly matters, with intention and purpose. This chapter calls for a **Rhythm Revolution**—a radical shift in how we design our work, our lives, and our communities. By moving away from the myth of infinite scale and embracing time-conscious systems, we can build a future that values well-being, connection, and creativity just as much as productivity and efficiency.

This vision doesn't merely ask for minor tweaks to existing systems, but calls for a **revolutionary rethinking** of how we structure our time, our priorities, and our understanding of success. It is time to recognise that **harmony**—not hustle—is the true measure of a flourishing life.

Ecotemporal Intelligence: Navigating Life's Rhythms

In a world that glorifies constant acceleration, the idea of slowing down can seem counterintuitive—perhaps even undesirable. Yet, as our society wrestles with burnout, environmental degradation, and the overwhelming pace of technological change, the concept of *ecotemporal intelligence* emerges as a crucial skill for the future. This new form of intelligence doesn't just help us manage our time more efficiently; it allows us to attune ourselves to the broader rhythms of life—knowing when to speed up, when to slow down, and how to maintain a sustainable, harmonious balance in both our personal and collective lives.

In this chapter, we will explore the profound implications of ecotemporal intelligence, proposing it as the key to fostering well-being, creativity, and long-term sustainability in our increasingly time-starved world. By cultivating an awareness of both individual and collective temporalities, we can transform not only how we work and live but also how we coexist with the natural world. At its core, ecotemporal intelligence invites us to reconsider our relationship with time, shifting from the industrial-era focus on productivity at all costs to a more ecological understanding of time as a dynamic, ever-shifting resource that must be stewarded carefully.

Understanding Ecotemporal Intelligence: A New Paradigm

The term *ecotemporal intelligence* combines two important concepts: *eco*, the Greek root for "house" or "environment", and *temporal*, related to time. Put together, it suggests an intelligence that not only recognises the cyclical and interconnected nature of time but also values the wisdom of knowing when to act and when to wait. Just as ecosystems depend on the intricate balance of various species interacting within a habitat, human beings too need to align their rhythms—personal and collective—with the broader rhythms of the environment and society.

Historically, time has been viewed through a linear lens, governed by the ticking clock and the imperative of productivity. This model, deeply embedded in capitalist and industrial thinking, tells us that more is better: more work, more output, more speed. However, as we push against the limits of human endurance and the planet's ecological boundaries, it's becoming increasingly clear that this model no longer serves us. In its place, we need a new form of time awareness—one that respects *natural limits*, embraces periods of rest, and acknowledges that not all moments are suitable for high-speed productivity.

At its most basic level, ecotemporal intelligence challenges us to recognise that time is not simply a tool for measurement and optimisation. It is a force that can nurture or deplete us, depending on how we engage with it. The practice of ecotemporal intelligence is about more than just managing time; it's about becoming fluent in the language of rhythms—whether those rhythms are personal, social, or ecological—and learning how to harmonise with them.

The Rhythms of Life: Knowing When to Speed Up and When to Slow Down

Ecotemporal intelligence requires the ability to perceive the subtle shifts in our environment, bodies, and minds that signal when action is needed and when stillness is required. Understanding the rhythms of life means recognising that time itself is not a singular, homogenous entity but a series of overlapping cycles that demand our attention and respect. Some of these rhythms are *internal*, such as our circadian rhythms, which dictate our sleep-wake cycles, and our hormonal cycles, which govern everything from energy levels to emotional well-being. Other rhythms are *external*, tied to the natural world, societal structures, and technological systems.

When we are out of sync with these rhythms, whether through overwork, lack of rest, or neglect of our environment, we experience a disconnect—a kind of temporal dissonance that leads to stress, anxiety, and burnout. But when we are in tune with these rhythms, we access a deep well of vitality and creativity.

For example, research has shown that **our bodies naturally align with natural cycles** like the day-night rhythm, with energy levels peaking in the morning and waning in the evening. Likewise, in modern societies, we must learn when to push forward in a burst of productivity and when to honour the stillness of a break or a sabbatical. This isn't just about resting to recover but about recognising that downtime is not the opposite of work; it is the partner to it. Just as the earth needs time to regenerate through cycles of rest and growth, so too do we.

Ecotemporal Intelligence and Sustainability: Harmonising with Nature's Cycles

The environmental crisis we face today is rooted in an economic model that ignores the limits of natural systems in favour of endless growth. The resulting depletion of resources, pollution, and climate change are all consequences of our collective failure to recognise the boundaries of our environment and, by extension, the boundaries of time itself. As much as we have tried to optimise time, we have neglected to consider the ecological costs of that optimisation.

Incorporating **ecotemporal intelligence** into our personal and collective decision-making is an essential step in reversing this trend. It is not enough to simply reduce our carbon footprint; we must also learn to *live within the rhythms* of the planet's cycles, respecting both the short-term and long-term implications of our actions. This means shifting from a model of *exploitation* to one of *stewardship*, where we take the time to ensure that our actions contribute to the regeneration and flourishing of the environment, rather than its depletion.

In practice, this could involve a range of shifts. On an individual level, it might mean taking conscious breaks to *attune* to the environment, spending time in nature, or adjusting our work schedules to better align with our natural rhythms. At a societal level, it means rethinking systems of production, energy consumption, and resource management, aiming for balance rather than growth at all costs. The question is no longer how to optimise every second for maximum output but how to create sustainable systems that allow both people and the planet to thrive.

Cultivating Ecotemporal Intelligence: A Practical Approach

If we are to adopt ecotemporal intelligence as a guiding principle, it requires both personal and collective shifts in how we engage with time. On a personal level, this means learning to listen to our own rhythms and slowing down when necessary. Whether that involves spending a day offline, participating in a community sabbath, or dedicating time to a restorative practice like yoga or meditation, we must first cultivate an awareness of how we experience time.

On a broader scale, ecotemporal intelligence demands a shift in the way we design our societies, workplaces, and technologies. It asks for **restructuring work** around sustainable, human-centred rhythms, and designing technology that supports human well-being rather than exploiting it. It calls for businesses to value quality over quantity, and for communities to celebrate shared time, fostering collective well-being.

We are already seeing early signs of this shift. **The four-day workweek**, **remote working**, and **flexible schedules** are becoming increasingly common as businesses recognise the importance of work-life balance. Similarly, movements advocating for slower living, such as the **Slow Food movement** or **Slow Cities**, are gaining traction, encouraging people to embrace quality experiences over speed.

The Future of Ecotemporal Intelligence

As we continue to confront the challenges of modern life, from climate change to mental health crises, the need for ecotemporal intelligence will become more pressing. The future of humanity depends not on how fast we can go but on how wisely we move. By tuning in to the rhythms of life—both individual and collective—we will discover that the *quality* of time, not its quantity, is what truly sustains us. It is only by learning when to speed up and when to slow down, when to act and when to rest, that we can hope to thrive in harmony with the natural world and each other.

Ecotemporal intelligence is, then, not just a new form of time management. It is a way of *being* that allows us to connect with life's deeper rhythms, fostering a world where both humanity and the earth can flourish together. In this new era, time becomes a resource to be respected, not a commodity to be exploited—a tool not just for productivity, but for well-being, sustainability, and connection.

The Myth of Infinite Scale: The Limits of Growth and the Wisdom of Thresholds

In an era dominated by the logic of startup cultures and an obsession with *scale*, it's easy to forget that growth has its limits. The prevalent narrative in business today—a narrative often reinforced by Silicon Valley and capitalist ideologies—is that bigger is always better. It suggests that scale is the ultimate metric of success, promising that expansion, acceleration, and exponential growth are the keys to long-term sustainability and prosperity. But beneath the surface of this prevailing myth lies a powerful, often overlooked truth: growth—when pursued without balance—can be unsustainable, damaging, and ultimately unfulfilling.

The myth of infinite scale isn't just an issue for businesses and entrepreneurs. It shapes the very fabric of our society, dictating how we measure success, organise labour, and interact with the planet's finite resources. In this subchapter, we will critically examine the myth of infinite growth, challenging the assumptions that fuel it, exploring the wisdom found in the concept of *thresholds*, and reimagining what a truly sustainable, meaningful approach to success might look like in a world increasingly focused on balance rather than boundless expansion.

Scaling: The Capitalist Obsession with More

The cult of scaling is not new, but it has intensified with the rise of the digital economy. From tech startups to multinational corporations, the idea that growth is synonymous with success has become deeply ingrained in the fabric of modern business culture. Silicon Valley entrepreneurs, with their fixation on *hockey-stick growth* and *unicorn valuations*, serve as the archetypes of this ethos, often hailed as visionary leaders who can scale their ideas to a global stage.

This obsession with scaling often leads to the belief that bigger is always better, that more capital, more customers, more employees, and more output are inherently good. Companies such as Uber, Facebook, Amazon, and Google have all demonstrated the power of rapid scaling, and their success has reinforced the narrative that larger corporations and expansive reach equate to higher profits and market dominance. From a financial perspective, this is undoubtedly true—expanding a customer base, increasing product offerings, and entering new markets generally leads to more revenue.

However, there is a darker side to this ideology, one that is less visible but equally important: the consequences of scaling beyond a certain point. The more an organisation expands, the harder it becomes to maintain a connection to its original values and vision. With each additional employee, the quality of relationships and communication tends to deteriorate. Systems that once operated with agility and creativity become bogged down by bureaucracy and inefficiency. In short, the obsession with scaling can undermine the very essence of a company's culture and purpose.

The Fallacy of Infinite Growth: Limits of Scale in Nature and Business

At its core, the myth of infinite scale is rooted in a misunderstanding of both the ecological and economic systems that underpin our world. In the natural world, infinite growth is not a sustainable concept. Ecosystems thrive not by expanding indefinitely, but by maintaining a balance that allows for regeneration, sustainability, and evolution within limits. Every species, habitat, and organism operates within a specific set of boundaries, defined by the resources available to them. The idea of infinite growth, whether in nature or business, contradicts this basic principle of balance.

Yet, this ideal of infinite growth is baked into the capitalist framework that has shaped modern economies. Economic models based on *unlimited growth* ignore the concept of *carrying capacity*—the maximum population size an environment can sustain given its resources. This is evident in our global economic systems, where the drive for perpetual expansion often leads to the overexploitation of natural resources, environmental degradation, and rising inequality.

This belief in unlimited growth also fails to account for human well-being. The relentless pursuit of success through growth can lead to burnout, stress, and a distorted sense of purpose. It dehumanises the labour force, reducing workers to mere cogs in a machine that churns out productivity at an unsustainable rate. This myth of infinite growth ultimately reinforces a value system that prioritises profit above people, efficiency over sustainability, and consumption over quality of life.

The Wisdom of Thresholds: Embracing Limits for Sustainable Success

If infinite growth is a myth, then what lies on the other side? The answer, in part, lies in *thresholds*. Rather than seeing limits as something to be feared or avoided, we can view them as guiding principles for creating sustainable, meaningful success. In contrast to the obsession with scaling, the concept of thresholds encourages us to consider the limits of our systems, resources, and capacities as opportunities for balance and wisdom.

Thresholds are natural boundaries that help us recognise when we have reached a point where further expansion would begin to erode quality, well-being, or sustainability. In business, this could mean scaling to a point where growth stabilises—when a company achieves the optimal size for its mission, culture, and values. It doesn't have to become a giant corporation to be successful; it can maintain a sustainable, thriving existence by embracing its limits. In other words, thresholds represent a healthy stopping point, after which the goal is not to grow larger, but to grow better.

One of the clearest examples of thresholds in action is found in the **B-Corp movement**, which recognises businesses that meet certain standards of social and environmental performance, accountability, and transparency. These businesses may not grow indefinitely in size, but they thrive by operating within ethical boundaries that prioritise sustainability, community, and environmental impact over sheer profit maximisation.

The Counter-Narrative: Creating from Overflow, Not Lack

The mythology of infinite growth is also deeply intertwined with the narrative of scarcity. We have been conditioned to believe that success requires us to work harder, faster, and more relentlessly, often at the expense of our health, relationships, and happiness. But this narrative, built on the assumption that there is always something to be earned, acquired, or accomplished, is deeply flawed. True creativity, innovation, and well-being emerge not from scarcity, but from *overflow*—from the abundance of time, space, and energy to think, reflect, and create.

When we embrace thresholds, we shift from a mindset of *lack* to one of *surplus*. This surplus is not about amassing more resources, but about making space for creativity, reflection, and connection. For example, when we let go of the need to constantly scale up our operations, we free ourselves to focus on what truly matters: producing high-quality work, fostering meaningful relationships, and contributing to the well-being of others. Creating from a place of overflow leads to deeper, more fulfilling results than pushing for growth without regard for the consequences.

This approach to creation is evident in movements like the **slow food movement** or **local business initiatives**, where the focus is not on global expansion but on building sustainable, community-oriented enterprises that respect limits and values quality over quantity. The message here is clear: success is not about doing more; it's about doing what we do with purpose, integrity, and mindfulness.

Designing Time-Conscious Systems: Moving Beyond the Myth of Growth

Ultimately, the myth of infinite growth is not just about money or size—it is embedded in the systems we create. As we reconsider the obsession with scaling, we must also rethink the structures that govern our personal and collective lives. From business to education, healthcare, and beyond, we need to design systems that respect time—the most precious and finite resource we have.

What does this mean in practice? For one, it requires businesses to create environments where work is aligned with human rhythms, not external pressures for endless productivity. It means designing work structures that emphasise balance over burnout, creativity over competition, and collaboration over hierarchical expansion. It involves rethinking education and healthcare systems to prioritise holistic development, well-being, and long-term sustainability over short-term results.

This can also extend to the digital world. As technology advances, we must ensure that it supports rather than exploits human time. Software and tools can be designed to enhance our efficiency in meaningful ways, not by pushing us to do more, but by helping us focus on what truly matters. In this way, even technology can be part of the solution, helping to preserve human time, creativity, and attention.

Conclusion: The Future Lies in Harmonising, Not Hustling

The myth of infinite scale, so deeply entrenched in capitalist culture, has shaped much of the modern business world and societal values. But it's time to question this myth and embrace a new model based on sustainability, balance, and limits. By recognising the wisdom of thresholds, creating from overflow rather than lack, and designing time-conscious systems, we can build a future that values quality over quantity, purpose over profit, and well-being over endless growth. The true path to success is not in scaling endlessly, but in harmonising with the rhythms of life, work, and nature.

Creating from Overflow, Not Lack: How Creativity Thrives in Surplus Time and Emotional Spaciousness

In today's fast-paced world, creativity is often associated with hustle and urgency. The myth of the starving artist—the belief that true creativity requires struggle, stress, and scarcity—has pervaded our culture for centuries. This idea tells us that pressure, tight deadlines, and limited resources are the fuel that powers innovation and originality. Yet, the reality is quite the opposite: creativity thrives not in the frenzy of scarcity, but in the spaciousness of abundance—abundant time, emotional space, and mental clarity. To unlock our full creative potential, we must learn to create from overflow, not from lack.

This paradigm shift is essential not only for artists but for professionals, entrepreneurs, and individuals across all fields. The relentless pressure to perform, produce, and "hustle" often leads to burnout, stifling the very creativity we are trying to harness. By reframing our approach to creativity—one that acknowledges the importance of emotional well-being, sufficient time, and mental relaxation—we can foster deeper, more impactful innovations and solutions. The question then becomes: how can we create from a place of overflow?

The Hustle Fallacy: Scarcity as a Creative Block

For decades, the idea that scarcity breeds creativity has dominated popular thinking. Countless narratives glorify the image of the overworked entrepreneur, the late-night coder, the artist working tirelessly in isolation, pushing themselves beyond their limits to create something exceptional. But this cultural narrative, while romanticised, is ultimately a myth.

Research has shown that working under constant pressure or scarcity does not enhance creativity. In fact, it hampers it. The brain, under stress, enters a state of *fight-or-flight*, diverting energy from creative problem-solving processes to survival mechanisms. The result is a decrease in cognitive flexibility, a key component of creativity. Instead of thinking broadly and making new connections, a stressed brain becomes fixated on solving immediate, pressing issues.

Moreover, the culture of hustle undermines long-term sustainability. The illusion that productivity and success are best achieved through non-stop work is both harmful and counterproductive. Rather than generating breakthrough ideas or innovative solutions, this mindset often leads to burnout, a decline in mental health, and a loss of creative passion.

The Surplus of Time and Space: A New Creative Paradigm

Creating from overflow begins by recognising that creativity is not something to be forced or rushed—it is something that emerges when we allow ourselves the time and emotional space to breathe. This surplus of time does not mean that we are idle or lazy, but that we are engaged in a more intentional, thoughtful process of creation.

Research in positive psychology has shown that when individuals are given more time to explore, reflect, and engage in creative thinking without pressure, their ability to generate novel ideas increases. When there is no urgent deadline looming, the brain can operate in a state of curiosity, free from the anxiety that typically accompanies the need for rapid production. This mental freedom leads to deeper, more original thinking.

Additionally, emotional space plays a crucial role in creative processes. Emotional well-being—marked by relaxation, fulfilment, and joy—creates an environment where new ideas can take root. When we are not burdened by negative emotions like stress or anxiety, our cognitive processes are more fluid, and we can connect disparate ideas in innovative ways. *Creativity thrives on emotional spaciousness*—the ability to process feelings, explore thoughts, and engage with the world in a way that is not hindered by emotional baggage.

Creating from Overflow in Practice: The Power of Rest and Reflection

So, how can we actively create an environment where we can generate ideas from overflow rather than scarcity? The key lies in cultivating practices of rest, reflection, and strategic disengagement. Here are some strategies to achieve this:

1. **Prioritising Rest and Recovery**: In many fields, rest is often viewed as a luxury or a distraction from productivity. However, research shows that sleep and rest are crucial for cognitive function and creativity. Studies on memory consolidation, for instance, have demonstrated that sleep strengthens creative problem-solving abilities. By prioritising rest, we allow our brains to process information, build connections, and make new insights that are crucial for creative breakthroughs.

2. **The Power of Downtime**: Contrary to the hustle mentality, creative breakthroughs often occur when we step away from our work. Engaging in activities that are not directly related to the task at hand—whether it's a walk in nature, a quiet moment of

meditation, or simply daydreaming—can provide the mental space necessary for new ideas to surface. This downtime is not wasted; it is an investment in the creative process. As the writer and philosopher Milan Kundera once noted, "The struggle of man against power is the struggle of memory against forgetting." In moments of pause, the mind works behind the scenes, allowing forgotten ideas to resurface and take shape.

3. **Building Emotional Spaciousness**: Emotional spaciousness is about clearing mental clutter, reducing stress, and giving ourselves the permission to feel without judgement. Practices such as mindfulness, yoga, or simply being present in the moment allow us to create emotional space. This mental clarity is essential for creativity. When we are not bogged down by negative emotions or overwhelmed by external pressures, we are free to engage deeply with our work, connect with others, and produce innovative solutions.

4. **Setting Healthy Boundaries**: To create from a place of overflow, we must be willing to set boundaries around our time and energy. This might involve learning to say no to commitments that drain us, reducing our digital consumption, or carving out time for solitary reflection. By setting these boundaries, we create the mental and emotional space needed for creativity to flourish. Boundaries, when used intentionally, protect our time from being consumed by distractions or the demands of others, allowing us to invest it in ways that nourish our creativity.

A Case Study: The Slow Food Movement

A compelling example of creating from overflow rather than lack is the Slow Food movement. Born out of a desire to counter the fast-paced, industrialised food production systems, Slow Food promotes eating that is *mindful*, *sustainable*, and *enjoyable*. Rather than focusing on mass production, fast food, or quantity, the movement celebrates quality, seasonal ingredients, and the shared joy of preparing and consuming food at a pace that honours the rhythms of nature.

This philosophy extends far beyond the kitchen. Slow Food advocates for a shift in how we approach all aspects of life—encouraging people to slow down, savour experiences, and create from a place of abundance rather than scarcity. By rejecting the idea that faster is always better, Slow Food offers a powerful model for how we can embrace creativity, community, and sustainability in a world increasingly obsessed with speed and scale.

The Future of Creativity: Cultivating Overflow in Work and Life

As we move forward, the challenge is to design environments—both personal and professional—that support creativity from a place of overflow. This means reimagining workspaces, redefining productivity, and shifting societal values away from the cult of hustle towards a culture of balance, sustainability, and holistic well-being.

Corporations and organisations must embrace a more thoughtful approach to creativity by prioritising the well-being of their employees. This might involve offering more flexible work schedules, encouraging regular breaks, and fostering environments that allow for deep work and reflection. Rather than pushing employees to constantly *do more*, businesses should encourage them to *be more*—to reflect, rest, and engage deeply with their tasks without the pressure of endless productivity.

Individuals, too, must take responsibility for creating their own overflow. By prioritising rest, setting boundaries, and embracing downtime, we can foster environments—both within ourselves and in our communities—that support creativity, growth, and fulfilment.

Overflow as a Path to Sustainable Creativity

Creating from overflow, not lack, challenges the conventional narrative that creativity and productivity are born of pressure, scarcity, and endless hustle. By embracing the idea that surplus time and emotional space are essential for creativity, we can unlock deeper, more innovative ideas and experiences. In a world that often values speed and scale over quality and depth, learning to create from overflow offers a revolutionary approach that fosters not only individual creativity but also collective well-being and sustainability. To thrive in our work and personal lives, we must shift our focus from doing more to being more—embracing the spaciousness and abundance that fuel true creativity.

Designing Time-Conscious Systems: Building a Future Where Human Time is Respected and Preserved

In today's rapidly evolving world, time has become one of the most exploited and undervalued resources. Businesses, institutions, and even technologies operate under systems that demand ever-increasing amounts of time from their employees and users. The pressures of a 24/7 connected world, where the boundaries between work and personal life are constantly blurred, have led to widespread burnout, exhaustion, and dissatisfaction. Yet, there is an emerging realisation that we need to rethink how we design our businesses, communities, and even software systems—not as machines to extract maximum time from individuals, but as environments that respect, preserve, and optimise human time.

The concept of "time-conscious systems" is about creating structures—whether in business, technology, or community—that not only honour human time but also enable it to be used in ways that promote well-being, creativity, and meaningful engagement. Rather than exploiting time for the sole benefit of profit or productivity, these systems aim to foster balance, sustainable work habits, and respect for personal space. They ask: *how can we design environments that make time work for people, rather than against them?*

The Age of Time Exploitation

Time, once a luxury in many societies, has now become a commodity, traded and utilised with little regard for the well-being of individuals. The corporate drive for scalability, efficiency, and productivity has transformed our understanding of time into something that needs to be maximised and consumed. The rise of 'always-on' cultures, the expectation of constant availability, and the ever-expanding demands of the digital economy have created environments where people are expected to work more and rest less. This paradox has led to a paradoxical state where workers are busier than ever, yet productivity gains are stalling or only incrementally improving.

Modern businesses, particularly those in the startup and tech sectors, are obsessed with growth. The myth of 'infinite scale' has led to a culture where companies—especially in the gig economy—create systems that prioritise speed, expansion, and scale, often at the cost of human well-being. In this race, time is seen as a tool for acceleration rather than a finite resource to be used wisely.

Research shows that while technology has been a great enabler of progress, the way it has been integrated into our work lives has contributed to rising stress levels and a decline in mental health. As a result, there is a growing need for time-conscious systems that don't just focus on extracting more hours of work but focus on creating healthier environments where time is aligned with human needs.

Time-Conscious Systems: A Radical Rethinking of Design

A time-conscious system is one that actively works to preserve and optimise human time, rather than diminishing it. Such systems can exist in a variety of domains, including business, technology, and community structures. These systems are designed with human rhythms in mind, acknowledging that time is not just an economic resource but also a personal one, integral to our well-being, creativity, and satisfaction.

1. **Business: The Importance of Designing for Well-being**
Many companies today operate under models that see employees as interchangeable units of output. They impose rigid schedules, exploit

overtime, and rely on constant productivity metrics to measure success. This often leads to burnout, disengagement, and a depletion of creativity. To design time-conscious businesses, we must shift away from profit-at-all-costs and towards a model that values people's time and well-being as much as financial outcomes.

A notable example is **Patagonia**, a company known for its commitment to work-life balance, environmental sustainability, and employee well-being. The company has long provided its employees with flexible schedules, mental health support, and opportunities to take time off to focus on their passions. This approach, while not the norm in most industries, demonstrates that businesses can thrive by designing environments that encourage rest, creativity, and personal fulfilment.

Similarly, **Ben & Jerry's** is another example of a company that puts time-conscious values into practice. By prioritising a healthy work-life balance, offering generous paid leave, and maintaining a commitment to social responsibility, Ben & Jerry's has cultivated a work culture that not only increases employee satisfaction but also improves performance. Time-conscious systems don't have to conflict with profitability—they can enhance it.

2. Technology: Designing Systems that Honour Human Time

The software and tools we use daily can either support or sabotage our time-conscious lifestyles. Today, many digital platforms are designed to maximise engagement, often pulling users into endless cycles of scrolling or constant notifications. These systems, from social media to email, are built to occupy as much of our time as possible. As a result, people often feel trapped in their screens, with little ability to disengage and focus on other meaningful aspects of life.

For example, **Facebook** and **Instagram** have been criticised for their time-sapping features—such as endless scrolling and personalised notifications—that keep users hooked to the platform.

While these features are designed to keep engagement levels high, they do so at the expense of the users' time and attention. More recently, however, there has been a pushback from technology companies, with platforms like **Apple** introducing screen time-tracking features to help users become more aware of their digital consumption.

To design time-conscious software systems, developers must focus on creating platforms that allow for voluntary engagement without exploiting users' time. This could mean offering users more control over notifications, allowing for offline options, and designing interfaces that encourage productivity, well-being, and breaks. Moreover, tech companies should prioritise features that encourage meaningful interactions over mindless scrolling, such as promoting deep conversations, idea-sharing, and connections that aren't driven by data-mining or ads.

3. **Community: Building Space for Collective Well-being**

The rhythms of our communities—whether in physical spaces or through online networks—have a profound effect on how we experience time. In many modern cities, we are often caught in the hustle of urban life, where time is spent navigating the demands of work, commuting, and social obligations. However, in some cultures, time is intentionally designed to slow down, allowing space for community interaction, rest, and personal growth.

Siestas in Spain, **Sabbaths** in Jewish traditions, and even **community festivals** around the world provide structured times for rest, reflection, and collective engagement. These practices prioritise time as a valuable, finite resource and provide communities with moments of pause that restore well-being.

The concept of communal slowness is not just a nostalgic ideal but a practical, restorative approach that can be integrated into urban planning and social structures. Cities like **Copenhagen** and **Oslo** have become pioneers in designing time-conscious urban spaces. They incorporate pedestrian-friendly streets, public parks, and workspaces that allow for breaks and slow interactions. Rather than racing against time, these communities encourage mindful movement and thoughtful engagement, fostering a culture where well-being is just as important as efficiency.

The Power of Designing Time-Conscious Systems

Time-conscious systems provide a model where individuals, businesses, and communities thrive by working in harmony with human rhythms, not against them. These systems embrace the complexity of human time and recognise that creativity, productivity, and innovation are enhanced when people are allowed space to rest, reflect, and recharge. They reject the culture of "hustle" and "always-on" demands in favour of more sustainable, balanced approaches.

As the world moves forward, the demand for time-conscious systems will only increase. The evolution of the workplace, the redesign of digital platforms, and the creation of time-conscious communities all present opportunities for us to rethink how we structure our lives. By prioritising well-being, balance, and respect for human time, we can build a world where productivity and creativity are not driven by scarcity, but by abundance and mindful engagement.

Respecting Time as a Human Resource

At its core, designing time-conscious systems is about more than just improving efficiency. It is about recognising time as a human right—a resource to be respected and preserved, not exploited. In business, in technology, and in communities, creating systems that honour the rhythms of human life is essential for a future where people can flourish, create, and connect meaningfully. By rejecting the tyranny of constant productivity and embracing the wisdom of time, we can build a world that values human well-being as much as it does innovation and progress.

Chapter 10
Time Is Not a Resource—It's a Relationship

In a culture increasingly governed by output, speed, and the ceaseless quest for optimisation, time has been stripped of its mystery and rendered mechanical—something to measure, dissect, and consume. We speak of saving it, spending it, wasting it. The prevailing assumption is that time is a finite asset, slipping through our fingers as we attempt to harness it with apps, routines, and bullet-pointed goals. But pause, just for a moment—what if time isn't a resource at all?

What if, instead, time is a relationship? One we are always in, whether we notice or not. A relationship that reflects back to us not only how we move through the world but also how we inhabit ourselves.

This chapter invites a shift in perspective—a kind of gentle rebellion against the reduction of time to a line on a calendar or a set of digits on a clockface. It asks us to consider the idea that time, far from being a fixed unit of measurement, is something textured, relational, alive. Something to be tended, rather than managed.

We're often taught that time is out of reach—untouchable, unyielding. The one thing you cannot buy more of, no matter your status, your intelligence, your determination. And so we hustle. We fill every hour, convinced that a fuller schedule might somehow equal a fuller life. But this belief—the quiet panic that doing more equals having more time—has a cost. It divorces us from presence. From noticing. From simply being.

To reimagine time as a relationship is to question that frenzied pace. It is to listen for something subtler beneath the ticking of the clock: the quality of an afternoon's light, the hush between two thoughts, the resonance of a long silence shared with someone you love. These are not measurable, but they are meaningful. And they remind us that not all time is created equal.

When we begin to engage with time as something living and intimate—something that responds to our attention, our breath, our awareness—we slowly begin to alter the texture of our days. We become less focused on how much time we have, and more attuned to how we are within it.

This is not a call to reject structure or abandon ambition. Rather, it's an invitation to deepen, to slow just enough to feel the shape of your own life again. Time, as a relationship, holds within it the possibility of returning—to yourself, to others, to the quiet spaces that often go unnoticed. Not because they are unimportant, but because they ask more of us than efficiency ever could: they ask us to be present.

The Intimacy of Attention: Presence as the Gateway to Deeper Connection

The relationship we have with time is intrinsically tied to how we direct our attention. Modern life bombards us with distractions and demands, encouraging a fragmented attention span that pulls us away from the present moment. Yet, the more we engage with time through the lens of intention and presence, the more we come to realise that time, in its truest form, is not about endless tasks or obligations—it is about how we *show up* for the life unfolding before us.

True presence, the art of being fully engaged in the moment, transcends mere multitasking or superficial interaction. When we practice presence, we are no longer rushing through the experience of life, but rather allowing ourselves to deeply inhabit the time we are given. This kind of attention creates space for the fullness of life to unfold—not just in our work, but in our relationships, our connection to nature, and our interactions with art and culture. As we direct our attention more intentionally, we discover that time, when approached as a relationship, opens up deeper channels of connection with the people we love, the natural world, and even with ourselves.

Consider the transformative power of presence in the everyday moments we often overlook. When we are fully engaged with a conversation, we don't just hear words—we feel the emotional energy behind them, the subtle nuances of body language, the intention behind the dialogue. In the same way, when we experience a sunset or a piece of music, our relationship with time deepens. We become attuned to the present, and in that attunement, time seems to stretch, becoming vast rather than fleeting. *The intimacy of attention*—our ability to be present with time, in all its forms—connects us to life in a way that transforms mundane moments into profound experiences.

Soul Timelines: Crafting a Timeline of Awakening Moments

A traditional timeline of life often revolves around achievements: milestones such as graduating, getting married, landing a promotion, or having children. These external markers are valuable in their own right, but they are not the entirety of the human experience. The essence of life's journey is not measured solely by what we do or accomplish, but by how we grow, learn, and evolve.

In this chapter, we invite readers to create a different kind of timeline—one not marked by outward success, but by inward awakening. A *soul timeline* charts the moments when something in us shifted, when we felt a deepening of understanding or connection, or when we experienced an expansion of consciousness. These are the moments that define us, shaping our perceptions and actions far more than any outward achievement could. They are moments of *being*—moments when we truly inhabit the present and feel deeply connected to life.

This alternative timeline might include moments like the first time we felt deeply at peace with ourselves, or the time we realised the futility of striving for external validation. It might mark the moment we chose to step away from a life of constant busyness and instead embraced slowness, allowing creativity and reflection to flourish. These moments of awakening aren't defined by dates or external accomplishments, but by their transformative power to shift our understanding of who we are and how we relate to time.

When we focus on these awakening moments, we stop measuring time through the lens of what we achieve and instead begin to see time as a rich, evolving relationship to our inner selves. Rather than accumulating years of achievement, we accumulate wisdom, self-awareness, and connection to the present moment.

Living Inside the Now: The Abundance of the Present Moment

At the heart of this exploration is the realisation that the present moment is the only true abundance we possess. While the past has shaped us and the future holds potential, it is the *now*—the very moment we are experiencing—that holds the power to transform our relationship with time. This is the essence of mindfulness, contemplative practices, and the flow state that psychologists and philosophers have long studied.

Mindfulness, in particular, offers us a tool to step fully into the present moment. When we practice mindfulness, we learn to observe our thoughts, feelings, and sensations without judgment, letting go of the need to control or manipulate them. This practice allows us to cultivate a deep connection to time, not as a scarce or fleeting resource, but as a living presence that can be fully experienced. As the philosopher and spiritual teacher **Eckhart Tolle** writes, "Realize deeply that the present moment is all you ever have. Make the NOW the primary focus of your life."

The science of flow, too, highlights the transformative potential of living in the present. Flow, the state of heightened focus and engagement, is often described as the feeling of "being in the zone." When we experience flow, time seems to slow down or disappear entirely. We become so deeply immersed in the activity at hand that we lose track of time, and in doing so, we come closest to experiencing the true nature of time as a relationship. In these moments, we transcend the pressures of "doing" and instead focus on the richness of "being." The present moment becomes not a burden to be rushed through, but a source of creative potential and connection.

The Paradigm Shift: From Resource to Relationship

As we have explored throughout this chapter, time is not something we can simply consume, optimise, or exploit. Time is a relationship—one that we must approach with reverence, presence, and mindfulness. When we shift our understanding of time from a commodity to a relational experience, we begin to unlock the fullness of life itself. The key is not in doing more, but in *being more*—more present, more connected, and more aware of the subtle rhythms of life.

By redefining our relationship with time, we open ourselves to deeper connection with others, with nature, and with our own sense of purpose. This shift allows us to experience time not as something that runs out, but as something that expands and deepens when we engage with it fully.

This chapter invites you to step into a new relationship with time—one that honours the fullness of the present moment, where creativity, connection, and wisdom emerge not from scarcity or pressure, but from spaciousness and intention. Time is not a resource to be spent, but a relationship to be cultivated, nurtured, and cherished.

Rewilding Time: Reclaiming the Organic Rhythm of Life

In a world where time is regimented, measured, and commodified, it has become easy to forget the primal, wild nature of time. We treat it as a mechanical force to be tamed, optimised, and processed, much like the industrialised systems that now dictate every aspect of our existence. But time, at its core, is not a conveyor belt—it is a river, flowing, unpredictable, and brimming with potential. This subchapter invites us to rewild time—allowing it to flow freely again, beyond the rigid constraints that society has imposed on it. We are called to unshackle our experience of time from the machinery of modernity and let it breathe, pulsing with the same organic energy that governs the natural world.

The concept of time as something to be "managed" or "spent" is deeply embedded in contemporary culture. It is reflected in our addiction to productivity metrics, our relentless pursuit of efficiency, and the constant pressure to accelerate. From the demanding work schedule to the planned, scheduled, and timed lives we lead, time has been stripped of its organic, liberating essence. But what if time could be more than just a resource to be drained? What if we returned to the idea of time as something to be *lived*, to be experienced as a flowing, unstructured force? *Rewilding time* is about reclaiming time as our birthright, not as a commodity, but as a living, breathing part of who we are.

The Industrialisation of Time: From Wildness to Conformity

The industrial revolution marked a significant turning point in our relationship with time. Prior to that, time was measured by the rhythms of the sun, the seasons, and natural cycles. There were harvests to tend, tides to observe, and communal rhythms shaped by the land and the sky. But with the advent of factories, mechanisation, and mass production, time became a tool of control. It became something that could be quantified, broken down into units, and used as a means of economic productivity. *The clock*, once a tool of convenience, became a symbol of control, shaping not only work but also every aspect of daily life.

In modern society, this view of time continues to dominate. The 9-to-5 workday, the obsession with "time management", and the increasing demand for "always-on" availability are all by-products of a system that has prioritised uniformity and productivity over the organic rhythms of life. We are now encouraged to "make the most of every minute"—to wring every drop of value from our time, leaving little room for the spontaneity, creativity, or leisure that once came naturally.

This mechanisation of time has also led to the erosion of social and communal rhythms. Where once communal gatherings, festivals, and shared breaks marked time in a way that fostered connection, we now find ourselves fragmented by individualised schedules and the constant rush of daily life. The modern workweek, with its focus on output and deliverables, has made time something that must be controlled and optimised, rather than something that can be experienced in its fullness.

Reclaiming the Flow: The Case for Unstructured Time

Rewilding time is about returning to a more natural, intuitive way of living—one that prioritises presence, flow, and connectedness over output. This doesn't mean abandoning all structure or responsibility but recognising that there is wisdom in slowing down, in *not doing*, and in creating the space for time to unfold organically.

The idea of unstructured time might seem foreign to many, especially those who have grown accustomed to the relentless pace of modern life. But the truth is that human beings are inherently designed to be in rhythm with nature. Just as ecosystems function in delicate balance, so too does human experience. When we live in sync with our natural rhythms—allowing ourselves time to rest, create, and simply be—we become more attuned to our deeper needs and desires. This process of rewilding time invites us to *listen* to the flow of our inner worlds, as well as the rhythms of the environment around us. It is through this attunement that we are able to rediscover the deeper, more creative, and more connected parts of ourselves.

Consider the example of festivals, sabbaths, or siestas—all communal practices that have historically allowed individuals and societies to slow down, reconnect, and re-energise. These communal pauses offer more than just rest; they provide opportunities for reflection, joy, and community-building. In the absence of such rituals, individuals often find themselves rushing through life, disconnected from the world and others around them. The act of rewilding time, then, is not simply about the individual, but about collective well-being. When we reintroduce moments of stillness and unstructured time into our lives, we invite connection not only with ourselves but with our communities and our planet.

The River vs. The Conveyor Belt: A New Framework for Time

Time, when seen as a river rather than a conveyor belt, shifts our understanding of productivity and value. In a river, there is movement, but there is also space for pause—places where the flow is slower, where the water gathers in eddies and pools, creating space for reflection and renewal. In the same way, rewilding time is about acknowledging that periods of non-activity, rest, or leisure are not wasted but necessary for true creativity and growth. It is only when we give ourselves the room to breathe and to step away from the relentless pace of life that we are able to *create from overflow*, rather than from scarcity.

This new framework of time requires us to let go of the scarcity mindset—that time must be constantly "spent" or "filled" in order to be valuable. By releasing this need, we can reclaim the freedom to *experience* time, rather than merely managing it. This is where creativity flourishes: not in moments of pressure or urgency, but in the unhurried spaces where ideas can grow naturally, without being forced or rushed.

Take, for instance, the process of deep work or creative inspiration. It often emerges not from the structured hours of a 9-to-5 workday but from moments of unstructured time—when we step away from the screen, take a walk, or allow our minds to wander. The most profound insights often occur when we allow ourselves the space to be idle, to let time flow without constraints. Rewilding time means embracing the fact that true creativity is born from the *space* between actions, from the quiet moments where our minds are free to process, synthesise, and explore.

The Benefits of Rewilding Time: Restoring Balance, Reconnecting with Life

Rewilding time holds the potential for profound transformation, not only for individuals but for societies as a whole. When we embrace time as a river—something to flow with rather than control—we can rediscover a sense of harmony and balance. Rewilding time is an antidote to the toxic hustle culture that equates worth with output. It is a practice that restores our connection to the rhythms of nature, to our communities, and to our own inner peace.

Rewilding time also has the potential to foster more sustainable and compassionate economies and societies. If businesses, communities, and even governments were to reframe time as a relationship rather than a resource, we would see a shift towards practices that honour human well-being, creativity, and connection. We would build systems that allow for rest, reflection, and renewal—not just for the individual, but for society as a whole.

The need to rewild time has never been more urgent. As we continue to navigate the complexities of modern life—marked by environmental crises, social disconnection, and growing inequality—the call to return to a more organic, rhythmic way of living becomes louder. Rewilding time is not just a personal journey; it is a collective imperative. By embracing the flow of life, we can rebuild communities, foster creativity, and reconnect with the natural world in ways that honour the living, breathing essence of time itself.

In the end, rewilding time is not a rejection of progress or productivity, but a reclamation of the deeper, more meaningful ways of being that time offers. It is about restoring balance, restoring connection, and, ultimately, restoring ourselves.

The Intimacy of Attention: How Presence with Time Enhances Our Connection to the World

In a world that is increasingly distracted and fragmented, where every moment seems to be filled with stimuli competing for our attention, the concept of *presence* is becoming increasingly rare. Yet, it is precisely through cultivating a deep, sustained presence with time that we can build more meaningful connections—not only with the people around us, but with nature, art, and even the deeper currents of our own being. The act of paying attention, when truly practised, opens up spaces of intimacy that allow us to feel more fully alive, more connected to the world, and more attuned to the rhythms that govern life itself.

Attention, when stripped of its usual connotations of productivity and efficiency, becomes something far more profound—a doorway into a richer experience of life. In this subchapter, we explore the transformative power of attention, how it shapes our connections, and why its cultivation is one of the most potent tools for developing a deep, meaningful relationship with time. From the realms of psychology and neuroscience to the wisdom of contemplative traditions, this article will guide you through understanding how attention—when nurtured consciously—becomes not just an act of focus, but a portal to intimacy, clarity, and depth.

The Fragmentation of Attention in Modern Life

To understand the true significance of attention, we must first examine the ways in which it has been compromised in our modern world. The digital age, with its constant influx of notifications, messages, and multitasking demands, has led to what might be termed the *fragmentation* of attention. We are no longer able to focus deeply on one thing for long periods of time; rather, we are pulled in multiple directions simultaneously, often leaving us mentally exhausted, unfocused, and disconnected from the present moment.

Studies have shown that constant distractions reduce our cognitive capacity, making it harder for us to form deep, lasting connections or engage meaningfully with our surroundings. When attention is divided or fleeting, we miss the nuances of our experiences and fail to build the kinds of meaningful relationships that require deep focus and presence. The simple act of being *present*—of truly attending to what is happening right now—becomes increasingly elusive.

In the context of time, this fragmentation manifests as a feeling that time is slipping through our fingers, that we are always "running out of time" or "falling behind." The more our time is fractured by the demands of technology, work, and social obligations, the less we are able to savour the richness of each passing moment. Reclaiming attention, then, is not just about improving focus, but about restoring our ability to be *fully present*, to experience time as a living, flowing current rather than a series of fragmented, disjointed intervals.

Attention as the Bridge to Deeper Connection

So, what does it mean to bring attention to time? To slow down enough to notice how the hours unfold, how we experience each moment as it passes, without rushing through it in a haze of obligations and distractions? The answer lies in developing what could be called *ecotemporal intelligence*—the ability to read the rhythms of time, to be attuned to its fluctuations, and to adjust our own pace accordingly. In this process, attention becomes an intimate act, a way of creating a richer, more connected relationship with everything we encounter.

At its core, attention allows us to tune into the subtle vibrations of life. When we are truly present, we are not just observing the surface of things—we are engaging with their essence. In the context of people, this means being fully available to the nuances of conversation, to the unspoken signals in body language, and to the emotional currents that move between individuals. This type of deep listening fosters empathy, connection, and trust, creating bonds that go beyond the superficial exchanges typical of a distracted, fast-paced world.

Consider the act of truly listening to another person. To give someone your full, undivided attention is one of the greatest gifts you can offer them. It is in these moments of deep connection—when we are not thinking about the next thing we need to do, or mentally checking off our to-do list—that we create meaningful relationships. In a world where attention is often diluted, the ability to focus intently on another person is an act of radical intimacy.

Nature, Art, and Spirit: The Expansive Power of Attention

Attention also allows us to build deeper relationships with nature, art, and even the intangible aspects of existence, such as spirit or soul. In this context, attention moves beyond the transactional or the practical—it becomes a meditative practice, a way of engaging with the world that enriches our understanding and our sense of connection.

In nature, for instance, attention allows us to see the subtle changes in the landscape, the intricate patterns of the seasons, or the quiet rhythms of the natural world that often go unnoticed in the rush of modern life. A simple walk through the woods, when taken with full attention, becomes a profound act of engagement, where every leaf, every branch, every sound is a part of a larger, interconnected whole. This deepened awareness of the natural world is not only enriching for the soul but also nurtures a sense of responsibility, as we begin to recognise our place within the ecosystem.

Similarly, in the realm of art, attention is what allows us to experience the true depth of a work. Whether it's a painting, a piece of music, or a dance performance, art requires us to engage fully, to lose ourselves in the rhythms and nuances of the creative expression. In doing so, we are transported to a place where time seems to slow down, where we are connected to the artist's vision, and where the boundaries between self and art dissolve. In this state, we experience a form of transcendence—a union of time, self, and creativity that opens up new dimensions of experience.

Lastly, when it comes to spirit, attention plays a pivotal role in our connection to the divine or the transcendent. Whether through prayer, meditation, or contemplation, the act of turning our attention inward—or outward towards something greater than ourselves—becomes a deeply intimate practice. In these moments of focused attention, we are able to experience the presence of something beyond the ordinary, tapping into the timeless, the sacred, and the eternal. It is through cultivating attention that we deepen our relationship with the spiritual dimensions of life, finding meaning, purpose, and connection in ways that go beyond the material world.

Mindfulness and Presence: The Practices of Attention

The cultivation of attention as intimacy is not something that happens overnight; it is a practice that requires discipline, awareness, and intention. Mindfulness, a concept drawn from Buddhist philosophy, offers one of the most powerful tools for enhancing attention. At its core, mindfulness is the art of being fully present in the moment, without judgment or distraction. By focusing on the breath, the body, or the present moment, mindfulness trains the mind to be still, to let go of the constant chatter, and to focus on the here and now.

This practice, when applied to daily life, becomes a form of rewilding time. We stop seeing time as a resource to be used up or controlled, and instead see it as something to be inhabited—something to experience fully. Whether we are eating, walking, listening, or simply resting, we can bring mindfulness to each moment, finding richness in the simplest activities.

Similarly, contemplative traditions offer wisdom on how to deepen our relationship with time through attention. From the slow, deliberate movements of Tai Chi to the stillness of silent retreats, these practices help us slow down, reconnect with the present, and cultivate the intimacy of attention.

Conclusion: Reclaiming the Gift of Presence

The intimacy of attention is one of the most profound ways in which we can re-engage with time. When we bring our full presence to our relationships, to nature, to art, and to spirit, we not only deepen our connections but also open ourselves to the fullness of life. In a world that often values speed, efficiency, and multitasking, the ability to be present, to listen deeply, and to experience life with intention becomes a radical act.

Reclaiming our attention is not just about improving focus—it is about restoring our humanity, our capacity for deep connection, and our ability to live fully in the present moment. As we cultivate this intimacy with time, we discover that the quality of our experience is far more important than its quantity. Time, when embraced with full attention, becomes not a burden to be managed, but a precious gift to be fully lived.

Soul Timelines: Charting the Growth of the Inner Self

In a world that often measures success by milestones—degrees, promotions, possessions, and titles—there is a growing need to rethink how we track and celebrate our journeys. We are conditioned to believe that our worth and progress are defined by external achievements, but what if we shifted that perspective to focus on something deeper? Instead of counting the number of things we've accumulated or the accolades we've collected, what if we charted our personal growth by the moments when we woke up to something new within ourselves?

This concept, which we call *Soul Timelines*, invites us to rethink how we measure our lives—not by what we have accomplished, but by the inner moments of awakening, insight, and transformation that shape us over time. In a society obsessed with linear, quantifiable progress, crafting a Soul Timeline encourages us to focus on the intangible forces of self-awareness, emotional growth, and spiritual deepening. By doing so, we gain a richer understanding of our personal evolution and the profound ways in which we are shaped by our internal, rather than external, experiences.

The Myth of External Achievement as True Progress

For most of human history, societies have measured success by what could be seen and touched—tangible, external markers of achievement. From building monuments to creating empires, progress was often measured by what was visible, measurable, and impactful in the external world. The modern era has not strayed far from this framework. Educational institutions, workplaces, and even social media platforms reward external accomplishments, creating a culture where we often equate our self-worth with how we perform in the outside world.

But as we delve deeper into the concept of a *Soul Timeline*, we begin to question the validity of this narrow measurement. Achievements can be fleeting, and titles can lose their meaning over time. The real growth, the kind that shapes our inner being and redefines our relationship to ourselves and others, often lies in the subtler, less quantifiable moments. These are the moments when we choose authenticity over conformity, when we break patterns, when we overcome personal limitations, or when we learn to embrace our vulnerability. These moments of inner awakening are what truly define us—and yet, they are seldom recognised on the standard timeline of success.

The Awakening Moments That Define Us

The beauty of a Soul Timeline is that it moves beyond the linear progression of the ego-driven goals to capture the nonlinear, often unpredictable nature of inner growth. This timeline is not focused on external events but rather on the moments of transformation—those pivotal, often small, shifts that change our relationship to the world around us and to ourselves. These moments might include the first time we truly forgave ourselves, the day we realised that our worth was not tied to our productivity, or the instance we learned to trust our intuition over societal expectations.

Each of these awakenings forms a milestone in a Soul Timeline, a personal record of inner evolution. These milestones may not always be recognised in the outside world, but they are no less important than any external achievement. In fact, they may well be more significant in defining who we are at the deepest level.

For instance, consider the moment when a person realises that they are more than their job title—that they are worthy, valuable, and complete as they are, regardless of their career trajectory. This is not a moment that can be measured with a pay raise or a promotion, yet it can have a profound impact on the way that person interacts with the world. It might lead them to seek a more fulfilling job, to improve their relationships, or to cultivate more time for creative pursuits. This shift in perception is a crucial moment in a Soul Timeline, one that changes the course of the person's life, even though it might not be reflected in the traditional milestones of success.

Crafting Your Soul Timeline

Creating a Soul Timeline is a deeply personal and introspective process. It involves reflecting on the most meaningful moments of growth, insight, and transformation in your life—moments that may not have been captured in the official records of your accomplishments. Instead of measuring your worth by degrees or job titles, ask yourself: *What were the moments that truly shifted my perception of myself? When did I learn something about my character, my values, or my purpose that changed the way I live?*

To craft your own Soul Timeline, you can start by identifying key moments in your life that felt transformative, even if they were not recognised by others as significant. These might be moments of self-realisation, such as recognising a deep-seated fear and learning to overcome it, or acknowledging a limiting belief and choosing to release it. It could also include times when you experienced a profound connection with others, nature, or a creative pursuit, moments that led you to a deeper understanding of yourself or your place in the world.

The key is to view your timeline through the lens of personal growth. Each milestone represents a shift in consciousness—a moment where you learned something about who you are, what you believe, and how you relate to the world. These moments are often not celebrated in the traditional sense, but they are what ultimately shape your inner life and your sense of peace.

The Power of Reflection: Reclaiming Inner Wisdom

In creating your Soul Timeline, you also engage in the process of *reclaiming wisdom.* So often, we rush through life without pausing to reflect on our journey, and in doing so, we miss the quiet yet profound insights that emerge from within. The act of reflecting on your Soul Timeline allows you to slow down and reconsider how each experience has contributed to your growth.

The process of reflecting on your own growth is deeply healing. By recognising and honouring the moments that have shaped you, you give yourself permission to fully embrace the person you have become. These awakenings are not things you need to prove to others—they are part of the sacred work of becoming yourself.

Moreover, reflecting on your Soul Timeline can also allow you to recognise patterns in your life. Perhaps there are recurring themes or lessons that you have repeatedly encountered—whether it's learning to let go of control, cultivating deeper compassion, or discovering the value of silence. By charting these moments, you can see how they have influenced your current trajectory and begin to better understand how your inner growth has unfolded over time.

The Wisdom of Thresholds

One of the most profound aspects of the Soul Timeline is its emphasis on *thresholds*. While the modern world tends to focus on external markers of success, a Soul Timeline highlights the importance of *thresholds*—those moments when we cross from one stage of awareness or understanding to another. Thresholds mark a shift, a boundary, a new beginning. They may occur in quiet, subtle ways, but they signal growth that has the potential to change the course of our lives.

In the same way that nature moves through cycles—spring, summer, autumn, winter—our own growth moves through thresholds of self-discovery. These moments are not about doing more, achieving more, or accumulating more. Instead, they are about aligning more deeply with who we truly are. They are invitations to step into a new chapter of life, where we leave behind outdated beliefs, relationships, or patterns that no longer serve our evolution.

The Soul Timeline as a Roadmap for Inner Fulfilment

What makes the Soul Timeline so powerful is that it offers an alternative way of measuring success—one that aligns with our truest, most authentic self. It reminds us that growth is not linear, and it cannot be measured by the external milestones society values most. Our inner evolution is a deeply personal journey that is marked by moments of awakening, rather than moments of attainment.

When we take the time to reflect on and honour the milestones of our Soul Timeline, we begin to realise that the most fulfilling and meaningful achievements are not those that can be seen on paper or celebrated by the masses, but those that live quietly within us. These are the moments when we truly awaken to our fullest potential and become more deeply connected to our true selves.

A Soul Timeline is, in essence, a roadmap to inner fulfilment—a guide to understanding not just who we are, but who we are becoming. By recognising and charting our growth in this way, we reclaim our time as our own. We shift from a life lived for external validation to one lived for internal satisfaction and peace.

Living Inside the Now: Embodying the Present as True Abundance

In an age dominated by perpetual motion, multitasking, and a constant barrage of distractions, the idea of truly *living in the present* might seem almost absurd. Time, we are taught, is something to be used efficiently, managed to its fullest potential, and squeezed for every drop of productivity. Yet, this race towards the future often comes at the expense of fully inhabiting the now. The present moment—the only time that is truly ours—often slips away unnoticed, leaving us with a life that feels fragmented, rushed, and unsatisfying. But what if we shifted our focus from time management to *time embodiment*? What if the secret to lasting fulfilment, creativity, and joy lay not in how we chase time, but in how we embrace it—right now, as it is?

This is the essence of *living inside the now*—the profound art of presence that connects deeply to our internal world, to others, and to the world around us. By drawing on mindfulness, contemplative traditions, and flow science, we can learn not just to experience the present moment, but to *embody* it, transforming our relationship with time from one of scarcity and stress to one of abundance and clarity.

The Elusive Nature of Time

At first glance, time may seem to be a linear, quantifiable resource. It is measured in seconds, minutes, and hours, and tracked through clocks, calendars, and deadlines. Yet, despite our obsession with measuring and managing time, it remains an elusive concept. Time can feel too slow when we're bored, too fast when we're stressed, or too stagnant when we're waiting for something to change. This contradiction points to a deeper truth: our experience of time is not defined by the passing of minutes but by how we engage with the present moment.

Philosophers, poets, and spiritual traditions alike have long recognised that time is not just an external force but a deeply internal experience. In Western thought, this insight was most famously captured by St. Augustine, who remarked, "What then is time? If no one asks me, I know; if I wish to explain it to him who asks, I know not." His reflection acknowledges the paradox of time: though we all experience it, it remains fundamentally difficult to define or pin down.

The Mindfulness Revolution: A Return to Presence

In the past few decades, the rise of mindfulness practices has brought attention back to this elusive quality of time. Mindfulness, a core element of many contemplative traditions, asks us to turn our awareness towards the present moment—without judgment, without attachment to outcomes, and without the need to constantly analyse or plan. In doing so, we are able to reconnect with the richness of life as it unfolds. Research has shown that mindfulness can reduce stress, improve emotional regulation, and enhance overall well-being, making it one of the most accessible tools for engaging fully with the now.

Jon Kabat-Zinn, a pioneer in the field of mindfulness, famously defined mindfulness as "the awareness that arises through paying attention, on purpose, in the present moment, and nonjudgmentally." This simple definition holds profound implications for how we experience time. When we engage in mindfulness, we stop trying to control time and instead allow ourselves to be *with* it—living in the present, where life happens, and where we have the greatest potential for true joy, connection, and creativity.

However, mindfulness is not just about being in the present moment; it's about inhabiting it with our full being. This is where the concept of *embodiment* comes in. By paying attention to our thoughts, emotions, and bodily sensations, we can anchor ourselves in the present moment—not as an abstract concept, but as a lived experience.

Flow: The Science of Total Presence

Another powerful lens through which we can understand the concept of living inside the now comes from the field of positive psychology, specifically Mihaly Csikszentmihalyi's concept of *flow*. Flow is a state of optimal experience in which a person is fully immersed in an activity, with complete focus and without the need for external rewards. Time, in these moments, becomes malleable—minutes feel like hours or vice versa. More importantly, flow creates a sense of deep satisfaction, as we experience the process of creation, work, or play as an end in itself.

Csikszentmihalyi's research has shown that flow states are associated with increased happiness, productivity, and creativity. However, the key to entering flow is not about forcing ourselves into a productive frenzy. Rather, it is about letting go of the constant pressure to achieve and, instead, allowing ourselves to be fully present in whatever we are doing. This is where *living inside the now* and *flow* converge: both are about engaging with time in such a way that it loses its usual constraints and transforms into an experience of pure, unbroken presence.

Time as the Ultimate Abundance

Perhaps the most radical shift in perspective comes when we move away from viewing time as a finite resource that needs to be managed, scheduled, or spent efficiently. In this view, time is something that is constantly running out, forcing us to chase it relentlessly. However, when we embrace *living inside the now*, we start to see time not as something we need to control but as something we can embody. Time becomes a space of abundance, not scarcity.

When we stop rushing, when we stop trying to fill every second with activity or achievement, we begin to experience the *fullness* of time. Each moment becomes rich with possibility, offering us opportunities for reflection, creativity, and connection that we might otherwise miss in our constant pursuit of the next thing. By living in the now, we allow time to flow freely, without resistance, and in doing so, we become attuned to the rhythms of life—both within ourselves and in the world around us.

The Practice of Living Inside the Now

Living inside the now requires intentional practice, and it involves several key elements:

1. **Presence over Performance**: Rather than focusing on how much we can achieve in a given time, we focus on the quality of our engagement with the present moment. This shift requires us to slow down, pause, and reconnect with what is happening in the here and now.

2. **Self-Awareness**: To fully inhabit the present, we must also be attuned to our inner world. Mindfulness practices, meditation, and simply paying attention to our emotional and physical state can help us stay grounded in the present.

3. **Letting Go of Control**: Living in the now also means releasing the need to control outcomes. This is a form of surrender,

where we accept that we can only influence the present moment, not predict or force the future.

4. **Embracing Flow**: Whether through creative pursuits, work, or leisure, allowing ourselves to enter flow states is a powerful way to become immersed in the now. This involves engaging in activities that challenge us just enough to keep us focused, without overwhelming us.

5. **Gratitude and Reflection**: The practice of reflecting on the present moment and cultivating gratitude can reinforce our awareness of time's abundance. By acknowledging the beauty and richness of the now, we deepen our connection to life itself.

The True Abundance of the Now

In a world that perpetually pushes us to focus on what's next, the art of *living inside the now* offers us a powerful alternative. Rather than measuring time by how much we do, achieve, or possess, we begin to measure it by how deeply we experience it. Time becomes a relationship—a fluid, organic process in which we are not passive observers but active participants, fully immersed in the present moment. When we engage with time in this way, we discover that the present is not a fleeting, finite resource but a source of endless abundance, offering us all the richness we need for creativity, connection, and fulfilment.

Conclusion
Wealth Was Always a Feeling

In a culture relentlessly driven by acquisition and achievement, our collective understanding of wealth has been subtly—yet profoundly—distorted. We've been conditioned to measure it by the digits in our accounts, the square footage of our homes, the sheen of outward accomplishments. These are the signs we've come to chase, the yardsticks we hold up against one another. And yet, curiously—or perhaps tellingly—the more we gather, the more a kind of hollowness tends to creep in. Not immediately, perhaps, but inevitably. It begs the question: if all the trophies of success fail to make us feel genuinely rich inside, have we misunderstood what wealth really is?

Here, we're invited to trace a different path, one that turns away from the gleam of material markers and looks, instead, inward. What if wealth isn't something to be counted or displayed, but something to be felt? Not a number on a screen, but a state of being—a sense of sufficiency, of quiet contentment, of belonging not just to a world of things, but to a life that feels whole?

This chapter proposes a quiet yet radical redefinition: that true wealth lives not in accumulation, but in appreciation. In the ability to dwell fully in the present rather than constantly striving for what lies just out of reach. It invites us to examine our relationship not just with money, but with longing itself—with that subtle ache that whispers, *not yet*, no matter how much we acquire.

To reimagine wealth in this way is not to dismiss the value of financial stability or the comforts it affords. That would be naïve. But it is to challenge the assumption that more is always better, and to ask instead whether *enough*—when recognised and honoured—might be the real source of freedom. Might even be, in the truest sense, abundance.

This kind of wealth does not glitter. It does not shout. It does not rely on validation or comparison. Rather, it shows itself quietly, in moments: the ability to exhale without urgency, the deep exhale of sufficiency, the sense that nothing more is needed in this very moment for life to feel whole.

And perhaps that is the paradox we've been circling all along. That what we most long for isn't *more*, but *ease*. Not accumulation, but connection. Not the endless pursuit of better, but the gentle, grounded awareness that this—right here—might already be enough.

The Illusion of External Wealth

We live in a world that measures wealth through numbers: salaries, net worth, assets, and investments. The more we accumulate, the more society reinforces the idea that we are succeeding. But if we look more closely, we realise that these external markers often fail to deliver lasting satisfaction. The endless cycle of *wanting more* leaves many feeling empty, anxious, and unfulfilled, no matter how much they accumulate.

It is in this context that the concept of "wealth" becomes increasingly fragmented. Many individuals, despite their material possessions, find themselves in a constant state of striving—whether for the next promotion, the next acquisition, or the next accomplishment. They are *wealthy* by conventional standards, but they live in a state of perpetual dissatisfaction. The more they gain, the more they feel the pull of *lack*—a longing for something that can never quite be attained. This paradoxical existence begs the question: is true wealth really about how much we have, or is it about how much we *feel* we have?

The Inner Dimensions of Wealth

Wealth, when understood as a *feeling*, becomes an internal experience rather than an external condition. It is less about accumulating resources and more about cultivating an inner sense of abundance. This shift in perspective redefines wealth, positioning it as a state of *inner sufficiency*—the ability to experience joy, contentment, and peace, regardless of our external circumstances.

What would it mean to live with a sense of inner wealth? It would mean living from a place of fullness, recognising that true abundance arises not from what we accumulate, but from our capacity to experience life fully and with gratitude. This shift in perspective allows us to *feel* wealthy in the present moment—without the need for endless accumulation or external validation.

In philosophical traditions such as Stoicism, this idea is central. The Stoics believed that the greatest wealth comes not from material possessions but from cultivating inner virtue, clarity, and contentment. They understood that true abundance lies not in having more, but in wanting less—recognising the richness of life even in the most modest circumstances. As the Roman emperor and philosopher Marcus Aurelius once wrote, "Wealth consists not in having great possessions, but in having few wants."

Shifting the Focus from External Metrics to Inner Values

This chapter will guide you through a process of rediscovering wealth as an internal, relational experience. Rather than measuring wealth through external markers, you will be encouraged to *define* wealth on your own terms—by the richness of your relationships, the depth of your experiences, and your ability to appreciate the present moment. The central idea is that wealth should be a reflection of the life you choose to live, not an accumulation of things you're told you should desire.

This new approach to wealth is more than just an intellectual exercise—it has profound practical implications. For instance, rather than focusing on increasing income or expanding one's material holdings, this perspective encourages individuals to invest in the areas of their lives that contribute most to *inner abundance*: relationships, health, personal development, and connection to nature. The emphasis shifts from the external quest for more to the internal cultivation of less—less stress, less competition, less striving, and more presence, more love, more connection.

Time as the Ultimate Wealth

One of the most profound realisations in this context is that *time* is, in fact, the ultimate form of wealth. Time is the one resource that cannot be stored or accumulated; it can only be spent in the present. Yet, it is often the most undervalued and overlooked aspect of our lives. People work tirelessly to earn money, yet they sacrifice time—the one thing that could actually allow them to experience the richness of life. In this sense, the pursuit of external wealth is often an illusion, masking the deeper need for time well spent.

True wealth, then, may not lie in accumulating more hours in the day or filling those hours with endless activities, but in creating time for what matters most: personal connection, reflection, creativity, and rest. As we begin to shift our relationship with time, we find that *time* becomes the most precious resource we possess—an investment not in future accumulation, but in present fulfilment.

The Path to Inner Abundance

The goal of this chapter is not merely to challenge conventional definitions of wealth, but to offer a practical path for those who wish to *live* their wealth, not just *accumulate* it. By the end of this exploration, you will have gained a new framework for understanding wealth—not as something external to be chased, but as something internal to be cultivated. This will involve learning how to cultivate emotional spaciousness, how to embrace sufficiency rather than scarcity, and how to create from a place of overflow rather than lack.

The journey towards true wealth is a process of recognising that abundance is not a future goal to be achieved, but a present state to be realised. It is the realisation that wealth is not a static condition, but a dynamic relationship—one that invites us to be present, to be mindful, and to recognise the richness in every moment, regardless of what we have or do not have.

Reimagining Success: Living Abundantly in the Now

By the end of this chapter, you will have come to understand that the myth of infinite accumulation, endless achievement, and constant striving is just that—a myth. True wealth is a *feeling*, an internal experience of abundance that arises when we free ourselves from the external pressures of comparison, competition, and consumption. It is the ability to live fully, to appreciate the beauty of the present moment, and to embrace the richness of life as it is, rather than always seeking more.

Ultimately, wealth was always a feeling. When we shift our focus from external accumulation to internal satisfaction, we unlock a deeper, more meaningful relationship with time, with life, and with ourselves. This, in essence, is the true path to wealth—and it is available to us all, right now.

Rather than Summarising, the Conclusion Offers a Moment of Still Reflection—a Gentle Space for Integration

In the fast-paced world we inhabit, it's all too easy to fall into the trap of relentless forward motion. We are conditioned to seek the next step, the next achievement, the next destination. Even when we make strides towards a more balanced and mindful relationship with time, we often find ourselves asking, *What comes next?* We find comfort in the structure of linear progression: after all, there's always something to strive for, always something to improve. But perhaps the most profound invitation we can extend to ourselves is to stop, to rest, to recognise that the journey is as significant as the destination—and sometimes, the destination is already here.

This is not a typical conclusion; it is an invitation to pause. In a world driven by outcomes, this final space is designed not to offer a new step forward, but to prompt reflection on what it means to truly inhabit the present. It is a chance to integrate everything we have discussed thus far, not by seeking more or doing more, but by being fully here. By embracing the stillness that exists between the 'doing' and the 'becoming', we allow ourselves the opportunity to create from a place of fullness rather than emptiness.

The Illusion of the Next Step

Modern life tells us that there is always a next step—a more efficient way to organise our time, a more lucrative way to invest it, a more productive way to measure it. We are raised on the belief that time is something to be maximised, not cherished, and that every moment must contribute towards an ever-expanding future. Yet, within this seemingly infinite march forward, we often lose sight of the value of simply *being*. We rush from one goal to the next, ever distant from the present moment that holds so much potential.

It's in this context that we must ask ourselves: *What would happen if we were to stop?* Not stop because we are burnt out, not stop because we are defeated, but stop intentionally—simply to *be*. What if, instead of seeking the next step, we recognised that we are already where we need to be? This is the paradox of time—it moves inexorably forward, yet when we allow ourselves to pause, we may discover that the present is already rich with the potential we seek elsewhere.

The Present Moment as Abundance

In a society that glorifies scarcity, it is almost revolutionary to consider the notion that the present moment is abundant. We are conditioned to focus on what is lacking—whether it's time, resources, or opportunities. Yet, the present moment, when fully embraced, holds all that we need. It is here that true wealth resides, not in what we acquire or achieve but in what we experience and allow ourselves to feel.

Wealth, in its most profound sense, is not an external state—it is internal. It arises not from accumulation, but from *presence*. Presence with the world around us, with those we love, with the work we do, and with ourselves. By allowing ourselves to dwell in this present moment, we release the grip of striving and open ourselves to the richness of what already is.

This chapter has invited us to reconsider time, not as something to be controlled or manipulated, but as a living, breathing entity—one that is intimately connected to our sense of presence, connection, and creativity. By reframing our relationship with time, we create space for deeper meaning and joy in our everyday lives.

A Gentle Invitation to Reflect

Now, as we approach the end of this exploration, we move not into the realm of "what comes next" but into a quieter, more introspective space. There is no need for a grand conclusion or a list of final steps. Instead, this moment invites you to reflect—not on what you must do, but on what you *already* are doing. It invites you to notice the ways in which you have already begun to shift your relationship with time, and to recognise that these small, everyday moments of mindfulness are far more powerful than the grand gestures of achievement we often idolise.

As you sit with this idea, you may notice a subtle shift in how you feel. There is no urgency to rush, no demand to accomplish. You are invited simply to be. In this space, time is no longer a burden to be managed or a commodity to be traded. Instead, it becomes a rich, fertile ground from which creativity, joy, and connection can grow.

If Time is Yours Again, What Will You Create That Money Never Could?

This is the question that lingers as we close this chapter. It is a question that is not asking for another goal to chase or another achievement to measure. Instead, it invites you to step into a new relationship with time. To ask, "If I were not rushing to the next milestone, if I were not consumed by the demands of external productivity, what would I create?"

Perhaps it is a deeper connection with loved ones, a more authentic form of self-expression, or simply the space to enjoy the beauty of life without the pressure of measuring it. Time, when reclaimed, has the power to bring forth creations that money and ambition never could. What could you build from a place of fullness, of rest, of alignment with the rhythms of the world around you? What might emerge when you allow time to become a relationship—one that nourishes, rather than depletes?

This final provocation is not a call to action, but a call to presence. It's an invitation to recognise that time, as we have known it, is not a finite resource to be managed but a living, breathing experience to be savoured. And in this space, we can create something far more valuable than any material success: a life rich in meaning, connection, and joy.

About the Author

Elian Varo is a thought leader at the intersection of future economics, technology, and philosophical living. With a background in systems design, cultural theory, and human potential studies, Varo explores how automation, decentralised income, and post-capitalist frameworks are transforming what it means to live a meaningful life. His work invites readers to rethink their relationship with time, work, and selfhood in a rapidly evolving world. Combining clarity with depth, Varo's writing guides individuals toward a life not just of freedom, but of presence, purpose, and true wealth.

www.ingramcontent.com/pod-product-compliance
Lightning Source LLC
Chambersburg PA
CBHW031339230926
51848CB00002B/306
9789371342469